Custom Textbook prepared for

DEPARTMENT OF INDUSTRIAL ENGINEERING AND OPERATIONS RESEARCH

Columbia University

Volume II

Includes Materials from:

Professor Soulaymane Kachani

for

IEOR E4003 & IEOR E4403

Columbia University

FINANCIAL ACCOUNTING: A Valuation Emphasis
Hughes–Ayres–Hoskin

ADVANCED ENGINEERING ECONOMICS
Park–Sharp–Bette

VALUATION: Measuring and Managing the Value of Companies
McKinsey & Company–Koller–Goedhart–Wessels

WILEY *Custom*
LEARNING SOLUTIONS

Cover images: © Columbia University.

Preface

New York, July 16th, 2012

This book is intended for students in the Industrial Economics (IEOR E4003) and the Advanced Engineering & Corporate Economics (IEOR E4403) courses at Columbia University.

The fifth edition of this custom book better covers the broad range of topics discussed in these courses using four different sources as well as a subset of the lecture slides that I developed here at Columbia University, and that leverage my experience at McKinsey.

I would like to thank Alan Most at Wiley for his continued assistance in the publishing process. I would also like to thank Professor Ali Sadighian and my former students for their feedback.

I look forward to your suggestions as, together, we continue to improve these courses and this custom book.

Sincerely,

Soulaymane Kachani
Department of Industrial Engineering & Operations Research

Table of Contents

Outline

Part III: Corporate Finance

- Lecture slides on dividend policy, debt policy, WACC and optimal capital structure

- Chapters 6, 7, 8, 10, 11 and 12 of "Valuation: Measuring and Managing the Value of Companies" by McKinsey & Company, Koller, Goedhart and Wessels

Dividend Policy

➢ **The Dividend Controversy**

➢ **The Rightists**

➢ **Taxes and the Radical Left**

➢ **The Middle of the Roaders**

The Dividend Decision

Lintner's "stylized facts" on how dividends are determined)

1. **Companies have long term target dividend payout ratios**

2. **Managers focus more on dividend changes than on absolute dividend levels**

3. **Dividend changes follow shifts in long-run sustainable levels of earnings**

4. **Managers are reluctant to make dividend changes that could be reversed**

Dividend Policy is Irrelevant

Modigliani & Miller

Since investors do not need dividends to convert shares to cash, they will not pay a premium for firms with higher dividend payouts. In other words, dividend policy has no impact on firms' value

Dividends Increase Value

Dividends as Signals

Dividend increases send good news about earnings and cash flows. On the other hand, dividend cuts send bad news

Dividends Decrease Value

Tax Issues

Companies can convert dividends into capital gains by shifting their dividend policies. If dividends are taxed more heavily than capital gains, investors should favor capital gains

Debt Policy

➢ **Leverage in a Tax Free Environment**

➢ **How Leverage Affects Returns**

➢ **The Traditional Position**

Modigliani - Miller

Modigliani & Miller

When there are no taxes and capital markets function well, it makes no difference whether the firm borrows or individual shareholders borrow. Therefore, the market value of a company does not depend on its capital structure

Weighted Average Cost of Capital

Why Do We Use WACC

- **WACC of an asset is the weighed opportunity cost of all investors for putting their money into the asset given the risk of the asset. It therefore reflects:**

  ➤ **The riskiness of the asset, and**

  ➤ **The way the asset is financed**

Weighted Average Cost of Capital

$$WACC = k_d(1-t)\frac{B}{V} + k_e\frac{S}{V} + k_p\frac{P}{V} + k_l(1-t)\frac{L}{V}$$

- ➢ k_d: cost of debt
- ➢ t: tax rate
- ➢ B: market value of debt
- ➢ V: market value of assets of company
- ➢ k_e: cost of equity
- ➢ S: market value of stocks
- ➢ k_p: cost of preferred stock
- ➢ P: market value of preferred stock
- ➢ k_l: cost of leases
- ➢ L: market value of leases

Weighted Average Cost of Capital

WACC Tree

$$WACC = k_d(1-t)\frac{B}{B+S} + k_e\frac{S}{B+S}$$

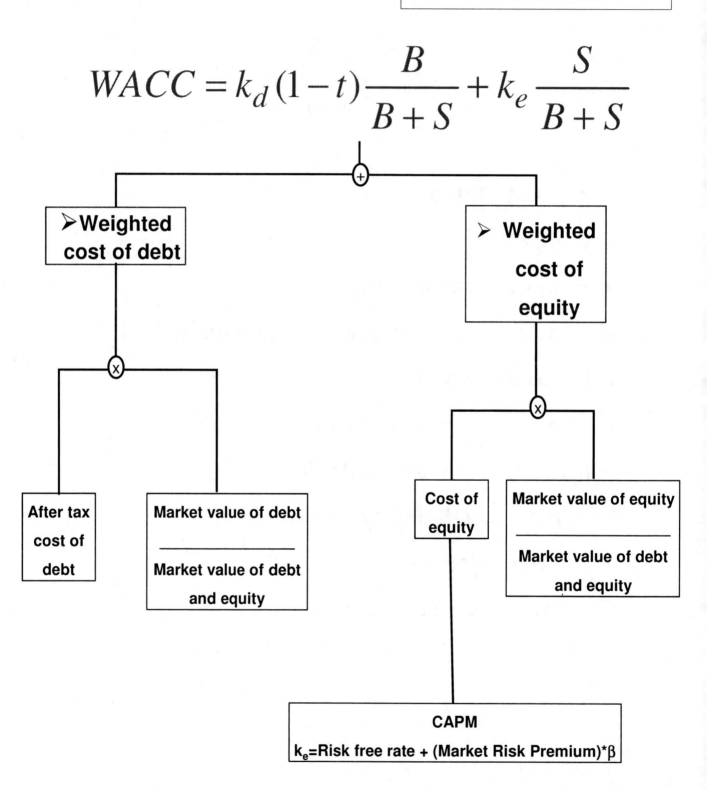

Weighted Average Cost of Capital

➢ **For any security (including corporate debt and equity), the nominal rate required by the investors is a function of:**

- **The expected inflation over the life of the security**

- **The expected real rate over the life of the security**

- **The expected interest rate risk premium (if any)**

- **The expected risk premiums**

- **The expected illiquidity premium**

Weighted Average Cost of Capital

➢ **Average rates of return of various securities, 1926-1997**

(%/year)

Inflation	**3.2%**
Treasury Bills (3-month bills)	**3.8%**
Government Bonds	**5.3%**
Corporate Bonds	**5.8%**
Common Stocks (S&P 500)	**11.2%**
Small-firm Common Stocks	**12.9%**

Weighted Average Cost of Capital

Cost of Equity and CAPM

➤ **Cost of equity:**

$$k_e = E[r_e] = r_f + \beta_e.(E[r_m] - r_f)$$

$$\text{where } \beta_e = \frac{Cov(R_e, R_m)}{Var(R_m)}$$

- **It takes into account the first four components in our security return decomposition (riskless rate takes into account the first three)**

- **For the riskless rate, use a long-term government bond rate and for the market risk premium, use the long-term realized risk premium of 3.5-4% (McK)**

Weighted Average Cost of Capital (Finer Points)

- **Levering-Unlevering relationship:**

$$\beta_e = \beta_a + [\beta_a - \beta_d](1 - t_c) \cdot \frac{B}{S}$$

This is the crucial formula as now, we can compute a new β_e (and k_e) if we want to use a new capital structure (**B/S**). This is true because:

  ✓ β_{assets} stays the same even if the capital structure changes as long as the projects (=assets) of the company do not change

  ✓ However, we should realize that in dramatic capital structure changes, β_{assets} changes

Cost of Financial Distress

Costs of Financial Distress: Costs arising from bankruptcy or distorted business decisions when close to bankruptcy

Market Value =   *Value if firm is all equity financed*

+ PV tax shield

- PV costs of financial distress

Cost of Financial Distress

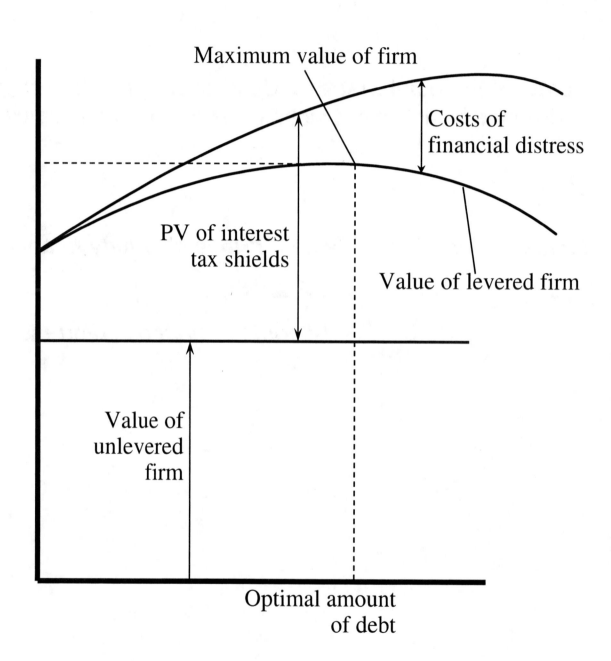

Maximum value of firm

Costs of financial distress

PV of interest tax shields

Value of levered firm

Value of unlevered firm

Optimal amount of debt

Debt

6

Frameworks for Valuation

In Part One, we built a conceptual framework to show what drives value. In broad terms, a company's value is driven by its ability to earn a healthy return on invested capital (ROIC) and by its ability to grow. Healthy rates of return and growth result in high cash flows, the ultimate source of value.

Part Two offers a step-by-step guide for analyzing and valuing a company in practice, including technical details for properly measuring and interpreting the drivers of value. Among the many ways to value a company (see Exhibit 6.1 for an overview), we focus particularly on two: enterprise discounted cash flow (DCF) and discounted economic profit. When applied correctly, both valuation methods yield the same results; however, each model has certain benefits in practice. Enterprise DCF remains a favorite of practitioners and academics because it relies solely on the flow of cash in and out of the company, rather than on accounting-based earnings. The discounted economic-profit valuation model is gaining in popularity because of its close link to economic theory and competitive strategy. Economic profit highlights whether a company is earning its cost of capital and how its financial performance is expected to change over time. Given that the two methods yield identical results and have different but complementary benefits, we recommend creating *both* enterprise DCF and economic-profit models when valuing a company.

Both the enterprise DCF and economic-profit models discount future income streams at the weighted average cost of capital (WACC). WACC-based models work best when a company maintains a relatively stable debt-to-value ratio. If a company's debt-to-value ratio is expected to change, WACC-based models can still yield accurate results but are more difficult to apply. In such cases, we recommend an alternative to WACC-based models: adjusted present value (APV). APV specifically forecasts and values any cash flows associated with capital structure separately, rather than embedding their value in the cost of capital.

The chapter also includes a discussion of capital cash flow and equity cash flow valuation models. Because these two valuation models mix together

EXHIBIT 6.1 **Frameworks for DCF-Based Valuation**

Model	Measure	Discount factor	Assessment
Enterprise discounted cash flow	Free cash flow	Weighted average cost of capital	Works best for projects, business units, and companies that manage their capital structure to a target level.
Discounted economic profit	Economic profit	Weighted average cost of capital	Explicitly highlights when a company creates value.
Adjusted present value	Free cash flow	Unlevered cost of equity	Highlights changing capital structure more easily than WACC-based models.
Capital cash flow	Capital cash flow	Unlevered cost of equity	Compresses free cash flow and the interest tax shield in one number, making it difficult to compare operating performance among companies and over time.
Equity cash flow	Cash flow to equity	Levered cost of equity	Difficult to implement correctly because capital structure is embedded within the cash flow. Best used when valuing financial institutions.

operating performance and capital structure in cash flow, they lead more easily to mistakes. For this reason, we avoid capital cash flow and equity cash flow valuation models, except when valuing banks and other financial institutions, where capital structure is an inextricable part of operations (for how to value banks, see Chapter 36).

ENTERPRISE DISCOUNTED CASH FLOW MODEL

The enterprise DCF model discounts free cash flow, meaning the cash flow available to all investors—equity holders, debt holders, and any other nonequity investors—at the weighted average cost of capital, meaning the blended cost for all investor capital. The claims on cash flow of debt holders and other nonequity investors are subtracted from enterprise value to determine equity holders' value.[1] Equity valuation models, in contrast, value only the equity holders' claims against operating cash flows. Exhibit 6.2 demonstrates the relationship between enterprise value and equity value. For this company, equity holders' value can be calculated either directly at $227.5 million or by estimating enterprise value ($427.5 million) and subtracting debt ($200.0 million).

Although both methods lead to identical results when applied correctly, the equity method is difficult to apply, since matching equity cash flows with the correct cost of equity is particularly challenging (for more on this, see the section

---

[1] Throughout this chapter, we refer to debt and other nonequity claims. Other nonequity claims arise when stakeholders have a claim against the company's future cash flow but do not hold traditional interest-bearing debt or common equity. Nonequity claims include debt equivalents (e.g., operating leases and unfunded pension liabilities) and hybrid securities (e.g., convertible debt and employee options).

EXHIBIT 6.2 **Enterprise Valuation of a Single-Business Company**

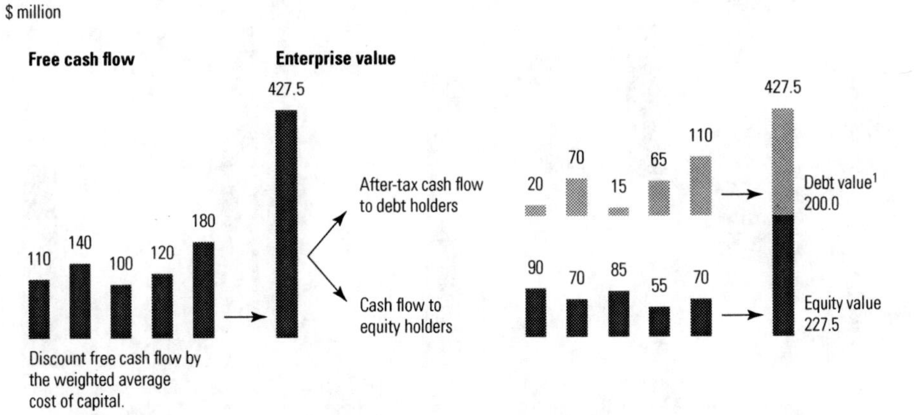

$ million

Free cash flow

Enterprise value

427.5

110   140   100   120   180

Discount free cash flow by
the weighted average
cost of capital.

427.5

After-tax cash flow
to debt holders

20   70   15   65   110

Debt value[1]
200.0

Cash flow to
equity holders

90   70   85   55   70

Equity value
227.5

[1] Debt value equals discounted after-tax cash flow to debt holders plus the present value of interest tax shield.

on equity valuation later in this chapter). Consequently, to value a company's equity, we recommend valuing the *enterprise* first and then subtracting the value of any nonequity financial claims.

The enterprise method is especially useful when applied to a multibusiness company. As shown in Exhibit 6.3, the enterprise value equals the summed value of the individual operating units less the present value of the corporate-center costs, plus the value of nonoperating assets.[2] If you use enterprise discounted cash flow instead of the equity cash flow model, you can value individual projects, business units, and even the entire company with a consistent methodology.

Valuing a company's common equity using enterprise DCF is a four-part process:

1. Value the company's operations by discounting free cash flow at the weighted average cost of capital.

2. Identify and value nonoperating assets, such as excess marketable securities, nonconsolidated subsidiaries, and other equity investments. Summing the value of operations and nonoperating assets gives enterprise value.

3. Identify and value all debt and other nonequity claims against the enterprise value. Debt and other nonequity claims include (among others)

[2] Many investment professionals define enterprise value as interest-bearing debt plus the market value of equity minus excess cash, whereas we define enterprise value as the value of operations plus nonoperating assets. The two definitions are equivalent for companies without nonoperating assets (e.g., excess cash and nonconsolidated subsidiaries) and debt equivalents (e.g., unfunded pension liabilities).

EXHIBIT 6.3 **Enterprise Valuation of a Multibusiness Company**

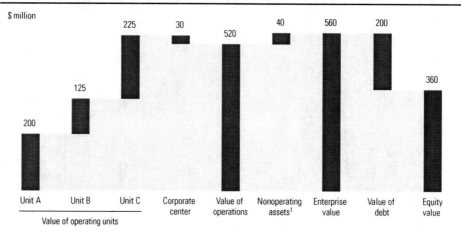

[1] including excess cash and marketable securities.

fixed-rate and floating-rate debt, unfunded pension liabilities, employee options, and preferred stock.

4. Subtract the value of nonequity financial claims from enterprise value to determine the value of common equity. To estimate price per share, divide equity value by the number of current shares outstanding.

Exhibit 6.4 presents the results of an enterprise DCF valuation for Home Depot, the world's largest retailer of home improvement products. We use Home Depot throughout the chapter to compare valuation methods. To value Home Depot, discount each annual projected cash flow by the company's weighted average cost of capital.[3] Next, sum the present values of all the annual cash flows to determine the present value of operations. For simplicity, the first year's cash flow is discounted by one full year, the second by two full years, and so on. Since cash flows are generated throughout the year, and not as a lump sum, discounting in full-year increments understates the appropriate discount factor. Therefore, adjust the present value upward by half a year;[4] the resulting value of operations is $65.3 billion.

To this value, add nonoperating assets (e.g., excess cash and other nonoperating assets) to estimate enterprise value. For Home Depot, enterprise value ($65.8 billion) almost mirrors the value of operations ($65.3 billion) because its

[3] To generate identical results across valuation methods, we have not adjusted results for rounding error. Rounding errors occur in most exhibits.

[4] A half-year adjustment is made to the present value for Home Depot because we assume cash flow is generated symmetrically around the midyear point. For companies dependent on year-end holidays, cash flows will be more heavily weighted toward the latter half of the year. In this case, the adjustment should be smaller.

EXHIBIT 6.4 **Home Depot: Enterprise DCF Valuation**

Forecast year	Free cash flow ($ million)	Discount factor (@ 8.5%)	Present value of FCF ($ million)
2009	5,909	0.922	5,448
2010	2,368	0.850	2,013
2011	1,921	0.784	1,506
2012	2,261	0.723	1,634
2013	2,854	0.666	1,902
2014	3,074	0.614	1,889
2015	3,308	0.567	1,874
2016	3,544	0.522	1,852
2017	3,783	0.482	1,822
2018	4,022	0.444	1,787
Continuing value	92,239	0.444	40,966
Present value of cash flow			62,694
Midyear adjustment factor			1.041
Value of operations			65,291
Value of excess cash			–
Value of long-term investments			361
Value of tax loss carry-forwards			112
Enterprise value			65,764
Less: Value of debt			(11,434)
Less: Value of capitalized operating leases			(8,298)
Equity value			46,032
Number of shares outstanding (December 2008)			1.7
Equity value per share			27.1

nonoperating assets are negligible. From enterprise value, subtract the present value of debt and other nonequity claims. Departing from its historically conservative capital structure, the company issued a considerable amount of debt ($11.4 billion) following the acquisition of Hughes Supply in 2006. Similar to most retailers, Home Depot uses off-balance-sheet operating leases ($8.3 billion) to finance its stores. Dividing the resulting equity value by the number of shares outstanding (1.7 billion) leads to an estimate of per-share value of $27.10. During the first half of 2009, Home Depot's stock price traded in the mid-$20s.

Over the next few pages, we outline the enterprise DCF valuation process. Although we present it sequentially, valuation is an iterative process. To value operations, we reorganize the company's financial statements to separate operating items from nonoperating items and capital structure; we then analyze the company's historical performance; define and project free cash flow over the short, medium, and long run; and discount the projected free cash flows at the weighted average cost of capital.

Valuing Operations

The value of operations equals the discounted value of future free cash flow. Free cash flow equals the cash flow generated by the company's operations, less any reinvestment back into the business. As defined at the beginning of this section, free cash flow is the cash flow available to all investors—equity holders, debt holders, and any other nonequity investors—so it is independent of capital structure. Consistent with this definition, free cash flow must be discounted using the weighted average cost of capital, because the WACC represents rates of return required by the company's debt and equity holders blended together, and as such is the company's opportunity cost of funds.

Reorganizing the financial statements A robust valuation model requires a clear account of financial performance. Although return on invested capital (ROIC) and free cash flow (FCF) are critical to the valuation process, they cannot be computed directly from a company's reported financial statements. Whereas ROIC and FCF are intended to measure the company's operating performance, financial statements mix operating performance, nonoperating performance, and capital structure. Therefore, to calculate ROIC and FCF, we must first reorganize the accountant's financial statements into new statements that separate operating items, nonoperating items, and financial structure.

This reorganization leads to two new terms: invested capital and net operating profit less adjusted taxes (NOPLAT). Invested capital represents the investor capital required to fund operations, without distinguishing how the capital is financed. NOPLAT represents the total after-tax operating income generated by the company's invested capital, available to all financial investors.

Exhibit 6.5 presents the historical NOPLAT and invested capital for Home Depot and one of its direct competitors, Lowe's. To calculate ROIC, divide NOPLAT by average invested capital. In 2008, Home Depot's return on invested capital equaled 8.0 percent (based on a two-year average of invested capital), which almost matches its 2008 weighted average cost of capital of 8.3 percent.

Next, use the reorganized financial statements to calculate free cash flow, which will be the basis for our valuation. Defined in a manner consistent with ROIC, free cash flow is derived directly from NOPLAT and the change in invested capital. Unlike the accountant's cash flow from operations (provided in the company's annual report), free cash flow is independent of nonoperating items and capital structure.

Exhibit 6.6 presents historical free cash flow for both Home Depot and Lowe's. As seen in the exhibit, Home Depot generated $3.7 billion in free cash flow in 2008, whereas the free cash flow of Lowe's is considerably smaller. This isn't necessarily a problem for Lowe's. Its free cash flow is small because the company is reinvesting most of its gross cash flow to grow its business.

Analyzing historical performance Once the company's financial statements are reorganized, analyze the company's historical financial performance. By

EXHIBIT 6.5 **Home Depot and Lowe's: Historical ROIC Analysis**

$ million

	Home Depot			Lowe's		
	2006	**2007**	**2008**	**2006**	**2007**	**2008**
Net sales	90,837	77,349	71,288	46,927	48,283	48,230
Cost of merchandise sold	(61,054)	(51,352)	(47,298)	(30,729)	(31,556)	(31,729)
Selling, general, and administrative	(18,348)	(17,053)	(17,846)	(9,884)	(10,656)	(11,176)
Depreciation	(1,645)	(1,693)	(1,785)	(1,162)	(1,366)	(1,539)
Add: Operating lease interest	441	536	486	185	169	199
Adjusted EBITA	10,231	7,787	4,845	5,337	4,874	3,985
Operating cash taxes	(3,986)	(3,331)	(1,811)	(2,071)	(1,973)	(1,496)
NOPLAT	6,245	4,456	3,033	3,266	2,901	2,489
Invested capital						
Operating working capital	4,556	3,490	3,490	1,725	1,792	2,084
Net property and equipment	26,605	27,476	26,234	18,971	21,361	22,722
Capitalized operating leases	9,141	7,878	8,298	3,034	3,528	3,913
Other operating assets, net of operating liabilities	(1,027)	(1,635)	(2,129)	(126)	(461)	(450)
Invested capital (excluding goodwill)[1]	39,275	37,209	35,893	23,604	26,220	28,269
Goodwill and acquired intangibles	7,092	1,309	1,134	–	–	–
Cumulative amortization and unreported goodwill	177	49	49	730	730	730
Invested capital (including goodwill)[1]	46,543	38,567	37,075	24,334	26,950	29,000
Return on invested capital (percent)						
ROIC excluding goodwill (average)[1]	16.7	11.7	8.3	14.5	11.6	9.1
ROIC including goodwill (average)[1]	14.5	10.5	8.0	14.0	11.3	8.9

[1] Goodwill includes goodwill, acquired intangibles, cumulative amortization, and unreported goodwill.

thoroughly analyzing the past, we can document whether the company has created value, whether it has grown, and how it compares with its competitors. A good analysis needs to focus on the key drivers of value: return on invested capital, revenue growth, and free cash flow. Understanding how these drivers behaved in the past will help you make more reliable estimates of future cash flow.

Exhibit 6.7 presents a 10-year summary of Home Depot's pretax operating margin, a critical component of return on invested capital. Before Robert Nardelli was hired as CEO in 2002, the company spent roughly 70 percent of revenue on merchandise and 19 percent on selling expenses, leading to an operating profit near 10 percent. During his tenure, Nardelli focused the organization on reducing the cost of merchandise. This led to a 2 percent increase in operating margin. In 2007, Frank Blake replaced Nardelli as CEO and stated he would make improved customer service a core part of the future strategy.[5] As a result, profitability dropped as selling expenses increased from 20 percent

[5] "Home Depot to Scale Back Growth: Back-to-Basics Plan Projected to Cut Earnings," *Atlanta Journal Constitution*, March 1, 2007.

EXHIBIT 6.6 **Home Depot and Lowe's: Historical Free Cash Flow**

$ million

	Home Depot			Lowe's		
	2006	**2007**	**2008**	**2006**	**2007**	**2008**
NOPLAT	6,245	4,456	3,033	3,266	2,901	2,489
Depreciation	1,645	1,693	1,785	1,162	1,366	1,539
Gross cash flow	7,890	6,149	4,818	4,428	4,267	4,028
Change in operating working capital	(936)	(739)	–	168	(67)	(292)
Net capital expenditures	(3,349)	(3,577)	(543)	(3,779)	(3,756)	(2,900)
Decrease (increase) in capitalized operating leases	(1,214)	1,262	(419)	291	(494)	(385)
Investments in goodwill and acquired intangibles	(3,525)	–	175	–	–	–
Decrease (increase) in net other operating assets	224	457	494	52	335	(11)
Increase (decrease) in accumulated other comprehensive income	(99)	445	(832)	–	7	(14)
Gross investment	(8,899)	(2,152)	(1,125)	(3,268)	(3,975)	(3,602)
Free cash flow	(1,009)	3,998	3,693	1,160	292	426
After-tax nonoperating income	(6)	334	(72)	52	42	44
Decrease (increase) in nonoperating assets	2	8,384	283	134	(376)	311
Cash flow available to investors	(1,013)	12,716	3,904	1,346	(42)	781
Reconciliation of cash flow to investors						
After-tax interest expense	244	432	390	127	148	199
After-tax operating lease interest expense	274	333	303	114	105	124
Decrease (increase) in debt	(7,576)	(1,769)	1,996	(905)	(2,244)	620
Decrease (increase) in capitalized operating leases	(1,214)	1,262	(419)	291	(494)	(385)
Flows to debt holders	(8,272)	258	2,269	(373)	(2,485)	557
Decrease (increase) in nonoperating deferred taxes	(282)	302	270	–	–	–
Dividends	1,395	1,709	1,521	276	428	491
Repurchased and retired shares	5,889	10,336	(190)	1,400	2,007	(267)
Adjustments to retained earnings	257	111	34	43	8	–
Flows to equity holders	7,259	12,458	1,635	1,719	2,443	224
Cash flow available to investors	(1,013)	12,716	3,904	1,346	(42)	781

to 24 percent of revenue. A reliable estimate of future sales expenses is critical for an accurate assessment of enterprise value based on future cash flow.

Projecting revenue growth, ROIC, and free cash flow   The next task in building an enterprise DCF valuation is to project revenue growth, return on invested capital, and free cash flow. Exhibit 6.8 graphs historical ROIC, projected ROIC, and revenue growth for Home Depot. As the graphs demonstrate, the company's revenue growth and ROIC fell dramatically with the collapse of the U.S. housing market. Sell-side research analysts forecast a gradual recovery by 2011 but do not project growth and return on invested capital to return to their historical levels, given the maturity of the market.

EXHIBIT 6.7 **Home Depot: Operating Margin Analysis**

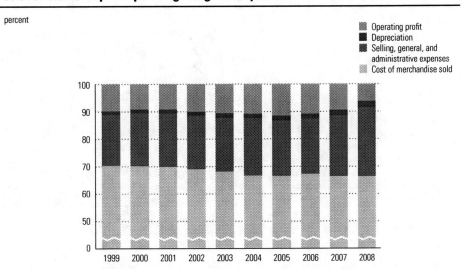

Note: SG&A and operating profit adjusted for operating leases.

EXHIBIT 6.8 **Home Depot: Projected Revenue Growth and ROIC**

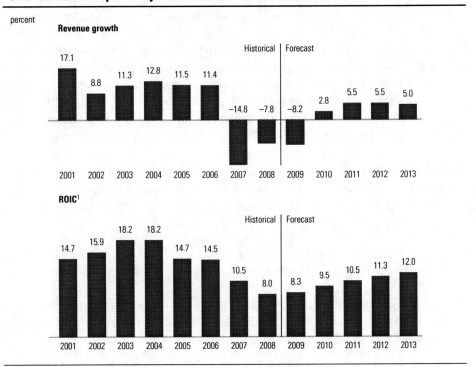

[1] ROIC measured using two-year average invested capital with goodwill and acquired intangible assets.

EXHIBIT 6.9 **Home Depot: Projected Free Cash Flow**

$ million

	Historical			Forecast		
	2006	2007	2008	2009	2010	2011
NOPLAT	6,245	4,456	3,033	2,971	3,269	3,780
Depreciation	1,645	1,693	1,785	1,639	1,685	1,778
Gross cash flow	7,890	6,149	4,818	4,610	4,954	5,558
Change in operating working capital	(936)	(739)	–	292	(73)	(163)
Net capital expenditures	(3,349)	(3,577)	(543)	503	(2,355)	(3,151)
Decrease (increase) in capitalized operating leases	(1,214)	1,262	(419)	678	(212)	(434)
Investments in goodwill and acquired intangibles	(3,525)	–	175	–	–	–
Decrease (increase) in net other operating assets	224	457	494	(174)	54	111
Increase (decrease) in accumulated other comprehensive income	(99)	445	(832)	–	–	–
Gross investment	(8,899)	(2,152)	(1,125)	1,299	(2,586)	(3,637)
Free cash flow	(1,009)	3,998	3,693	5,909	2,368	1,921

Free cash flow, which is driven by revenue growth and ROIC, provides the basis for an enterprise DCF valuation. Exhibit 6.9 shows a summarized free cash flow calculation for Home Depot.[6] To forecast Home Depot's free cash flow, start with forecasts of NOPLAT and invested capital. Over the short run (the first few years), forecast each financial-statement line item, such as gross margin, selling expenses, accounts receivable, and inventory (see Chapter 9 for detail on how to forecast cash flows). Moving further out, individual line items become difficult to project. Therefore, over the medium horizon (5 to 10 years), focus on the company's key value drivers, such as operating margin, the operating tax rate, and capital efficiency. At some point, though, projecting even key drivers on a year-by-year basis becomes meaningless. To value cash flows beyond this point, use a continuing-value formula, described next.

Estimating continuing value At the point where predicting the individual key value drivers on a year-by-year basis becomes impractical, do not vary the individual drivers over time. Instead, use a perpetuity-based continuing value, such that:

$$\text{Value of Operations} = \frac{\text{Present Value of Free Cash Flow}}{during \text{ Explicit Forecast Period}} + \frac{\text{Present Value of Free Cash Flow}}{after \text{ Explicit Forecast Period}}$$

Although many continuing-value models exist, we prefer the key value driver model presented in Chapter 2. The key value driver formula is superior

---

[6] Free cash flow does not incorporate any financing-related cash flows such as interest expense or dividends. A good stress test for an enterprise valuation model is to change future interest rates or dividend payout ratios and observe free cash flow. Free cash flow forecasts should not change when you adjust the cost of debt or dividend policy.

EXHIBIT 6.10 **Home Depot: Continuing Value**

$ million

Key inputs[1]	
Projected NOPLAT in 2019	6,122
NOPLAT growth rate in perpetuity (g)	4.0%
Return on new invested capital (RONIC)	12.2%
Weighted average cost of capital (WACC)	8.5%

$$\text{Continuing value}_t = \frac{\text{NOPLAT}_{t+1}\left(1 - \frac{g}{\text{RONIC}}\right)}{\text{WACC} - g}$$

$$= 91,440$$

[1] Enterprise valuation based on $92,239 million; the precise calculation without rounding.

to alternative methodologies because it is based on cash flow and links cash flow directly to growth and ROIC. The key value driver formula is expressed as follows:

$$\text{Continuing Value}_t = \frac{\text{NOPLAT}_{t+1}\left(1 - \frac{g}{\text{RONIC}}\right)}{\text{WACC} - g}$$

The formula requires a forecast of net operating profit less adjusted taxes (NOPLAT) in the year *following* the end of the explicit forecast period, the long-run forecast for return on new capital (RONIC), the weighted average cost of capital (WACC), and long-run growth in NOPLAT (g).

Exhibit 6.10 presents an estimate for Home Depot's continuing value. Based on a final-year estimate of NOPLAT ($6.1 billion), return on new investment (12.2 percent) slightly above the cost of capital (8.5 percent), and a long-term growth rate of 4 percent, the continuing value is estimated at $92.2 billion. This value is then discounted into today's dollars and added to the value from the explicit forecast period to determine Home Depot's operating value. (Exhibit 6.4 discounts continuing value in 2018 back to 2009.)

Alternative methods and additional details for estimating continuing value are provided in Chapter 10.

Discounting free cash flow at the weighted average cost of capital   To determine the value of operations, discount each year's forecast of free cash flow for time and risk. When you discount any set of cash flows, make sure to define the cash flows and discount factor consistently. In an enterprise valuation, free cash flows are available to all investors. Consequently, the discount factor for free cash flow must represent the risk faced by all investors. The weighted average cost of capital (WACC) blends the rates of return required by debt holders (k_d) and equity holders (k_e). For a company financed solely with debt and equity, the WACC is defined as follows:

$$\text{WACC} = \frac{D}{D+E}k_d(1 - T_m) + \frac{E}{D+E}k_e$$

where debt (*D*) and equity (*E*) are measured using market values. Note how the cost of debt has been reduced by the marginal tax rate (T_m). The reason for doing this is that the interest tax shield (ITS) has been excluded from free cash flow. Since the interest tax shield has value, it must be incorporated in the valuation. Enterprise DCF values the tax shield by reducing the weighted average cost of capital.

Why move interest tax shields from free cash flow to the cost of capital? By calculating free cash flow as if the company were financed entirely with equity, we can compare operating performance across companies and over time without regard to capital structure. By focusing solely on operations, we can develop a clearer picture of historical performance, and this leads to better performance measurement and forecasting.

Although applying the weighted average cost of capital is intuitive and relatively straightforward, it has some drawbacks. If you discount all future cash flows with a constant cost of capital, as most analysts do, you are implicitly assuming the company keeps its capital structure constant at a target ratio of debt to equity. But if a company plans, say, to increase its debt-to-value ratio, the current cost of capital will understate the expected tax shields. The WACC can be adjusted to accommodate a changing capital structure. However, the process is complicated, and in these situations, we recommend an alternative method such as adjusted present value (APV).

The weighted average cost of capital for Home Depot is presented in Exhibit 6.11. Home Depot funds operations with a mix of debt and equity. Compared with earlier years, the company is using a substantial amount of debt to fund operations, making its net debt-to-value 31.5 percent. The higher debt-to-value is a result of the company's use of debt to fund acquisitions, use of excess cash to repurchase shares, and a drop in equity value resulting from the collapse of the U.S. housing market. The increase in leverage has led to a drop in the company's debt rating and an increase in equity risk. Even so, Home Depot's weighted average cost of capital remains quite low (8.5 percent), as interest rates are at historical lows.

This cost of capital is used to discount each year's forecasted cash flow, as well as the continuing value. The result is the value of operations.

EXHIBIT 6.11 **Home Depot: Weighted Average Cost of Capital**

percent

Source of capital	Proportion of total capital	Cost of capital	Marginal tax rate	After-tax cost of capital	Contribution to weighted average[1]
Debt	31.5	6.8	37.6	4.2	1.3
Equity	68.5	10.4		10.4	7.1
WACC	100.0				8.5

[1] Total does not sum due to rounding error.

Identifying and Valuing Nonoperating Assets

Many companies own assets that have value but whose cash flows are not included in accounting revenue or operating profit. As a result, the cash generated by these assets is not part of free cash flow and must be valued separately.

For example, consider equity investments, known outside the United States as nonconsolidated subsidiaries. When a company owns a small minority stake in another company, it will not record the company's revenue or costs as part of its own. Instead, the company will record only its proportion of the other company's net income as a separate line item.[7] Including net income from nonconsolidated subsidiaries as part of the parent's operating profit will distort margins, since only the subsidiaries' profit is recognized and not the corresponding revenues. Consequently, nonconsolidated subsidiaries are best analyzed and valued separately. The quality of this analysis, however, will depend on how much the other company discloses: typically, the workings of nonconsolidated subsidiaries are not clearly visible to the company's shareholders.

Other nonoperating assets include excess cash, tradable securities, and customer financing arms. A detailed process for identifying and valuing nonoperating assets can be found in Chapter 12.

Identifying and Valuing Nonequity Claims

To convert enterprise value into equity value, subtract any nonequity claims, such as short-term debt, long-term debt, unfunded retirement liabilities, capitalized operating leases, and outstanding employee options. Common equity is a residual claimant, receiving cash flows only *after* the company has fulfilled its other contractual claims. Careful analysis of all potential claims against cash flows is therefore critical.

In today's increasingly complex financial markets, nonequity claims are not always easy to spot. For example, throughout the first decade of the 2000s, numerous banks moved assets and the debt that financed them off the balance sheet into special investment vehicles (SIVs). Since SIVs are structured as separate legal entities, the originating banks are not contractually responsible for the debt. Yet to regain trust with bank clients who lent the SIV money, many banks decided to repurchase the assets and guarantee the corresponding debt. In November 2008, Citigroup repurchased $17 billion in SIV-owned assets. Its share price dropped 23 percent on the day of the announcement.[8]

---

[7] For minority stakes between 20 percent and 50 percent, the parent company will recognize its proportion of the subsidiary's income. A parent that owns less than a 20 percent stake in another company records only dividends paid as part of its own income. This makes valuation of stakes less than 20 percent extremely challenging.

[8] "Citi's Slide Deepens as Investors Bail Out: Shares Drop 23% as SIV Move, Analyst's Warning Spook Market; Pandit Points to Strengths," *Wall Street Journal*, November 20, 2008.

Although a comprehensive list of nonequity claims is impractical, here are the most common:

- *Debt:* If available, use the market value of all outstanding debt, including fixed- and floating-rate debt. If that information is unavailable, the book value of debt is a reasonable proxy, unless the probability of default is high or interest rates have changed dramatically since the debt was originally issued. Any valuation of debt, however, should be consistent with your estimates of enterprise value. (See Chapter 11 for more details.)

- *Operating leases:* These represent the most common form of off-balance-sheet debt. Under certain conditions, companies can avoid capitalizing leases as debt on their balance sheets, although required payments must be disclosed in the footnotes.

- *Unfunded retirement liabilities:* During the early 2000s, accounting bodies around the globe began requiring companies to report on the balance sheet the present value of unfunded retirement liabilities. If these liabilities are not explicitly visible (line items are often consolidated), check the company's note on pensions to determine the size of any unfunded liabilities and where they are reported on the balance sheet.

- *Preferred stock:* Although the name denotes equity, preferred stock in well-established companies more closely resembles unsecured debt.

- *Employee options:* Each year, many companies offer their employees compensation in the form of options. Since options give the employee the right to buy company stock at a potentially discounted price, they can have great value.

- *Minority interest:* When a company controls a subsidiary but does not own 100 percent, the investment must be consolidated on the parent company's balance sheet. The funding other investors provide is recognized on the parent company's balance sheet as minority interest. When valuing minority interest, it is important to realize the minority interest holder does not have a claim on the company's assets, but rather a claim on the subsidiary's assets.

The identification and valuation of nonequity financial claims are covered in detail in Chapter 12. A detailed discussion of how to analyze operating leases, unfunded pension liabilities, and employee options is presented in Chapter 27.

A common mistake made when valuing companies is to double-count claims already deducted from cash flow. Consider a company with a pension shortfall. You have been told the company will make extra payments to eliminate the liability. If you deduct the present value of the liability from enterprise value, you should not model the extra payments within free cash flow; that would mean double-counting the shortfall (once in cash flow and once as a claim), leading to an underestimate of equity value.

Valuing Equity

Once you have identified and valued all nonequity claims, subtract the claims from enterprise value to determine equity value. Home Depot has traditional debt ($11.4 billion) and capitalized operating leases ($8.3 billion). To value Home Depot's common equity, subtract each of these claims from Home Depot's enterprise value (see Exhibit 6.4).

To determine Home Depot's share price, divide the estimated common-stock value by the number of *undiluted* shares outstanding. Do not use diluted shares. We have already valued convertible debt and employee stock options separately. If we were to use diluted shares, we would be double-counting the options' value.

At the end of fiscal year 2008, Home Depot had 1.7 billion shares outstanding. Dividing the equity estimate of $46.0 billion by 1.7 billion shares generates an estimated value of $27 per share. The estimated share value assumes Home Depot can rebound from the 2008 recession, with returns slightly above its cost of capital and growth back in line with gross domestic product (GDP). During the first half of 2009, Home Depot's actual stock price traded between $20 and $25 per share.

ECONOMIC-PROFIT-BASED VALUATION MODELS

The enterprise DCF model is a favorite of academics and practitioners because it relies solely on how cash flows in and out of the company. Complex accounting can be replaced with a simple question: Does cash change hands? One shortfall of enterprise DCF, however, is that each year's cash flow provides little insight into the company's economic performance. Declining free cash flow can signal either poor performance or investment for the future. The economic-profit model highlights how and when the company creates value yet leads to a valuation that is identical to that of enterprise DCF.

Economic profit measures the value created by the company in a single period and is defined as follows:

$$\text{Economic Profit} = \text{Invested Capital} \times (\text{ROIC} - \text{WACC})$$

Since ROIC equals NOPLAT divided by invested capital, we can rewrite the equation as follows:

$$\text{Economic Profit} = \text{NOPLAT} - (\text{Invested Capital} \times \text{WACC})$$

In Exhibit 6.12, we present economic-profit calculations for Home Depot using both methods. Historically, Home Depot earned significant economic profits. But as the housing boom waned in 2007, ROIC fell below the company's cost of capital, and as a result economic profit became negative. Research

EXHIBIT 6.12 **Home Depot: Economic Profit Summary**

$ million

	Historical			Forecast		
	2006	2007	2008	2009	2010	2011
Method 1:						
Return on invested capital (percent)[1]	15.9	9.6	7.9	8.0	9.6	10.8
Weighted average cost of capital (percent)	8.4	8.2	8.3	8.5	8.5	8.5
Economic spread (percent)	7.5	1.4	−0.4	−0.4	1.1	2.3
× Invested capital (beginning of year)	39,389	46,543	38,567	37,075	34,137	35,038
= Economic profit (loss)	2,950	629	(162)	(164)	383	818
Method 2:						
Invested capital (beginning of year)	39,389	46,543	38,567	37,075	34,137	35,038
× Weighted average cost of capital (percent)	8.4	8.2	8.3	8.5	8.5	8.5
Capital charge	3,295	3,827	3,195	3,135	2,886	2,962
NOPLAT	6,245	4,456	3,033	2,971	3,269	3,780
Capital charge	(3,295)	(3,827)	(3,195)	(3,135)	(2,886)	(2,962)
Economic profit (loss)	2,950	629	(162)	(164)	383	818

[1] ROIC measured using beginning of year capital.

analysts expected economic profit to become positive again in 2009, but nowhere near its level before the housing boom.

To demonstrate how economic profit can be used to value a company—and to demonstrate its equivalence to enterprise DCF, consider a stream of growing cash flows valued using the growing-perpetuity formula:

$$\text{Value}_0 = \frac{\text{FCF}_1}{\text{WACC} - g}$$

In Chapter 2, we transformed this cash flow perpetuity into the key value driver model. The key value driver model is superior to the simple cash flow perpetuity model, because it explicitly models the relationship between growth and required investment. Using a few additional algebraic steps (see Appendix A) and the assumption that the company's ROIC on new projects equals historical ROIC, we can transform the cash flow perpetuity into a key value driver model based on economic profits:

$$\text{Value}_0 = \text{Invested Capital}_0 + \frac{\text{Invested Capital}_0 \times (\text{ROIC} - \text{WACC})}{\text{WACC} - g}$$

Finally, we substitute the definition of economic profit:

$$\text{Value}_0 = \text{Invested Capital}_0 + \frac{\text{Economic Profit}_1}{\text{WACC} - g}$$

As can be seen in the economic-profit-based key value driver model, the operating value of a company equals its book value of invested capital plus the present value of all future value created. In this case, the future economic profits are valued using a growing perpetuity, because the company's economic profits are increasing at a constant rate over time. The formula also demonstrates that when future economic profit is expected to be zero, the value of operations will equal invested capital. If a company's value of operations exceeds its invested capital, be sure to identify the sources of competitive advantage that allows the company to maintain superior financial performance.

More generally, economic profit can be valued as follows:

$$\text{Value}_0 = \text{Invested Capital}_0 + \sum_{t=1}^{\infty} \frac{\text{Invested Capital}_{t-1} \times (\text{ROIC}_t - \text{WACC})}{(1 + \text{WACC})^t}$$

Since the economic-profit valuation was derived directly from the free cash flow model (see Appendix B for a general proof of equivalence), any valuation based on discounted economic profits will be identical to enterprise DCF. To assure equivalence, however, you must use the following values:

- Beginning-of-year invested capital (i.e., last year's value).

- The same invested-capital number for both economic profit and ROIC. For example, ROIC can be measured either with or without goodwill. If you measure ROIC without goodwill, invested capital must also be measured without goodwill. All told, it doesn't matter how you define invested capital, as long as you are consistent.

- A constant cost of capital to discount projections.

Exhibit 6.13 presents the valuation results for Home Depot using economic profit. Economic profits are explicitly forecast for 10 years; the remaining years are valued using an economic-profit continuing-value formula.[9] Comparing the equity value from Exhibit 6.4 with that of Exhibit 6.13, we see that the estimate of Home Depot's intrinsic value is the same, regardless of the method.

---

[9] To calculate continuing value, you can use the economic-profit-based key value driver formula, but only if RONIC equals historical ROIC in the continuing-value year. If RONIC going forward differs from the final year's ROIC, then the equation must be separated into current and future economic profits:

$$\text{Value}_t = \text{IC}_t + \underbrace{\frac{\text{IC}_t \, (\text{ROIC}_{t+1} - \text{WACC})}{\text{WACC}}}_{\text{Current Economic Profits}} + \underbrace{\frac{\text{PV}(\text{Economic Profit}_{t+2})}{\text{WACC} - g}}_{\text{Future Economic Profits}}$$

such that

$$\text{PV}(\text{Economic Profit}_{t+2}) = \frac{\text{NOPLAT}_{t+1} \left(\frac{g}{\text{RONIC}} \right) (\text{RONIC} - \text{WACC})}{\text{WACC}}$$

EXHIBIT 6.13 **Home Depot: Economic Profit Valuation**

Year	Invested capital[1] ($ million)	ROIC[1] (percent)	WACC (percent)	Economic profit ($ million)	Discount factor (@ 8.5%)	Present value of economic profit ($ million)
2009	37,075	8.0	8.5	(164)	0.922	(151)
2010	34,137	9.6	8.5	383	0.850	325
2011	35,038	10.8	8.5	818	0.784	641
2012	36,897	11.6	8.5	1,145	0.723	827
2013	38,900	12.3	8.5	1,487	0.666	991
2014	40,821	12.3	8.5	1,550	0.614	952
2015	42,748	12.2	8.5	1,611	0.567	913
2016	44,665	12.2	8.5	1,671	0.522	873
2017	46,568	12.2	8.5	1,731	0.482	834
2018	48,453	12.1	8.5	1,789	0.444	795
Continuing value				41,922	0.444	18,619
Present value of economic profit						25,619
Invested capital in 2008						37,075
Invested capital plus present value of economic profit						62,694
Midyear adjustment factor						1.041
Value of operations						65,291
Value of excess cash						–
Value of long-term investments						361
Value of tax loss carry-forwards						112
Enterprise value						65,764
Value of debt						(11,434)
Less: Value of capitalized operating leases						(8,298)
Equity value						46,032

[1] Invested capital is measured at the beginning of the year.

The benefits of economic profit become apparent when we examine the drivers of economic profit, ROIC and WACC, on a year-by-year basis in Exhibit 6.13. The current valuation is contingent on a small and gradual improvement in ROIC from 8.0 percent to 12.1 percent, conservative by most measures. This stands in stark contrast to our assessment in 2004, when the market valuation was dependent on maintaining high returns on capital:

> The valuation depends on Home Depot's ability to maintain current levels of ROIC (17.5 percent) well above the WACC (9.3 percent). If the company's markets become saturated, growth could become elusive, and some companies might compete on price to steal market share. If this occurs, ROICs will drop, and economic profits will revert to zero.[10]

[10] Tim Koller, Marc Goedhart, and David Wessels, *Valuation: Measuring and Managing the Value of Companies*, 4th ed. (Hoboken, NJ: John Wiley & Sons, 2005), 119.

Explicitly modeling ROIC as a primary driver of economic profit prominently displays expectations of value creation. Conversely, the free cash flow model fails to show this dynamic. Free cash flow could continue to grow, even as ROIC falls.

ADJUSTED PRESENT VALUE MODEL

When building an enterprise DCF or economic-profit valuation, most financial analysts discount all future flows at a constant weighted average cost of capital. Using a constant WACC, however, assumes the company manages its capital structure to a target debt-to-value ratio.

In most situations, debt grows in line with company value. But suppose the company planned to change its capital structure significantly. Indeed, companies with a high proportion of debt often pay it down as cash flow improves, thus lowering their future debt-to-value ratios. In these cases, a valuation based on a constant WACC would overstate the value of the tax shields. Although the WACC can be adjusted yearly to handle a changing capital structure, the process is complex. Therefore, we turn to an alternative model: adjusted present value (APV).

The adjusted present value model separates the value of operations into two components: the value of operations as if the company were all-equity financed and the value of tax shields that arise from debt financing:[11]

$$\text{Adjusted Present Value} = \text{Enterprise Value as if the Company Was All-Equity Financed} + \text{Present Value of Tax Shields}$$

The APV valuation model follows directly from the teachings of economists Franco Modigliani and Merton Miller, who proposed that in a market with no taxes (among other things), a company's choice of financial structure will not affect the value of its economic assets. Only market imperfections, such as taxes and distress costs, affect enterprise value.

When building a valuation model, it is easy to forget these teachings. To see this, imagine a company (in a world with no taxes) that has a 50–50 mix of debt and equity. If the company's debt has an expected return of 5 percent and the company's equity has an expected return of 15 percent, its weighted average cost of capital would be 10 percent. Suppose the company decides to issue more debt, using the proceeds to repurchase shares. Since the cost of

---

[11] In this book, we focus on the tax shields generated by interest expense. On a more general basis, the APV values any incremental cash flows associated with capital structure, such as tax shields, issue costs, and distress costs. Distress costs include direct costs, such as court-related fees, and indirect costs, such as the loss of customers and suppliers.

debt is lower than the cost of equity, it would appear that issuing debt to retire equity should lower the WACC, raising the company's value.

This line of thinking is flawed, however. In a world without taxes, a change in capital structure would not change the cash flow generated by operations, nor the risk of those cash flows. Therefore, neither the company's enterprise value nor its cost of capital would change. So why did we think it would? When adding debt, we adjusted the weights, but we failed to properly increase the cost of equity. Since debt payments have priority over cash flows to equity, adding leverage increases the risk to equity holders. When leverage rises, they demand a higher return. Modigliani and Miller postulated that this increase would perfectly offset the change in weights.

In reality, taxes play a role in determining capital structure. Since interest is tax deductible, profitable companies can lower taxes by raising debt. But if the company relies too heavily on debt, the company's customers and suppliers may fear bankruptcy and walk away, restricting future cash flow (academics call this distress costs or deadweight costs). Rather than model the effect of capital-structure changes in the weighted average cost of capital, APV explicitly measures and values the cash flow effects of financing separately.

To build an APV-based valuation, value the company as if it were all-equity financed. Do this by discounting free cash flow by the unlevered cost of equity (what the cost of equity would be if the company had no debt).[12] To this value, add any value created by the company's use of debt. Exhibit 6.14 values Home Depot using adjusted present value. Since we assume (for expositional purposes) that Home Depot will manage its capital structure to a target debt-to-value level of 35 percent, the APV-based valuation leads to the same value for equity as did enterprise DCF (see Exhibit 6.4) and economic profit (see Exhibit 6.13). A simplified proof of equivalence between enterprise DCF and adjusted present value can be found in Appendix C. The following subsections explain APV in detail.

Valuing Free Cash Flow at Unlevered Cost of Equity

When valuing a company using the APV, we explicitly separate the unlevered value of operations (V_u) from any value created by financing, such as tax shields (V_{txa}). For a company with debt (D) and equity (E), this relationship is as follows:

$$V_u + V_{txa} = D + E \qquad (6.1)$$

A second result of Modigliani and Miller's work is that the total risk of the company's assets, real and financial, must equal the total risk of the financial

---

[12] Free cash flow projections in the APV model are identical to those presented in Exhibit 6.4. Continuing value is computed using the key value driver formula. Only the cost of capital changes.

EXHIBIT 6.14 **Home Depot: Valuation Using Adjusted Present Value**

Year	Free cash flow ($ million)	Interest tax shield ($ million)	Discount factor (@ 9.3%)	Present value of FCF ($ million)	Present value of ITS ($ million)
2009	5,909	502	0.915	5,408	460
2010	2,368	498	0.838	1,984	417
2011	1,921	521	0.767	1,473	399
2012	2,261	549	0.702	1,587	385
2013	2,854	578	0.642	1,834	371
2014	3,074	604	0.588	1,807	355
2015	3,308	630	0.538	1,780	339
2016	3,544	657	0.493	1,746	323
2017	3,783	684	0.451	1,705	308
2018	4,022	711	0.413	1,660	293
Continuing value	78,175	14,064	0.413	32,256	5,803
Present value				53,240	9,454

Present value of FCF	53,240
Present value of interest tax shields	9,454
Present value of FCF and interest tax shields	62,694
Midyear adjustment factor	1.041
Value of operations	65,291
Value of excess cash	–
Value of long-term investments	361
Value of tax loss carry-forwards	112
Enterprise value	65,764
Less: Value of debt	(11,434)
Less: Value of capitalized operating leases	(8,298)
Equity value	46,032

claims against those assets. Thus, in equilibrium, the blended cost of capital for operating assets (k_u, which we call the unlevered cost of equity) and financial assets (k_{txa}) must equal the blended cost of capital for debt (k_d) and equity (k_e):

$$\underbrace{\frac{V_u}{V_u + V_{txa}}k_u}_{\text{Operating Assets}} + \underbrace{\frac{V_{txa}}{V_u + V_{txa}}k_{txa}}_{\text{Tax Assets}} = \underbrace{\frac{D}{D+E}k_d}_{\text{Debt}} + \underbrace{\frac{E}{D+E}k_e}_{\text{Equity}} \qquad (6.2)$$

In the corporate-finance literature, academics combine Modigliani and Miller's two equations to solve for the cost of equity—to demonstrate the relationship between leverage and the cost of equity. In Appendix C, we algebraically rearrange equation 6.2 to solve for the levered cost of equity:

$$k_e = k_u + \frac{D}{E}(k_u - k_d) - \frac{V_{txa}}{E}(k_u - k_{txa}) \qquad (6.3)$$

As this equation indicates, the cost of equity depends on the unlevered cost of equity plus a premium for leverage, less a reduction for the tax deductibility of debt. Note that when a company has no debt ($D = 0$) and subsequently no tax shields ($V_{txa} = 0$), k_e equals k_u. This is why k_u is referred to as the unlevered cost of equity.

Determining the unlevered cost of equity with market data To use the APV, discount projected free cash flow at the unlevered cost of equity, k_u. Unfortunately, k_u cannot be observed directly. In fact, none of the variables on the left side of equation 6.2 can be observed directly. Only the values on the right—that is, those related to debt and equity—can be estimated using market data. Because there are so many unknowns and only one equation, we must impose additional restrictions to build an implementable relationship between k_e and k_u.

Method 1: Assume k_{txa} equals k_u If you believe the company will manage its debt-to-value ratio to a target level (the company's debt will grow with the business), then the value of the tax shields will track the value of the operating assets. Thus, the risk of tax shields will equal the risk of operating assets ($k_{txa} = k_u$). Setting k_{txa} equal to k_u, equation 6.3 can be simplified as follows:

$$k_e = k_u + \frac{D}{E}(k_u - k_d) \tag{6.4}$$

The unlevered cost of equity can now be solved using the observed cost of equity, the cost of debt, and the market debt-to-equity ratio.

Method 2: Assume k_{txa} equals k_d If you believe the market debt-to-equity ratio will not remain constant, then the value of interest tax shields will be more closely tied to the value of forecasted debt, rather than operating assets. In this case, the risk of tax shields is equivalent to the risk of debt. (When a company is unprofitable, it cannot use interest tax shields, the risk of default rises, and the value of debt drops.) Setting k_{txa} equal to k_d, equation 6.3 can be simplified as follows:

$$k_e = k_u + \frac{D - V_{txa}}{E}(k_u - k_d) \tag{6.5}$$

In this equation, the relationship between k_e and k_u relies on observable variables, such as the market value of debt, market value of equity, cost of debt, and cost of equity, as well as one unobservable variable: the present value of tax shields (V_{txa}). To use equation 6.5, discount expected future tax shields at the cost of debt (to remain consistent with the underlying assumption), and then solve for the unlevered cost of equity.

To avoid having to value the tax shields explicitly, many practitioners further refine the preceding equation by imposing an additional restriction: that the absolute dollar level of debt is constant. If the dollar level of debt is constant, V_{txa} simplifies to $D \times T_m$ (the market value of debt times the marginal tax rate), and equation 6.5 becomes:

$$k_e = k_u + (1 - T_m)\frac{D}{E}(k_u - k_d) \qquad (6.6)$$

Although equation 6.6 is commonly used, its usefulness is limited because the assumptions are extremely restrictive.

Choosing the appropriate formula Which formula should you use to estimate the unlevered cost of equity, k_u? It depends on how you see the company managing its capital structure going forward and whether the debt is risk free. The majority of companies have relatively stable capital structures (as a percentage of expected value), so we strongly favor the first method.

In periods of high debt, such as financial distress and leveraged buyouts, the second method is appropriate. Yet even if a company's tax shields are predetermined for a given period, eventually they will track value. For instance, successful leveraged buyouts pay down debt for a period of time, but once the debt level becomes reasonable, debt will more likely track value than remain constant. Thus, even in situations where leverage is high, we recommend the first method.

Valuing Tax Shields and Other Capital Structure Effects

To complete an APV-based valuation, forecast and discount capital structure side effects such as tax shields, security issue costs, and distress costs. Since Home Depot has only a small probability of default, we estimated the company's future interest tax shields using the company's promised yield to maturity and marginal tax rate (see Exhibit 6.15). To calculate the expected interest payment in 2009, multiply the prior year's net debt of $19.7 billion by the expected yield of 6.8 percent (net debt equals reported debt plus capitalized operating leases minus excess cash). This results in an expected interest payment of $1.3 billion. Next, multiply the expected interest payment by the marginal tax rate of 37.6 percent, for an expected interest tax shield of $502 million in 2009. To determine the continuing value of interest tax shields beyond 2018, use a growth perpetuity based on 2019 interest tax shields, the unlevered cost of capital, and growth in NOPLAT.

For companies with significant leverage, the company may not be able to fully use the tax shields (it may not have enough profits to shield). If there is a significant probability of default, you must model expected tax shields, rather

EXHIBIT 6.15 **Home Depot: Forecast of Interest Tax Shields**

Forecast year	Prior-year net debt ($ million)	Expected interest rate (percent)	Interest payment ($ million)	Marginal tax rate (percent)	Interest tax shield ($ million)
2009	19,732	6.8	1,337	37.6	502
2010	19,540	6.8	1,324	37.6	498
2011	20,447	6.8	1,386	37.6	521
2012	21,571	6.8	1,462	37.6	549
2013	22,683	6.8	1,537	37.6	578
2014	23,702	6.8	1,606	37.6	604
2015	24,739	6.8	1,676	37.6	630
2016	25,790	6.8	1,748	37.6	657
2017	26,854	6.8	1,820	37.6	684
2018	27,934	6.8	1,893	37.6	711
Continuing value	29,030	6.8	1,967	37.6	739

than the tax shields based on promised interest payments. To do this, reduce each promised tax shield by the cumulative probability of default.

CAPITAL CASH FLOW MODEL

When a company actively manages its capital structure to a target debt-to-value level, both free cash flow (FCF) and the interest tax shield (ITS) are discounted at the unlevered cost of equity, k_u:

$$V = \sum_{t=1}^{\infty} \frac{\text{FCF}_t}{(1 + k_u)^t} + \sum_{t=1}^{\infty} \frac{\text{ITS}_t}{(1 + k_u)^t}$$

In 2000, Richard Ruback of the Harvard Business School argued that there is no need to separate free cash flow from tax shields when both flows are discounted by the same cost of capital.[13] He combined the two flows and named the resulting cash flow (FCF plus interest tax shields) capital cash flow (CCF):

$$V = \text{PV(Capital Cash Flows)} = \sum_{t=1}^{\infty} \frac{\text{FCT}_t + \text{ITS}_t}{(1 + k_u)^t}$$

Given that Ruback's assumptions match those of the weighted average cost of capital, the capital cash flow and WACC-based valuations will lead to identical results. In fact, we now have detailed three distinct but identical

[13] Richard S. Ruback, "Capital Cash Flows: A Simple Approach to Valuing Risky Cash Flows," Social Science Research Network (March 2000).

valuation methods created solely around how they treat tax shields: WACC (tax shield valued in the cost of capital), APV (tax shield valued separately), and CCF (tax shield valued in the cash flow).

Although FCF and CCF lead to the same result when debt is proportional to value, we believe free cash flow models are superior to capital cash flow models. Why? By keeping NOPLAT and FCF independent of leverage, we can cleanly evaluate the company's operating performance over time and across competitors. A clean measure of historical operating performance leads to better forecasts.

CASH-FLOW-TO-EQUITY VALUATION MODEL

Each of the preceding valuation models determined the value of equity indirectly by subtracting debt and other nonequity claims from enterprise value. The equity cash flow model values equity directly by discounting cash flows to equity at the cost of equity, rather than at the weighted average cost of capital.[14]

Exhibit 6.16 details the cash flow to equity for Home Depot. Cash flow to equity starts with net income. Next, add back noncash expenses, and subtract investments in working capital, fixed assets, and nonoperating assets. Finally, add any increases in debt and other nonequity claims, and subtract decreases in debt and other nonequity claims. Alternatively, you can compute cash flow to equity as dividends plus share repurchases minus new equity issues. The two methods generate identical results.[15]

To value Home Depot, discount projected equity cash flows at the cost of equity (see Exhibit 6.17). Unlike enterprise-based models, this method makes no adjustments to the DCF value for nonoperating assets, debt, or capitalized operating leases. Rather, they are embedded as part of the equity cash flow.

---

[14] The equity method can be difficult to implement correctly because capital structure is embedded in the cash flow, so forecasting is difficult. For companies whose operations are related to financing, such as financial institutions, the equity method is appropriate. We discuss valuing financial institutions in Chapter 36.

[15] When performing a stand-alone equity cash flow valuation, calculate the continuing value using an equity-based variant of the key value driver formula:

$$V_e = \frac{\text{Net Income}\left(1 - \frac{g}{\text{ROE}}\right)}{k_e - g}$$

To tie the free cash flow and equity cash flow models, you must convert free cash flow continuing-value inputs into equity cash flow inputs. We did this using the following equation:

$$\text{Net Income}\left(1 - \frac{g}{\text{ROE}}\right) = \frac{\text{NOPLAT}\left(1 - \frac{g}{\text{ROIC}}\right)}{1 + \frac{D}{E}\left(1 - \frac{k_e - (1 - T)k_d}{k_e - g}\right)}$$

EXHIBIT 6.16 **Home Depot: Equity Cash Flow Summary**

$ million

	Historical			Forecast		
	2006	2007	2008	2009	2010	2011
Net income	5,761	4,395	2,260	2,183	2,477	2,947
Depreciation	1,645	1,693	1,785	1,639	1,685	1,778
Amortization	117	9	–	–	–	–
Gross cash flow	7,523	6,097	4,045	3,822	4,162	4,725
Change in operating working capital	(936)	1,066	–	292	(73)	(163)
Decrease (increase) in net long-term operating assets	(7,006)	4,152	(740)	329	(2,300)	(3,040)
Decrease (increase) in nonoperating assets	5	(324)	306	–	–	–
Decrease (increase) in net deferred tax liabilities	122	(715)	(284)	226	3	6
Increase (decrease) in short-term debt	(1,395)	2,029	(280)	75	107	107
Increase (decrease) in long-term debt	8,971	(260)	(1,716)	411	588	583
Cash flow to equity	7,284	12,045	1,331	5,155	2,486	2,218
Reconciliation of cash flow to equity						
Dividends	1,395	1,709	1,521	1,436	1,629	1,939
Share repurchases (net of stock issued)	5,889	10,336	(190)	3,719	856	279
Cash flow to equity	7,284	12,045	1,331	5,155	2,486	2,218

EXHIBIT 6.17 **Home Depot: Cash-Flow-to-Equity Valuation**

Forecast year	Cash flow to equity[1] ($ million)	Discount factor (@ 10.4%)	Present value of CFE ($ million)
2009	5,044	0.906	4,569
2010	2,486	0.821	2,040
2011	2,218	0.743	1,649
2012	2,498	0.673	1,682
2013	2,952	0.610	1,800
2014	3,145	0.552	1,738
2015	3,349	0.500	1,676
2016	3,556	0.453	1,612
2017	3,764	0.411	1,546
2018	3,974	0.372	1,478
Continuing value	63,569	0.372	23,646
Present value of cash flow to equity			43,436
Midyear adjustment amount			2,597
Equity value			46,032

[1] Cash flow to equity in 2009 excludes $111 million change in nonoperating deferred tax liabilities, as their value is incorporated elsewhere.

Once again, note how the valuation, derived using equity cash flows, matches each of the prior valuations. This occurs because we have modeled Home Depot's debt-to-value ratio at a constant level. If leverage is expected to change, the cost of equity must be appropriately adjusted to reflect the change in risk imposed on equity holders. Although formulas exist to adjust the cost of equity (as we did in the APV section earlier in this chapter), many of the best-known formulas are built under restrictions that may be inconsistent with the way you are implicitly forecasting the company's capital structure via the cash flows. This will cause a mismatch between cash flows and the cost of equity, resulting in an incorrect valuation.

It is quite easy to change the company's capital structure without realizing it when using the cash-flow-to-equity model—and that is what makes implementing the equity model so risky. Suppose you plan to value a company whose debt-to-value ratio is 15 percent. You believe the company will pay extra dividends, so you increase debt to raise the dividend payout ratio. Presto! Increased dividends lead to higher equity cash flows and a higher valuation. Even though operating performance has not changed, the equity value has mistakenly increased. What happened? Using new debt to pay dividends causes a rise in net debt to value. Unless you adjust the cost of equity, the valuation will rise incorrectly.

Another shortcoming of the direct equity approach emerges when valuing a company by business unit. The direct equity approach requires allocating debt and interest expense to each unit. This creates extra work yet provides few additional insights.

OTHER APPROACHES TO DISCOUNTED CASH FLOW

In this chapter, we valued Home Depot by discounting nominal cash flows at a cost of capital based on observable interest rates. An alternative is to value companies by projecting cash flow in real terms (e.g., in constant 2009 dollars) and discounting this cash flow at a real discount rate (e.g., the nominal rate less expected inflation). But most managers think in terms of nominal rather than real measures, so nominal measures are often easier to communicate. In addition, interest rates are generally quoted nominally rather than in real terms (excluding expected inflation).

A second difficulty occurs when calculating and interpreting ROIC. The historical statements are nominal, so historical returns on invested capital are nominal. But if the projections for the company use real rather than nominal forecasts, returns on new capital are also real. Projected returns on total capital (new and old) are a combination of nominal and real, so they are impossible to interpret. The only way around this is to restate historical performance on a real basis—a complex and time-consuming task. The extra insights gained rarely equal the effort, except in extremely high-inflation environments, described in Chapter 29.

A second alternative to the enterprise DCF method outlined earlier is to discount pretax cash flows by a pretax hurdle rate (the market-based cost of capital multiplied by 1 plus the marginal tax rate) to determine a pretax value. This method, however, leads to three fundamental inconsistencies. First, the government calculates taxes on profits after depreciation, not on cash flow after capital expenditures. By discounting pretax cash flow at the pretax cost of capital, you implicitly assume capital investments are tax deductible when made, not as they are depreciated. Furthermore, short-term investments, such as accounts receivable and inventory, are never tax deductible. Selling a product at a profit is what leads to incremental taxes, not holding inventory. By discounting pretax cash flow at the pretax cost of capital, you incorrectly assume investments in operating working capital are tax deductible. Finally, it can be shown that even when net investment equals depreciation, the final result will be downward biased—and the larger the cost of capital, the larger the bias. This bias occurs because the method is only an approximation, not a formal mathematical relationship. Because of these inconsistencies, we recommend against discounting pretax cash flows at a pretax hurdle rate.

ALTERNATIVES TO DISCOUNTED CASH FLOW

To this point, we have focused solely on discounted cash flow models. Two additional valuation techniques exist: multiples (comparables) and real options.

Multiples

Assume that you have been asked to value a company that is about to go public. Although you project and discount free cash flow to derive an enterprise value, you worry that your forecasts lack precision. One way to place your DCF model in the proper context is to create a set of comparables. One of the most commonly used comparables is the enterprise value (EV)–to–earnings before interest, taxes, and amortization (EBITA) multiple. To apply the EV/EBITA multiple, look for a set of comparable companies, and multiply a representative EV/EBITA multiple by the company's EBITA. For example, assume the company's EBITA equals $100 million and the typical EV/EBITA multiple in the industry is 9 times. Multiplying 9 by $100 million leads to an estimated value of $900 million. Is the enterprise DCF valuation near $900 million? If not, what enables the company to earn better (or worse) returns or to grow faster (or slower) than other companies in the industry?

Although the concept of multiples is simple, the methodology is misunderstood and often misapplied. In Chapter 14, we demonstrate how to build and interpret forward-looking comparables, independent of capital structure and other nonoperating items.

Real Options Using Replicating Portfolios

In 1997 Robert Merton and Myron Scholes won the Nobel Prize in economics for developing an ingenious method to value derivatives that avoids the need to estimate either cash flows or the cost of capital. (Fischer Black would have been named as a third recipient, but the Nobel Prize is not awarded posthumously.) Their model relies on what today's economists call a "replicating portfolio." They argued that if there exists a portfolio of traded securities whose future cash flows perfectly mimic the security you are attempting to value, the portfolio and security must have the same price. As long as we can find a suitable replicating portfolio, we need not discount future cash flows.

Given the model's power, there have been many recent attempts to translate the concepts of replicating portfolios to corporate valuation. This valuation technique is commonly known as real options. Unlike those for financial options, however, replicating portfolios for companies and their projects are difficult to create. Therefore, although options-pricing models may teach powerful lessons, today's applications are limited. We cover valuation using options-based models in Chapter 32.

SUMMARY

This chapter described the most common DCF valuation models, with particular focus on the enterprise DCF model and the economic-profit model. We explained the rationale for each model and reasons why each model has an important place in corporate valuation. The remaining chapters in Part Two describe a step-by-step approach to valuing a company. These chapters explain the technical details of valuation, including how to reorganize the financial statements, analyze return on invested capital and revenue growth, forecast free cash flow, compute the cost of capital, and estimate an appropriate terminal value.

REVIEW QUESTIONS

1. Exhibit 6.18 presents the income statement and reorganized balance sheet for BrandCo, an $800 million consumer products company. Using the methodology outlined in Exhibit 6.5, determine NOPLAT for year 1. Assume an operating tax rate of 25 percent. Using the methodology outlined in Exhibit 6.6, determine free cash flow for year 1.

EXHIBIT 6.18 **BrandCo: Income Statement and Reorganized Balance Sheet**

$ million

Income statement				Reorganized balance sheet		
	Today	**Year 1**			**Today**	**Year 1**
Revenues	800.0	840.0		Operating working capital[1]	70.1	73.6
Operating costs	(640.0)	(672.0)		Property and equipment	438.4	460.3
Depreciation	(40.0)	(42.0)		Invested capital	508.5	533.9
Operating profit	120.0	126.0				
				Debt	200.0	210.0
Interest expense	(16.0)	(16.0)		Shareholders' equity	308.5	323.9
Earnings before taxes	104.0	110.0		Invested capital	508.5	533.9
Taxes	(26.0)	(27.5)				
Net income	78.0	82.5				

[1] Accounts payable has been netted against inventory to determine operating working capital.

2. BrandCo currently has 50 million shares outstanding. If BrandCo's shares are trading at $19.16 per share, what is the company's market capitalization (value of equity)? Assuming the market value of debt equals today's book value of debt, what percentage of the company's enterprise value is attributable to debt, and what percentage is attributable to equity? Using these weights, compute the weighted average cost of capital. Assume the pretax cost of debt is 8 percent, the cost of equity is 12 percent, and the marginal tax rate is 25 percent.

3. Using free cash flow computed in Question 1 and the weighted average cost of capital computed in Question 2, estimate BrandCo's enterprise value using the growing-perpetuity formula. Assume free cash flow grows at 5 percent.

4. Assuming the market value of debt equals today's book value of debt, what is the intrinsic equity value for BrandCo? What is the intrinsic value per share? Does it differ from the share price used to determine the cost of capital weightings?

5. What are the three components required to calculate economic profit? Determine BrandCo's economic profit in year 1.

6. Using economic profit calculated in Question 5 and the weighted average cost of capital computed in Question 2, value BrandCo using the economic-profit-based key value driver model. Does the calculation generate enterprise value or equity value? Should discounted economic profit be greater than, equal to, or less than discounted free cash flow? Hint: remember, prior-year invested capital must be used to determine ROIC and capital charge.

7. Using the methodology outlined in Exhibit 6.16, determine equity cash flow for year 1. Use the growing-perpetuity formula (based on equity cash flow) to compute BrandCo's equity value. Assume the cost of equity is 12 percent and cash flows are growing at 5 percent.

7

Reorganizing the
Financial Statements

Traditional financial statements—the income statement, balance sheet, and statement of cash flows—are not organized for robust assessments of operating performance and value. The balance sheet mixes together operating assets, nonoperating assets, and sources of financing. The income statement similarly combines operating profits with the costs of financing, such as interest expense.

To prepare the financial statements for analysis of economic performance, you need to reorganize the items on the balance sheet, income statement, and statement of cash flows into three categories of components: operating, nonoperating, and sources of financing. This will entail searching through the notes to separate accounts that aggregate operating and nonoperating items. Although this task seems mundane, it is crucial for avoiding the common traps of double-counting, omitting cash flows, or hiding leverage that artificially boosts reported performance.

Since the process of reorganizing the financial statements is complex, this chapter proceeds in three steps. In step 1, we present a simple example demonstrating how to build invested capital, net operating profit less adjusted taxes (NOPLAT), and free cash flow (FCF). In the second step, we apply this method to the financial statements for Home Depot and Lowe's, commenting on some of the intricacies of implementation. In the final step, we provide a brief summary of advanced analytical topics, including how to adjust for operating leases, pensions, capitalized expenses, and restructuring charges. An in-depth analysis of each of these topics can be found in Part Five.

REORGANIZING THE ACCOUNTING STATEMENTS: KEY CONCEPTS

To calculate return on invested capital (ROIC) and free cash flow (FCF), we need to reorganize the balance sheet to create invested capital and likewise reorganize the income statement to create net operating profit less adjusted taxes (NOPLAT). Invested capital represents the total investor capital required to fund operations, without regard to how the capital is financed. NOPLAT represents the total after-tax operating profit (generated by the company's invested capital) that is available to all financial investors.

Return on invested capital and free cash flow are both derived from NOPLAT and invested capital. ROIC is defined as:

$$\text{ROIC} = \frac{\text{NOPLAT}}{\text{Invested Capital}}$$

and free cash flow is defined as:

$$\text{FCF} = \text{NOPLAT} + \text{Noncash Operating Expenses}$$
$$- \text{Investment in Invested Capital}$$

By combining noncash operating expenses, such as depreciation, with investment in invested capital, we can also express FCF as:

$$\text{FCF} = \text{NOPLAT} - \text{Net Increase in Invested Capital}$$

Invested Capital: Key Concepts

To build an economic balance sheet that separates a company's operating assets from its nonoperating assets and financial structure, we start with the traditional balance sheet. The accountant's balance sheet is bound by the most fundamental rule of accounting:

$$\text{Assets} = \text{Liabilities} + \text{Equity}$$

Typically, assets consist primarily of operating assets (OA), such as receivables, inventory, and property, plant, and equipment. Liabilities consist of operating liabilities (OL), such as accounts payable and accrued salaries, and interest-bearing debt (D), such as notes payable and long-term debt. Equity (E) consists of common stock, possibly preferred stock, and retained earnings. Using this more explicit breakdown of assets, liabilities, and equity leads to an expanded version of the balance sheet relationship:

$$\text{Operating Assets} = \text{Operating Liabilities} + \text{Debt} + \text{Equity}$$

The traditional balance sheet equation, however, mixes operating liabilities and sources of financing on the right side of the equation. Moving operating liabilities to the left side of the equation leads to invested capital:

$$\text{Operating Assets} - \text{Operating Liabilities} = \text{Invested Capital} = \text{Debt} + \text{Equity}$$

With this new equation, we have rearranged the balance sheet to reflect more accurately capital used for operations and the financing provided by investors to fund those operations. Note how invested capital can be calculated using the operating method—that is, operating assets minus operating liabilities—or the financing method, which equals debt plus equity.

For many companies, the previous equation is too simple. Assets consist of not only core operating assets, but also nonoperating assets (NOA), such as marketable securities, prepaid pension assets, nonconsolidated subsidiaries, and other long-term investments. Liabilities consist of not only operating liabilities and interest-bearing debt, but also debt equivalents (DE), such as unfunded retirement liabilities, and equity equivalents (EE), such as deferred taxes and income-smoothing provisions (we explain equivalents in detail later in the chapter). Expanding our original balance sheet equation:

OA		NOA		OL		D + DE		E + EE
Operating	+	Nonoperating	=	Operating	+	Debt and	+	Equity and
Assets		Assets		Liabilities		Its Equivalents		Its Equivalents

Rearranging leads to total funds invested:

OA − OL		NOA		Total		D + DE		E + EE
Invested	+	Nonoperating	=	Funds	=	Debt and	+	Equity and
Capital		Assets		Invested		Its Equivalents		Its Equivalents

From an investing perspective, total funds invested equals invested capital plus nonoperating assets. From the financing perspective, total funds invested equals debt and its equivalents, plus equity and its equivalents. Exhibit 7.1 rearranges the balance sheet into invested capital for a simple hypothetical company with only a few line items. A more sophisticated example, using real companies, is developed later in the chapter.

Net Operating Profit Less Adjusted Taxes: Key Concepts

To determine a company's after-tax operating profit, you need to compute net operating profit less adjusted taxes (NOPLAT). NOPLAT is the after-tax profit generated from core operations, excluding any gains from nonoperating assets or financing expenses, such as interest. Whereas net income is the profit available to equity holders only, NOPLAT is the profit available to *all* investors,

EXHIBIT 7.1 **An Example of Invested Capital**

$ million

Accountant's balance sheet	Prior year	Current year		Invested capital	Prior year	Current year	
Assets				**Assets**			
Inventory	200	225		Inventory	200	225	Operating liabilities are netted against operating assets
Net PP&E	300	350		Accounts payable	(125)	(150)	
Equity investments	15	25		Operating working capital	75	75	
Total assets	515	600					
				Net PP&E	300	350	
Liabilities and equity				Invested capital	375	425	
Accounts payable	125	150					Nonoperating assets are not included in invested capital
Interest-bearing debt	225	200		Equity investments	15	25	
Common stock	50	50		Total funds invested	390	450	
Retained earnings	115	200					
Total liabilities and equity	515	600		**Reconciliation of total funds invested**			
				Interest-bearing debt	225	200	
				Common stock	50	50	
				Retained earnings	115	200	
				Total funds invested	390	450	

including providers of debt, equity, and any other types of investor financing. It is critical to define NOPLAT consistently with your definition of invested capital and include only those profits generated by invested capital.

To calculate NOPLAT, we reorganize the accountant's income statement (see Exhibit 7.2) in three fundamental ways. First, interest is not subtracted from operating profit, because interest is considered a payment to the company's financial investors, not an operating expense. By reclassifying interest as a financing item, we make NOPLAT independent of the company's capital structure.

Second, when calculating after-tax operating profit, exclude any nonoperating income generated from assets that were excluded from invested capital. Mistakenly including nonoperating income in NOPLAT without including the associated assets in invested capital will lead to an inconsistent definition of ROIC (the numerator and denominator will include unrelated elements).

Finally, since reported taxes are calculated after interest and nonoperating income, they are a function of nonoperating items and capital structure. Keeping NOPLAT focused solely on operations requires that the effects of interest expense and nonoperating income also be removed from taxes. To calculate operating taxes, start with reported taxes, add back the tax shield caused by interest expense, and remove the taxes paid on nonoperating income. The resulting operating taxes should equal the hypothetical taxes that would be reported by an all-equity, pure operating company.

Since interest is tax deductible, leverage has value. But rather than factor tax shields into NOPLAT, we will account for all financing costs (including interest

EXHIBIT 7.2 **An Example of NOPLAT**

$ million

Accountant's income statement		NOPLAT		
	Current year		Current year	
Revenues	1,000	Revenues	1,000	
Operating costs	(700)	Operating costs	(700)	
Depreciation	(20)	Depreciation	(20)	
Operating profit	280	Operating profit	280	
Interest	(20)	Operating taxes[1]	(70)	← Taxes are calculated on operating profits
Nonoperating income	4	NOPLAT	210	
Earnings before taxes	264			
		After-tax nonoperating income[1]	3	← Do not include income from any asset excluded from invested capital as part of NOPLAT
Taxes	(66)	Income available to investors	213	
Net income	198			
		Reconciliation with net income		
		Net income	198	← Treat interest as a financial payout to investors, not an expense
		After-tax interest expense[1]	15	
		Income available to investors	213	

[1] Assumes a marginal tax of 25% on all income.

and its tax shield) in the cost of capital. Similarly, taxes for nonoperating income must be accounted for and should be netted directly against nonoperating income, since they are not included as part of NOPLAT.

Free Cash Flow: Key Concepts

To value a company's operations, we discount projected free cash flow at an appropriate risk-adjusted cost of capital. Free cash flow is the after-tax cash flow available to all investors: debt holders and equity holders. Unlike "cash flow from operations" reported in a company's annual report, free cash flow is independent of financing and nonoperating items. It can be thought of as the after-tax cash flow—as if the company held only core operating assets and financed the business entirely with equity. Free cash flow is defined as:

$$FCF = NOPLAT + \text{Noncash Operating Expenses}$$
$$- \text{Investments in Invested Capital}$$

As shown in Exhibit 7.3, free cash flow excludes nonoperating flows and items related to capital structure. Unlike the accountant's cash flow statement, the free cash flow statement starts with NOPLAT (instead of net income). As discussed earlier, NOPLAT excludes nonoperating income and interest expense. Instead, interest (and its tax shield) is treated as a financing cash flow.

EXHIBIT 7.3 **An Example of Free Cash Flow**

$ million

Accountant's cash flow statement	Current year	Free cash flow	Current year	
Net income	198	NOPLAT	210	
Depreciation	20	Depreciation	20	
Decrease (increase) in inventory	(25)	Gross cash flow	230	Subtract investments in operating items from gross cash flow
Increase (decrease) in accounts payable	25			
Cash flow from operations	218	Decrease (increase) in inventory	(25)	
		Increase (decrease) in accounts payable	25	
Capital expenditures	(70)	Capital expenditures	(70)	
Decrease (increase) in equality investments	(10)	Free cash flow	160	Evaluate cash flow from nonoperating assets separately from core operations
Cash flow from investing	(80)			
		After-tax nonoperating Income	3	
Increase (decrease) in debt	(25)	Decrease (increase) in equity investments	(10)	
Increase (decrease) in common stock	–	Cash flow available to investors	153	
Dividends	(113)			
Cash flow from financing	(138)	**Reconciliation of cash flow available to investors**		Treat interest as a financial payout to investors, not an expense
		After-tax interest	15	
		Increase (decrease) in interest-bearing debt	25	
		Increase (decrease) in common stock	–	
		Dividends	113	
		Cash flow available to investors	153	

Net investments in nonoperating assets and the gains, losses, and income associated with these nonoperating assets are not included in free cash flow. Instead, nonoperating cash flows should be valued separately. Combining free cash flow and nonoperating cash flow leads to cash flow available to investors. As is true with total funds invested and NOPLAT, cash flow available to investors can be calculated using two methodologies: one starts from where the cash flow is generated, and the other starts with the recipients of the cash flow. Although the two methods seem redundant, checking that both give you the same result can help you avoid line item omissions and classification pitfalls.

REORGANIZING THE ACCOUNTING STATEMENTS: IN PRACTICE

Reorganizing the statements can be difficult, even for the savviest analyst. Which items are operating assets? Which are nonoperating? Which items should be treated as debt? As equity? In the following pages, we address these questions through an examination of Home Depot, the world's largest home improvement retailer, with stores located throughout North America, and comparison with Lowe's, a direct competitor of Home Depot. Home Depot has grown rapidly over the past 10 years, generating strong returns and cash flow. But its core markets have become increasingly saturated, the real estate market has soured, and the company now faces new challenges.

Invested Capital: In Practice

This section applies the process just outlined for reorganizing financial statements to the financial statements for Home Depot and Lowe's. It demonstrates how to compute invested capital and total funds invested, and how to reconcile the two methods for computing total funds invested.

Computing Invested Capital

To compute invested capital, first reorganize the company's balance sheet. In Exhibit 7.4, we present reorganized balance sheets for Home Depot and Lowe's. The reorganized versions we present are more detailed than the balance sheets reported in each company's respective annual reports, because we have searched the footnotes for information that enables us to disaggregate any accounts that mix together operating and nonoperating items. For instance, a search of Home Depot's 2007 notes reveals that the company aggregates equity investments, intangible assets, and long-term deferred taxes within the "other assets" line item (no description of other assets was provided in 2008).[1] Since "other assets" combines operating and nonoperating items, the balance sheet in its original form would be unusable for valuation purposes.

Invested capital sums operating working capital (current operating assets minus current operating liabilities); fixed assets (e.g., net property, plant, and equipment); intangible assets (e.g., goodwill); and net other long-term operating assets (net of long-term operating liabilities). Exhibit 7.5 demonstrates this line-by-line aggregation for Home Depot and Lowe's. In the following subsections, we examine each element in detail.

Operating working capital Operating working capital equals operating current assets minus operating current liabilities. Operating current assets comprise all current assets necessary for the operation of the business, including working cash balances, trade accounts receivable, inventory, and prepaid expenses. Specifically *excluded* are excess cash and marketable securities—that is, cash greater than the operating needs of the business. Excess cash generally

---

[1] According to Home Depot's 2007 10-K, "The Company purchased a 12.5% equity interest in the newly formed HD Supply for $325 million, which is included in Other Assets in the accompanying Consolidated Balance Sheets." Regarding acquired intangibles, "The Company's intangible assets at the end of fiscal 2007 and 2006, which are included in Other Assets in the accompanying Consolidated Balance Sheets, consisted of [$100 million in 2007] and [$778 million in 2006]."

EXHIBIT 7.4 **Home Depot and Lowe's: Historical Balance Sheets**

$ million

	Home Depot			Lowe's		
	2006	2007	2008	2006	2007	2008
Assets						
Cash and cash equivalents	614	457	525	796	530	661
Receivables, net	3,223	1,259	972	–	–	–
Merchandise inventories	12,822	11,731	10,673	7,144	7,611	8,209
Short-term deferred tax assets	561	535	491	161	247	166
Other current assets	780	692	701	213	298	215
Total current assets	18,000	14,674	13,362	8,314	8,686	9,251
Net property and equipment	26,605	27,476	26,234	18,971	21,361	22,722
Goodwill	6,314	1,209	1,134	–	–	–
Notes receivable	343	342	36	165	509	253
Other assets: Equity investments	–	325	325	–	–	–
Other assets: Acquired intangibles	778	100	–	–	–	–
Other assets: Long-term deferred tax assets	7	–	4	–	–	–
Other assets: Undisclosed	216	198	69	317	313	460
Total assets	52,263	44,324	41,164	27,767	30,869	32,686
Liabilities and equity						
Short-term debt	18	2,047	1,767	111	1,104	1,021
Accounts payable	7,356	5,732	4,822	3,524	3,713	4,109
Accrued salaries	1,295	1,094	1,129	372	424	434
Deferred revenue	1,634	1,474	1,165	731	717	674
Short-term deferred tax liabilities	30	10	5	–	–	–
Other accrued expenses	2,598	2,349	2,265	1,801	1,793	1,784
Total current liabilities	12,931	12,706	11,153	6,539	7,751	8,022
Long-term debt	11,643	11,383	9,667	4,325	5,576	5,039
Deferred income taxes	1,416	688	369	735	670	660
Other long-term liabilities	1,243	1,833	2,198	443	774	910
Common stock and paid-in capital	8,051	5,885	6,133	864	745	1,012
Retained earnings	33,052	11,388	12,093	14,860	15,345	17,049
Accumulated other comprehensive income	310	755	(77)	1	8	(6)
Treasury stock	(16,383)	(314)	(372)	–	–	–
Total liabilities and shareholders' equity	52,263	44,324	41,164	27,767	30,869	32,686

represents temporary imbalances in the company's cash position and is discussed later in this section.[2]

Operating current liabilities include those liabilities that are related to the ongoing operations of the firm. The most common operating liabilities are those related to suppliers (accounts payable), employees (accrued salaries),

[2] In a company's financial statements, accountants often distinguish between cash and marketable securities, but not between working cash and excess cash. We provide guidance on distinguishing working cash from excess cash later in this chapter.

EXHIBIT 7.5 **Home Depot and Lowe's: Invested Capital Calculations**

$ million

	Home Depot			Lowe's		
	2006	**2007**	**2008**	**2006**	**2007**	**2008**
Total funds invested: Uses						
Operating cash	614	457	525	796	530	661
Receivables, net	3,223	1,259	972	–	–	–
Merchandise inventories	12,822	11,731	10,673	7,144	7,611	8,209
Other current assets	780	692	701	213	298	215
Operating current assets	17,439	14,139	12,871	8,153	8,439	9,085
Accounts payable	(7,356)	(5,732)	(4,822)	(3,524)	(3,713)	(4,109)
Accrued salaries	(1,295)	(1,094)	(1,129)	(372)	(424)	(434)
Deferred revenue	(1,634)	(1,474)	(1,165)	(731)	(717)	(674)
Other accrued expenses	(2,598)	(2,349)	(2,265)	(1,801)	(1,793)	(1,784)
Operating current liabilities	(12,883)	(10,649)	(9,381)	(6,428)	(6,647)	(7,001)
Operating working capital	4,556	3,490	3,490	1,725	1,792	2,084
Net property and equipment	26,605	27,476	26,234	18,971	21,361	22,722
Capitalized operating leases[1]	9,141	7,878	8,298	3,034	3,528	3,913
Other long-term assets, net of liabilities	(1,027)	(1,635)	(2,129)	(126)	(461)	(450)
Invested capital (excluding goodwill and acquired intangibles)	39,275	37,209	35,893	23,604	26,220	28,269
Goodwill and acquired intangibles	7,092	1,309	1,134	–	–	–
Cumulative amortization and unrecorded goodwill[2]	177	49	49	730	730	730
Invested capital	46,543	38,567	37,075	24,334	26,950	29,000
Excess cash	–	–	–	–	–	–
Nonconsolidated investments	343	667	361	165	509	253
Tax loss carry-forwards[3]	66	101	124	(33)	(1)	(56)
Total funds invested	46,952	39,335	37,560	24,466	27,458	29,197
Total funds invested: Sources						
Short-term debt	18	2,047	1,767	111	1,104	1,021
Long-term debt	11,643	11,383	9,667	4,325	5,576	5,039
Capitalized operating leases[1]	9,141	7,878	8,298	3,034	3,528	3,913
Debt and debt equivalents	20,802	21,308	19,732	7,470	10,208	9,973
Deferred income taxes: operating[3]	480	105	114	541	422	438
Deferred income taxes: nonoperating[3]	464	159	(111)	–	–	–
Cumulative amortization and unrecorded goodwill[2]	177	49	49	730	730	730
Common stock and paid-in capital	8,051	5,885	6,133	864	745	1,012
Retained earnings	33,052	11,388	12,093	14,860	15,345	17,049
Accumulated other comprehensive income	310	755	(77)	1	8	(6)
Treasury stock	(16,383)	(314)	(372)	–	–	–
Equity and equity equivalents	26,151	18,027	17,829	16,996	17,250	19,223
Total funds invested	46,952	39,335	37,560	24,466	27,458	29,197

[1] Capitalized operating lease adjustments are detailed in Exhibit 7.14.
[2] Goodwill and cumulative amortization adjustments are detailed in Exhibit 7.6.
[3] Deferred tax adjustments are detailed in Exhibit 7.8.

customers (deferred revenue), and the government (income taxes payable).[3] If a liability is deemed operating rather than financial, it should be netted from operating assets to determine invested capital. Interest-bearing liabilities are nonoperating and should *not* be netted from operating assets.

Some argue that operating liabilities, such as accounts payable, are a form of financing and should be treated no differently than debt. However, this would lead to an inconsistent definition of NOPLAT and invested capital. NOPLAT is the income available to both debt and equity holders, so when you are determining ROIC, you should divide NOPLAT by debt plus equity. Although a supplier may charge customers implicit interest for the right to pay in 30 days, the charge is an indistinguishable part of the price, and hence an indistinguishable part of the cost of goods sold. Since cost of goods sold is subtracted from revenue to determine NOPLAT, operating liabilities must be subtracted from operating assets to determine invested capital.[4]

Net property, plant, and equipment   The book value of net property, plant, and equipment (e.g., production equipment and facilities) is always included in operating assets. Situations that require using the market value or replacement cost are discussed in Chapter 8.

Net other operating assets   If other long-term assets and liabilities are small—and not detailed by the company—we can assume they are operating. To determine net other long-term operating assets, subtract other long-term liabilities from other long-term assets. This figure should be included as part of invested capital. If, however, other long-term assets and liabilities are relatively large, you will need to disaggregate each account into its operating and nonoperating components before you can calculate net other long-term operating assets.

For instance, a relatively large other long-term assets account might include nonoperating items such as deferred tax assets, prepaid pension assets, intangible assets related to pensions, nonconsolidated subsidiaries, and other equity investments. Nonoperating items should not be included in invested capital. Long-term liabilities might similarly include operating and nonoperating items. Operating liabilities are liabilities that result directly from an ongoing operating activity. For instance, Home Depot warranties some products beyond one year, collecting customer funds today but recognizing the revenue (and resulting income) only gradually over the warranty period. However, most long-term liabilities are not operating liabilities, but rather what we

[3] Retailers, such as Home Depot and Lowe's, receive customer prepayments from gift cards, prepaid product installations, and anticipated customer returns (for which funds are received but revenue is not recognized).

[4] Alternatively, we could compute return on operating assets by adding back to NOPLAT the estimated financing cost associated with any operating liabilities. This approach, however, is unnecessarily complex, requires information not readily available, and fails to provide additional insight.

deem debt and equity equivalents. These include unfunded pension liabilities, unfunded postretirement medical costs, restructuring reserves, and deferred taxes.

Where can you find the breakdown of other assets and other liabilities? In some cases, companies provide a table in the footnotes. Most of the time, however, you must work through the footnotes, note by note, searching for items aggregated within other assets and liabilities. For instance, in 2007, Home Depot aggregated a nonoperating equity investment (HD Supply) within other assets. This was reported solely in the 2007 footnote titled, "Disposition and Acquisitions."

Goodwill and acquired intangibles   In Chapter 8, return on invested capital is analyzed both with and without goodwill and acquired intangibles. ROIC with goodwill and acquired intangibles measures a company's ability to create value after paying acquisition premiums. ROIC without goodwill and acquired intangibles measures the competitiveness of the underlying business. For instance, Belgian brewer InBev has a lower ROIC with goodwill and acquired intangibles than Dutch brewer Heineken, but this difference is attributable to premiums InBev paid to acquire breweries, not poor operating performance. When ROIC is computed without goodwill and acquired intangibles, InBev's operating performance is best in class. To prepare for both analyses, compute invested capital with and without goodwill and acquired intangibles.

To evaluate goodwill and acquired intangibles properly, you need to make two adjustments. Unlike other fixed assets, goodwill and acquired intangibles do not wear out, nor are they replaceable. Therefore, you need to adjust reported goodwill and acquired intangibles upward to recapture historical amortization and impairments.[5] (To maintain consistency, amortization and impairments will not be deducted from revenues to determine NOPLAT.) In Exhibit 7.6, amortization and impairments dating back to 1999 are added back to Home Depot's recorded goodwill and acquired intangibles. For instance, Home Depot reported $117 million in amortization in 2006. This amount was added to the 2005 cumulative amortization of $60 million to give a total of $177 million in cumulative amortization for 2006.[6] In 2007, Home Depot sold a subsidiary, HD Supply, to a consortium of investors. Subsequently, goodwill, acquired intangibles, and cumulative amortization all dropped. In 2008,

---

[5] The implementation of new accounting standards (in 2001 for the United States and 2005 for Europe) radically changed the way companies account for acquisitions. Today, whether paid in cash or in stock, acquisitions must be recorded on the balance sheet using the purchase methodology. Second, goodwill is not amortized. Instead, the company periodically tests the level of goodwill to determine whether the acquired business has lost value. If it has, goodwill is impaired (written down). Intangible assets (which differ from goodwill in that they are separable and identifiable) are amortized over the perceived life of the asset.

[6] The calculation of cumulative amortization and impairments will not always match cumulative amortization reported in the company's financial statements, since reported cumulative amortization does not include impairments.

EXHIBIT 7.6 **Home Depot and Lowe's: Adjustments to Goodwill and Acquired Intangibles**

$ million

	2004	2005	2006	2007	2008
Home Depot					
Goodwill	1,394	3,286	6,314	1,209	1,134
Acquired intangibles	–	398	778	100	–
Unrecorded goodwill related to pooling	–	–	–	–	–
Cumulative amortization and impairments	31	60	177	49	49
Adjusted goodwill and acquired intangibles	1,425	3,744	7,269	1,358	1,183
Lowe's					
Goodwill	–	–	–	–	–
Acquired intangibles	–	–	–	–	–
Unrecorded goodwill related to pooling	730	730	730	730	730
Cumulative amortization and impairments	–	–	–	–	–
Adjusted goodwill and acquired intangibles	730	730	730	730	730

Home Depot did not provide details on acquired intangibles or amortization, so cumulative amortization was left constant.

The second adjustment required is to add to recorded goodwill any unrecorded goodwill (due to the old pooling of interest/merger accounting). Consider Lowe's acquisition of Eagle Garden & Hardware in 1998. Since the acquisition was recorded using pooling, no goodwill was recognized. Had Lowe's used purchase accounting, the company would have recorded $730 million in goodwill.[7] To include pooling transactions, estimate and record the incremental goodwill while simultaneously adjusting equity to represent the value of shares given away. Exhibit 7.6 shows Lowe's recapitalized goodwill from the Eagle Garden & Hardware acquisition.

Not all intangible assets are generated through corporate acquisitions. Consider purchased customer contracts, for example. Companies sometimes purchase customer contracts from distributors or competitors. In these cases, the purchase cost is recognized as an intangible asset and amortized over the life of the contract.

Computing Total Funds Invested

Invested capital represents the capital necessary to operate a company's core business. In addition to invested capital, companies can also own nonoperating assets. Nonoperating assets include excess cash and marketable securities, certain financing receivables (e.g., credit card receivables), nonconsolidated

---

[7] On the final day of trading, Eagle had 29.1 million shares outstanding at a price of $37.75. Thus, Lowe's paid approximately $1.1 billion. According to its last 10-Q, Eagle had only $370 million in total equity. Pooled goodwill equals $1.1 billion less $370 million, or $730 million.

subsidiaries, and excess pension assets. Summing invested capital and nonoperating assets leads to total funds invested.

We next evaluate various types of nonoperating assets, beginning with excess cash and marketable securities.

Excess cash and marketable securities   Do not include excess cash in invested capital. By its definition, excess cash is unnecessary for core operations. Rather than mix excess cash with core operations, analyze and value excess cash separately. Given its liquidity and low risk, excess cash will earn very small returns. Failing to separate excess cash from core operations will incorrectly depress the company's apparent ROIC.

Companies do not disclose how much cash they deem necessary for operations. Nor does the accountant's definition of cash versus marketable securities distinguish working cash from excess cash. To estimate the size of working cash, we examined the cash holdings of the S&P 500 nonfinancial companies. Between 1993 and 2000, the companies with the smallest cash balances held cash just below 2 percent of sales. If this is a good proxy for working cash, any cash above 2 percent should be considered excess.[8] Neither Home Depot nor Lowe's carried excess cash in 2007, although they each held as much as $1.5 billion in the early 2000s.

Financial subsidiaries   Some companies, including IBM, Siemens, and Caterpillar, have financing subsidiaries that finance customer purchases. Because these subsidiaries charge interest on financing for purchases, they resemble banks. Since bank economics are quite different from those of manufacturing companies, you should separate line items related to the financial subsidiary from the line items for the manufacturing business. Then evaluate the return on capital for each type of business separately. Otherwise, significant distortions of performance will make comparison with other companies impossible.

Nonconsolidated subsidiaries and equity investments   Nonconsolidated subsidiaries and equity investments should be measured and valued separately from invested capital. When a company owns a minority stake in another company, it will record the investment as a single line item on the balance sheet and will not record the individual assets owned by the subsidiary. On the income statement, only income from the subsidiary will be recorded on the parent's income statement, not the subsidiary's revenues or costs. Since only income

---

[8] This aggregate figure, however, is not a rule. Required cash holdings vary by industry. For instance, one study found that companies in industries with higher cash flow volatility hold higher cash balances. To assess the minimum cash needed to support operations, look for a minimum clustering of cash to revenue across the industry. For more on predictive cash balances, see T. Opler, L. Pinkowitz, R. Stulz, and R. Williamson, "The Determinants and Implications of Corporate Cash Holdings," *Journal of Financial Economics* 52, no. 1 (1999): 3–46. For more on why companies hold excess cash, see F. Foley, J. Hartzell, S. Titman, and G. Twite, "Why Do Firms Hold So Much Cash? A Tax-Based Explanation," *Journal of Financial Economics* 86, no. 3 (December 2007): 579–607.

and not revenue is recorded, including nonconsolidated subsidiaries as part of operations will distort margins and capital turnover. Therefore, we recommend separating nonconsolidated subsidiaries from invested capital and analyzing and valuing nonconsolidated subsidiaries separately from core operations.

Prepaid and intangible pension assets If a company runs a defined-benefit pension plan for its employees, it must fund the plan each year. And if a company funds its plan faster than its pension expenses dictate, under U.S. Generally Accepted Accounting Principles (GAAP) and International Accounting/ Financial Reporting Standards (IAS/IFRS), the company can recognize a portion of the excess assets on the balance sheet. Pension assets are considered a nonoperating asset and not part of invested capital. Their value is important to the equity holder, so they will be valued later, but separately from core operations. We examine pension assets in detail in Chapter 27.

Tax loss carry-forwards Treat tax loss carry-forwards—also known as net operating losses (NOLs)—as a nonoperating asset. The treatment of deferred taxes is discussed in more detail in a subsequent subsection.

Other nonoperating assets Other nonoperating assets, such as excess real estate and discontinued operations, also should be excluded from invested capital.

Reconciling total funds invested Total funds invested can be calculated as invested capital plus nonoperating assets, as in the previous section, or as the sum of net debt, equity, and their equivalents. The totals produced by the two approaches should reconcile. A summary of sources of financing is presented in Exhibit 7.7. We next examine each of these sources of capital contributing to total funds invested.

EXHIBIT 7.7 **Sources of Financing**

Source of capital	Description
Debt	Interest-bearing debt from banks and public capital markets
Debt equivalents	Off-balance-sheet debt and one-time debts owed to others that are not part of ongoing operations (e.g., severance payments as part of a restructuring, an unfunded pension liability, or expected environmental remediation following a plant closure)
Hybrid securities	Claims that have equity characteristics but are not yet part of owner's equity (e.g., convertible debt and employee options)
Minority interest	External shareholder that owns a minority position in one of the company's consolidated subsidiaries
Equity	Common stock, additional paid-in capital, retained earnings, and accumulated other comprehensive income
Equity equivalents	Balance sheet accounts that arise because of noncash adjustments to retained earnings; similar to debt equivalents but not deducted from enterprise value to determine equity value (e.g., most deferred-tax accounts and income-smoothing provisions)

Debt Debt includes any short-term or long-term interest-bearing liability. Short-term debt includes commercial paper, notes payable, and the current portion of long-term debt. Long-term debt includes fixed debt, floating debt, and convertible debt with maturities of more than a year.

Debt equivalents such as retirement liabilities and restructuring reserves If a company's defined-benefit plan is underfunded, it must recognize the underfunding as a liability. The amount of underfunding is not an operating liability. Rather, we treat unfunded pension liabilities and unfunded postretirement medical liabilities as a debt equivalent (and treat the net interest expense associated with these liabilities as nonoperating). It is as if the company must borrow money to fund the plan. Treating unfunded retirement expenses as debt might seem hypothetical, but for some companies, the issue has become real. In June 2003, General Motors issued $17 billion in debt, using the proceeds to reduce its pension shortfall, not to fund operations.[9]

Other debt equivalents, such as reserves for plant decommissioning and restructuring, are discussed in Chapter 26.

Hybrid securities Hybrid securities are claims against enterprise value that have characteristics similar to equity but are not part of current equity. The three most common hybrid securities are convertible debt, preferred stock, and employee options.

Minority interest A minority interest occurs when a third party owns some percentage of one of the company's consolidated subsidiaries. If a minority interest exists, treat the balance sheet amount as an equity equivalent. Treat the earnings attributable to any minority interest as a financing cash flow similar to dividends.

Equity Equity includes original investor funds, such as common stock and additional paid-in capital, as well as investor funds reinvested into the company, such as retained earnings and accumulated other comprehensive income (OCI). In the United States, accumulated OCI consists primarily of currency adjustments and aggregate unrealized gains and losses from liquid assets whose value has changed but that have not yet been sold. IFRS also includes accumulated OCI within shareholders' equity but reports each reserve separately. Any stock repurchased and held in the treasury should be deducted from total equity.

Equity equivalents such as deferred taxes Equity equivalents are balance sheet accounts that arise because of noncash adjustments to retained

---

[9] R. Barley and C. Evans, "GM Plans Record Bond Sale Thursday to Plug Pension Gap," Reuters News, June 26, 2003.

earnings. Equity equivalents are similar to debt equivalents; they differ only in that they are not deducted from enterprise value to determine equity value.

The most common equity equivalent, deferred taxes, arises from differences in how investors and the government account for taxes. For instance, the government typically uses accelerated depreciation to determine a company's tax burden, whereas the accounting statements are prepared using straight-line depreciation. This leads to cash taxes that are lower than reported taxes during the early years of an asset's life. For growing companies, this difference will cause reported taxes consistently to overstate the company's actual tax burden. To avoid this bias, use cash taxes to determine NOPLAT. Since reported taxes will now match cash taxes, the deferred tax account is no longer necessary. This is why the original deferred tax account is referred to as an equity equivalent. It represents the adjustment to retained earnings that would be made if the company reported cash taxes to investors.

Not every deferred tax account should be incorporated into cash taxes, but only deferred tax assets (DTAs) and liabilities (DTLs) *associated with ongoing operations*.[10] Nonoperating tax liabilities, such as deferred taxes related to pensions, should instead be valued as part of the corresponding liability. To compute operating cash taxes accurately, separate deferred taxes into the following three categories, and treat them as recommended:

1. *Tax loss carry-forwards:* Nonoperating tax assets such as tax loss carry-forwards should be treated as nonoperating assets.

2. *Operating deferred tax assets and liabilities:* Deferred tax liabilities (net of deferred tax assets) related to the ongoing operation of the business should be treated as equity equivalents. They will be used to compute operating cash taxes in the next section.

3. *Nonoperating deferred tax assets and liabilities:* Treat deferred tax liabilities (net of deferred tax assets) related to accounting conventions (such as acquired intangibles), nonoperating assets (such as pensions), or financial liabilities (such as convertible debt) as equity equivalents, but do *not* include them in cash taxes.

Exhibit 7.8 uses Home Depot's deferred tax footnote to disaggregate deferred taxes into tax loss carry-forwards, operating DTLs, and nonoperating DTLs. Tax loss carry-forwards totaled $124 million in 2008. Tax loss carry-forwards are a nonoperating asset and are treated as such when reorganizing the balance sheet in Exhibit 7.5. Operating deferred tax liabilities totaled $114 million in 2008. These liabilities include accounts related to accelerated

---

[10] Separating deferred taxes into operating and nonoperating items is a complex task and requires advanced knowledge of accounting conventions. For an in-depth discussion of deferred taxes, see Chapter 25.

EXHIBIT 7.8 **Home Depot: Deferred-Tax Assets and Liabilities**

$ million

Reported in Home Depot 10-K notes				Reorganized financials			
	2006	2007	2008		2006	2007	2008
Assets				**Tax loss carry-forwards**			
Accrued self-insurance liabilities	419	440	460	Net operating losses	66	108	136
State income taxes	–	105	118	Valuation allowance	–	(7)	(12)
Other accrued liabilities	603	601	490	Tax loss carry-forwards	66	101	124
Net operating losses	66	108	136				
Other deferred-tax assets	–	54	307	**Operating deferred taxes**			
Deferred-tax assets	1,088	1,308	1,511	Accelerated depreciation	(1,365)	(1,133)	(1,068)
				Accelerated inventory deduction	(137)	(118)	(114)
Valuation allowance	–	(7)	(12)	Accrued self-insurance liabilities	419	440	460
Net deferred-tax assets	1,088	1,301	1,499	State income taxes	–	105	118
				Other accrued liabilities	603	601	490
Liabilities				Operating deferred-tax assets (liabilities)	(480)	(105)	(114)
Accelerated depreciation	(1,365)	(1,133)	(1,068)				
Accelerated inventory deduction	(137)	(118)	(114)	**Nonoperating deferred taxes**			
Goodwill and other intangibles	(361)	(69)	(78)	Goodwill and other intangibles	(361)	(69)	(78)
Other deferred-tax liabilities	(103)	(144)	(118)	Other deferred-tax liabilities	(103)	(144)	(118)
Deferred-tax liabilities	(1,966)	(1,464)	(1,378)	Other deferred-tax assets	–	54	307
				Nonoperating deferred-tax assets (liabilities)	(464)	(159)	111
Deferred-tax assets (liabilities)	(878)	(163)	121	Deferred-tax assets (liabilities)	(878)	(163)	121

Source: Home Depot 10-K notes, 2006–2008.

depreciation, inventory valuation, and self-insurance. Operating DTLs are treated as an equity equivalent in Exhibit 7.5, and the change in operating DTLs will be the basis for computing cash taxes later in this chapter. The remaining items are classified as nonoperating deferred tax liabilities.

NOPLAT: In Practice

This section details how to calculate net operating profits less adjusted taxes (NOPLAT) and how to reconcile this figure with net income. NOPLAT represents total income generated from operations available to all investors.

Calculating NOPLAT

To determine NOPLAT for Home Depot and Lowe's, we turn to their respective income statements (see Exhibit 7.9) and convert the income statement into NOPLAT (see Exhibit 7.10).

Net operating profit (NOP or EBITA) NOPLAT starts with earnings before interest, taxes, and amortization of acquired intangibles (EBITA), which equals

EXHIBIT 7.9 **Home Depot and Lowe's: Historical Income Statement**

$ million

	Home Depot			Lowe's		
	2006	2007	2008	2006	2007	2008
Net sales	90,837	77,349	71,288	46,927	48,283	48,230
Cost of merchandise sold	(61,054)	(51,352)	(47,298)	(30,729)	(31,556)	(31,729)
Selling, general, and administrative	(18,348)	(17,053)	(17,846)	(9,884)	(10,656)	(11,176)
Depreciation	(1,645)	(1,693)	(1,785)	(1,162)	(1,366)	(1,539)
Amortization	(117)	(9)	–	–	–	–
EBIT	9,673	7,242	4,359	5,152	4,705	3,786
Interest and investment income	27	74	18	52	45	40
Interest expense	(392)	(696)	(624)	(206)	(239)	(320)
Nonrecurring charge	–	–	(163)	–	–	–
Earnings before taxes	9,308	6,620	3,590	4,998	4,511	3,506
Income taxes	(3,547)	(2,410)	(1,278)	(1,893)	(1,702)	(1,311)
Earnings from continuing operations	5,761	4,210	2,312	3,105	2,809	2,195
Discontinued operations	–	185	(52)	–	–	–
Net income	5,761	4,395	2,260	3,105	2,809	2,195

revenue less operating expenses (e.g., cost of goods sold, selling costs, general and administrative costs, depreciation).

Why use EBITA and not EBITDA? When a company purchases a physical asset such as equipment, it capitalizes the asset on the balance sheet and depreciates the asset over its lifetime. Since the asset loses economic value over time, depreciation must be included as an operating expense when determining NOPLAT.

Why use EBITA and not EBIT? After all, the same argument could be made for the amortization of acquired intangibles: They, too, have fixed lives and lose value over time. But the accounting for intangibles differs from the accounting for physical assets. Unlike capital expenditures, organic investment in intangibles such as brands are *expensed* and not capitalized. Thus, when the acquired intangible loses value and is replaced through further investment, the reinvestment is expensed, and the company is penalized twice: once through amortization and a second time through reinvestment. Using EBITA avoids double-counting amortization expense in this way.

Adjustments to EBITA   In some companies, nonoperating gains and expenses are embedded within EBITA. To ensure that EBITA arises solely from operations, dig through the notes to weed out nonoperating items. The most common nonoperating items are gains (or losses) related to pensions, embedded interest expenses from operating leases, and restructuring charges hidden in the cost of sales. Each of these is briefly addressed at the end of this chapter and in detail in the chapters in Part Five covering advanced valuation issues.

EXHIBIT 7.10 **Home Depot and Lowe's: NOPLAT Calculation**

$ million

	Home Depot			Lowe's		
	2006	**2007**	**2008**	**2006**	**2007**	**2008**
Income statement						
Net sales	90,837	77,349	71,288	46,927	48,283	48,230
Cost of merchandise sold	(61,054)	(51,352)	(47,298)	(30,729)	(31,556)	(31,729)
Selling, general, and administrative	(18,348)	(17,053)	(17,846)	(9,884)	(10,656)	(11,176)
Depreciation	(1,645)	(1,693)	(1,785)	(1,162)	(1,366)	(1,539)
EBITA	9,790	7,251	4,359	5,152	4,705	3,786
Add: Operating lease interest[3]	441	536	486	185	169	199
Adjusted EBITA	10,231	7,787	4,845	5,337	4,874	3,985
Operating cash taxes	(3,986)	(3,331)	(1,811)	(2,071)	(1,973)	(1,496)
NOPLAT	6,245	4,456	3,033	3,266	2,901	2,489
Operating cash taxes						
Operating taxes[1]	3,873	2,956	1,820	2,043	1,854	1,512
Increase (decrease) in operating deferred taxes[2]	113	375	(9)	28	119	(16)
Operating cash taxes	3,986	3,331	1,811	2,071	1,973	1,496
Reconciliation with net income						
Net income	5,761	4,395	2,260	3,105	2,809	2,195
Decrease (increase) in operating deferred taxes[2]	(113)	(375)	9	(28)	(119)	16
Adjusted net income	5,648	4,020	2,269	3,077	2,690	2,211
After-tax interest expense	244	432	390	127	148	199
After-tax operating lease interest expense[3]	274	333	303	114	105	124
Total income available to investors	6,166	4,784	2,962	3,318	2,943	2,533
Nonoperating taxes	23	(103)	(71)	(20)	(14)	(19)
Loss (gain) from discontinued operations	–	(185)	52	–	–	–
After-tax nonrecurring charges	–	–	102	–	–	–
After-tax amortization of intangibles	73	6	–	–	–	–
After-tax interest income	(17)	(46)	(11)	(32)	(28)	(25)
NOPLAT	6,245	4,456	3,033	3,266	2,901	2,489

[1] Operating taxes calculation detailed in Exhibit 7.12.
[2] Operating deferred tax liabilities, net of operating deferred tax assets.
[3] Operating lease interest detailed in Exhibit 7.14.

Operating cash taxes Since nonoperating items also affect reported taxes, they must be *adjusted* to an all-equity, operating level. Since interest expense is deductible before taxes, highly leveraged companies will have smaller tax burdens. Although a smaller tax burden will lead to a higher valuation, we recommend valuing financing effects in the weighted average cost of capital (WACC) or valuing them separately using adjusted present value (APV)—but not as part of after-tax operating profit.

The reasons for adjusting taxes are quite complex. In Chapter 25, we provide an in-depth explanation of the process we recommend for computing operating cash taxes. In this chapter, we focus on the simplest method. To estimate operating taxes, proceed in three steps:

1. Search the footnotes for the tax reconciliation table. For tables presented in dollars, build a second reconciliation table in percent, and vice versa. Data from both tables are necessary to complete the remaining steps.
2. Using the percent-based tax reconciliation table, determine the marginal tax rate. Multiply the marginal tax rate by adjusted EBITA to determine marginal taxes on EBITA.
3. Using the dollar-based tax reconciliation table, adjust operating taxes by other operating items not included in the marginal tax rate. The most common adjustment is related to differences in foreign tax rates.

To demonstrate the three-step process, let's examine the operating tax rate for Home Depot. Start by converting the reported tax reconciliation table to percentages. The results of this conversion are presented in the right-hand half of Exhibit 7.11. To convert a line item from dollars to percent, divide the line item by *earnings before taxes* ($3,590 million in 2008). Earnings before taxes are reported on the income statement.

Next, use the percentage-based tax reconciliation table to determine the marginal tax rate. You can use the company's statutory rate plus state or local taxes to calculate a proxy for the marginal rate. In 2008, Home Depot paid 37.6 percent in federal (35.0 percent) and state (2.6 percent) taxes. Use this marginal rate to compute taxes on adjusted EBITA. Exhibit 7.12 presents the calculation of marginal taxes on adjusted EBITA for Home Depot. In 2008, taxes on adjusted EBITA equaled $1,820 million (37.6 percent times $4,845 million in EBITA).

After computing taxes on adjusted EBITA, search the dollar-based reconciliation table for other operating taxes. For Home Depot, the only operating taxes

EXHIBIT 7.11 **Home Depot: Tax Reconciliation Tables**

$ million	2006	2007	2008		percent	2006	2007	2008
Tax reconciliation				**Step 1:**	**Reformatted tax reconciliation**			
Income taxes at statutory rate	3,258	2,317	1,257		Income taxes at statutory rate	35.0	35.0	35.0
State income taxes, net of federal	261	196	92		State income taxes, net of federal	2.8	3.0	2.6
Foreign rate differences	5	–	–		Foreign rate differences	0.1	–	–
Other, net	23	(103)	(71)		Other, net	0.2	(1.6)	(2.0)
Reported taxes	3,547	2,410	1,278		Reported taxes	38.1	36.4	35.6
Earnings before taxes	9,308	6,620	3,590					

Source: Home Depot 2008 10-K, note 6.

EXHIBIT 7.12 **Home Depot: Operating Taxes and Operating Cash Taxes**

$ million

		2004	2005	2006	2007	2008
Operating taxes						
Step 2:	Marginal tax rate (percent)	37.7	38.0	37.8	38.0	37.6
	× Adjusted EBITA	8,214	9,731	10,231	7,787	4,845
	= Marginal taxes on EBITA	3,098	3,698	3,868	2,956	1,820
Step 3:	Other operating taxes	(17)	(10)	5	–	–
	Operating taxes	3,081	3,688	3,873	2,956	1,820
Operating cash taxes						
	Operating taxes	3,081	3,688	3,873	2,956	1,820
	Increase in operating deferred taxes[1]	(548)	668	113	375	(9)
	Operating cash taxes	2,533	4,356	3,986	3,331	1,811

[1] Increase in operating deferred tax liabilities, net of operating deferred tax assets, as reported in Exhibit 7.8.

paid beyond marginal taxes were foreign rate differences.[11] In 2006, foreign rate differences resulted in $5 million of additional operating taxes. Therefore, increase taxes on adjusted EBITA by $5 million to determine operating taxes in 2006.

The tax reconciliation table for Home Depot is quite simple and requires few adjustments. For large multinationals, however, the tax footnote can be complex and may require multiple adjustments.

Adjusting for cash taxes　We recommend using operating cash taxes actually paid, if possible, rather than accrual-based taxes reported.[12] The simplest way to calculate cash taxes is to subtract the increase in *net operating deferred tax liabilities* (DTLs) from operating taxes. Exhibit 7.8 separates Home Depot's net operating DTLs from its nonoperating DTLs. Home Depot's net operating DTLs have been falling over the past few years, so reported taxes understate actual cash taxes. Subtracting (or adding) the annual increase (or decrease) in deferred taxes gives cash taxes. In 2008, operating taxes were decreased by $9 million because *operating* deferred tax liabilities rose from $105 million to $114 million, as reported in Exhibit 7.8.

Using changes in deferred taxes to compute cash taxes requires special care. As discussed in the section on invested capital, only changes in *operating-based* deferred taxes are included in cash taxes. Otherwise, changes in deferred

[11] Countries have different statutory tax rates on income. Thus, when a company's foreign income is taxed at a rate lower than its domestic income, a deduction appears on the tax reconciliation table. When foreign income is repatriated, a company's home country typically requires it to pay the difference between the two rates.

[12] Not every company discloses enough information to separate operating deferred taxes, such as accelerated depreciation, from nonoperating deferred taxes, such as those related to prepaid pension assets. When this information is unavailable, we recommend using operating taxes without a cash adjustment.

taxes might be double-counted: once in NOPLAT and potentially again as part of the corresponding item.[13] Also, deferred tax accounts rise and fall as a result of acquisitions and divestitures. However, only organic increases in deferred taxes should be included in cash taxes, not increases resulting from consolidation. For companies involved in multiple mergers and acquisitions, a clean measure of cash taxes may be impossible to calculate. When this is the case, use operating taxes rather than cash taxes.

Reconciliation to Net Income

To ensure that the reorganization is complete, we recommend reconciling net income to NOPLAT (see the lower half of Exhibit 7.10). To reconcile NO-PLAT, start with net income, and add back (or subtract) the increase (or decrease) in operating deferred tax liabilities. Next, add back after-tax interest expense from both debt and capitalized operating leases. This determines the income available to all investors. To calculate NOPLAT, add back nonoperating expenses (such as nonoperating taxes, after-tax nonrecurring charges, and the after-tax amortization of intangibles), and subtract after-tax gains and income from nonoperating assets. We do this for Home Depot and Lowe's in Exhibit 7.10.

Nonoperating income, gains, and losses   To remain consistent with the calculation of invested capital, calculate NOPLAT without interest income and without gains or losses from the corresponding assets that have been excluded. Historical returns on excess cash and other nonoperating assets should be calculated and evaluated separately.

Free Cash Flow: In Practice

This subsection details how we build free cash flow from Home Depot and Lowe's reorganized financial statements. It shows how to add in cash flow from nonoperating assets to arrive at cash flow available to investors and how to reconcile that sum with the total flow of financing.

Calculating Free Cash Flow

Free cash flow is defined as:

$$FCF = NOPLAT + Noncash\ Operating\ Expenses$$
$$- Investments\ in\ Invested\ Capital$$

---

[13] For instance, cash flow related to future taxes on pension shortfalls should be computed using projected contributions, not on the historical deferred tax account.

EXHIBIT 7.13 **Home Depot and Lowe's: Free Cash Flow Calculation**

$ million

	Home Depot			Lowe's		
	2006	2007	2008	2006	2007	2008
NOPLAT	6,245	4,456	3,033	3,266	2,901	2,489
Depreciation	1,645	1,693	1,785	1,162	1,366	1,539
Gross cash flow	7,890	6,149	4,818	4,428	4,267	4,028
Change in operating working capital	(936)	(739)	–	168	(67)	(292)
Net capital expenditures	(3,349)	(3,577)	(543)	(3,779)	(3,756)	(2,900)
Decrease (increase) in capitalized operating leases	(1,214)	1,262	(419)	291	(494)	(385)
Investments in goodwill and acquired intangibles	(3,525)	–	175	–	–	–
Decrease (increase) in net long-term operating assets	224	457	494	52	335	(11)
Increase (decrease) in accumulated other comprehensive income	(99)	445	(832)	–	7	(14)
Gross investment	(8,899)	(2,152)	(1,125)	(3,268)	(3,975)	(3,602)
Free cash flow	(1,009)	3,998	3,693	1,160	292	426
After-tax interest income	17	46	11	32	28	25
After-tax nonrecurring charge	–	–	(102)	–	–	–
Loss (gain) from discontinued operations	–	185	(52)	–	–	–
Nonoperating taxes	(23)	103	71	20	14	19
Decrease (increase) in excess cash	–	–	–	11	–	–
Decrease (increase) in long-term investments	5	(324)	306	129	(344)	256
Decrease (increase) in net loss carry-forwards	(3)	(35)	(23)	(6)	(32)	55
Sale of HD Supply	–	8,743	–	–	–	–
Nonoperating cash flow	(4)	8,718	211	186	(334)	355
Cash flow available to investors	(1,013)	12,716	3,904	1,346	(42)	781
After-tax interest expense	244	432	390	127	148	199
After-tax operating lease interest expense	274	333	303	114	105	124
Decrease (increase) in short-term debt	1,395	(2,029)	280	(79)	(993)	83
Decrease (increase) in long-term debt	(8,971)	260	1,716	(826)	(1,251)	537
Decrease (increase) in capitalized operating leases	(1,214)	1,262	(419)	291	(494)	(385)
Flows to debt holders	(8,272)	258	2,269	(373)	(2,485)	557
Decrease (increase) in nonoperating deferred taxes	(282)	302	270	–	–	–
Dividends	1,395	1,709	1,521	276	428	491
Repurchased and retired shares	5,889	10,336	(190)	1,400	2,007	(267)
Adjustments to retained earnings	257	111	34	43	8	–
Flows to equity holders	7,259	12,458	1,635	1,719	2,443	224
Cash flow available to investors	(1,013)	12,716	3,904	1,346	(42)	781

[1] Increase in nonoperating deferred tax liabilities, net of nonoperating deferred tax assets.

Exhibit 7.13 builds the free cash flow calculation and reconciles free cash flow to cash flow available to investors for both Home Depot and Lowe's. The components of free cash flow are gross cash flow, investments in invested capital, and effects of acquisitions and divestitures.

Gross cash flow Gross cash flow represents the cash flow generated by the company's operations. It represents the cash available for investment and investor payout without the company having to sell nonoperating assets (e.g., excess cash) or raise additional capital. Gross cash flow has two components:

1. *NOPLAT:* As previously defined, net operating profits less adjusted taxes are the after-tax operating profits available to all investors.

2. *Noncash operating expenses:* Some expenses deducted from revenue to generate NOPLAT are noncash expenses. To convert NOPLAT into cash flow, add back noncash expenses. The two most common noncash expenses are depreciation and noncash employee compensation. Do not add back intangibles amortization and impairments to NOPLAT; they were not subtracted in calculating NOPLAT.

Investments in invested capital   To maintain and grow their operations, companies must reinvest a portion of their gross cash flow back into the business. To determine free cash flow, subtract gross investment from gross cash flow. We segment gross investment into five primary areas:

1. *Change in operating working capital:* Growing a business requires investment in operating cash, inventory, and other components of working capital. Operating working capital excludes nonoperating assets, such as excess cash, and financing items, such as short-term debt and dividends payable.

2. *Net capital expenditures:* Net capital expenditures equals investments in property, plant, and equipment (PP&E), less the book value of any PP&E sold. Net capital expenditures are estimated by adding the increase in net PP&E to depreciation. Do not estimate capital expenditures by taking the change in gross PP&E. Since gross PP&E drops when companies retire assets (which has no cash implications), the change in gross PP&E will often understate the actual amount of capital expenditures.

3. *Change in capitalized operating leases:* To keep the definitions of NOPLAT, invested capital, and free cash flow consistent, include investments in capitalized operating leases in gross investment.

4. *Investment in goodwill and acquired intangibles:* For acquired intangible assets, where cumulative amortization has been added back, we can estimate investment by computing the change in net goodwill and acquired intangibles. For intangible assets that are being amortized, use the same method as for determining net capital expenditures (by adding the increase in net intangibles to amortization).

5. *Change in other long-term operating assets, net of long-term liabilities:* Subtract investments in other net operating assets. As with invested capital, do not confuse other long-term operating assets with other long-term nonoperating assets, such as equity investments and excess pension

assets. Changes in equity investments need to be evaluated—but should be measured separately.

Since companies translate foreign balance sheets into their home currencies, changes in accounts will capture both true investments (which involve cash) and currency-based restatements (which are merely accounting adjustments and not the flow of cash in or out of the company). Removing the currency effects line item by line item is impossible. But we can partially undo their effect by subtracting the increase in the equity item titled "foreign currency translation effect," which under U.S. GAAP and IFRS is found within the "accumulated other comprehensive income" (OCI) account.[14] By subtracting the increase, we undo the effect of changing exchange rates.

Effect of acquisitions and divestitures   Another effect that contributes to the change in balance sheet accounts is restatements due to acquisitions and divestitures. For instance, Home Depot divested its HD Supply business in 2007 for approximately $8 billion. This caused an artificial drop in many accounts on the balance sheet, such as inventory, even though the company continued to invest in these accounts. As an example, consider merchandise inventories reported in Exhibit 7.4. The account decreased by $1.1 billion from $12,822 million in 2006 to $11,731 million in 2007. From a cash perspective, however, the company reported (in their 2007 cash flow from operating activities) an investment of $491 million in inventory. To reconcile the change in accounts with the actual cash expenditures, the difference of $1,582 million was reallocated to "sale of HD Supply" and recorded as a nonoperating cash flow.[15] Although not shown, adjustments related to the sale of HD Supply in 2007 are made to a number of accounts, including receivables, inventories, accounts payable, deferred revenues, PP&E, goodwill, and acquired intangibles.

Cash Flow Available to Investors

Although not included in free cash flow, cash flows related to nonoperating assets are valuable in their own right. They must be evaluated and valued separately and then added to free cash flow to give the total cash flow available to investors:

$$\begin{array}{ccc} \text{Present Value} & \text{Value of} & \text{Total Value} \\ \text{of Company's} + \text{Nonoperating} = & \text{of} \\ \text{Free Cash Flow} & \text{Assets} & \text{Enterprise} \end{array}$$

[14] In the 2008 annual report, Home Depot reported that "Accumulated Other Comprehensive Income consists primarily of foreign currency translation adjustments." Therefore, the change in accumulated other comprehensive income is included in gross investment in Exhibit 7.13.

[15] Adjusting for acquisitions and divestitures is a time-consuming process. Therefore, adjust cash flow to allow for the effects of both only when the resulting adjustments will be substantial.

To reconcile free cash flow with total cash flow available to investors, include the following nonoperating cash flows:

- *Cash flow related to excess cash and marketable securities:* Excess cash and marketable securities generate cash flow through interest income and asset sales. When you add investment income to cash flow, it must be added back on an after-tax basis, using the marginal tax rate.

- *Cash flow from other nonoperating assets:* Add other nonoperating income and gains (or subtract losses) less increases in other nonoperating assets (or plus decreases). It is best to combine nonoperating income and changes in nonoperating assets; otherwise, a distorted picture could emerge. Consider a company that impaired a $100 million equity investment. If we examine the change in equity investments alone, it appears that the company sold $100 million in nonoperating assets. But this assessment is misleading because no cash actually changed hands; the asset was merely marked down. If we combine the $100 million change (positive cash flow) with the $100 million reported loss (negative cash flow) from the income statement, we see the true impact is zero.

Reconciling Cash Flow Available to Investors

Cash flow available to investors should be identical to total financing flow. By modeling cash flow to and from investors, you will catch mistakes otherwise missed. Financial flows include flows related to debt, debt equivalents, and equity:

- *After-tax interest expenses:* After-tax interest should be treated as a financing flow. When computing after-tax interest, use the same marginal tax rate used for NOPLAT.

- *Debt issues and repurchases:* The change in debt represents the net borrowing or repayment on all the company's interest-bearing debt, including short-term debt, long-term debt, and capitalized operating leases.

- *Dividends:* Dividends include all cash dividends on common and preferred shares. Dividends paid in stock have no cash effects and should be ignored.

- *Share issues and repurchases:* When new equity is issued or shares are repurchased, four accounts will be affected: common stock, additional paid-in capital, treasury shares, and retained earnings (for shares that are retired). Although different transactions will have varying effects on the individual accounts, we focus on the aggregate change of the four accounts combined. In Exhibit 7.13, we refer to the aggregate change as "repurchased and retired shares."

- *Change in debt equivalents:* Since accrued pension liabilities and accrued postretirement medical liabilities are considered debt equivalents (see Chapter 27 for more on issues related to pensions and other postretirement benefits), their changes should be treated as a financing flow. Equity equivalents such as operating deferred taxes should not be included in the financing flow, because they are already included as part of NOPLAT.

ADVANCED ANALYTICAL ISSUES

Until now, we have focused on the issues you will typically encounter when analyzing a company. Depending on the company, you may come across difficult (and technical) accounting issues that can affect the estimation of NOPLAT, invested capital, and free cash flow. In this section, we summarize a set of advanced analytical topics, including operating leases, pensions, capitalized research and development (R&D), restructuring charges, and restructuring reserves. Although we provide a brief summary of these topics here, each one is discussed in depth in the chapters of Part Five, "Advanced Valuation Issues." Note, however, that not every issue will lead to material differences in ROIC, growth, and free cash flow. Before collecting extra data and estimating required unknowns, decide whether the adjustment will further your understanding of a company and its industry.

Operating Leases

When a company leases an asset under certain conditions, it need not record either an asset or a liability. Instead, it records the asset's rental charge as an expense and reports future commitments in the notes. To compare asset intensity meaningfully across companies with different leasing policies, include the value of the lease as an operating asset, with a corresponding debt recorded as a financing item. Otherwise, companies that lease assets will appear "capital light" relative to identical companies that purchase the assets.

Companies typically do not disclose the value of their leased assets. Chapter 27 evaluates alternatives for estimating value. We focus on one in particular: multiplying rental expense by an appropriate capitalization factor, based on the cost of debt (k_d) and average asset life.[16] As shown in Chapter 27, the asset value can be estimated as:

$$\text{Asset Value}_{t-1} = \left(\frac{\text{Rental Expense}_t}{k_d + \frac{1}{\text{Asset Life}}} \right)$$

[16] Chapter 27 derives an appropriate capitalization factor based on the cost of secured debt and average asset life.

EXHIBIT 7.14 **Home Depot and Lowe's: Capitalizing Operating Leases**

$ million

	Home Depot			Lowe's		
	2006	**2007**	**2008**	**2006**	**2007**	**2008**
EBITA						
EBITA	9,790	7,251	4,359	5,152	4,705	3,786
Implied interest[1]	441	536	486	185	169	199
Adjusted EBITA	10,231	7,787	4,845	5,337	4,874	3,985
Operating cash taxes						
Operating cash taxes	3,819	3,128	1,629	2,000	1,909	1,420
Tax shield on operating lease interest expense	167	204	182	71	64	76
Adjusted operating cash taxes	3,986	3,331	1,811	2,071	1,973	1,496
NOPLAT						
NOPLAT (using rental expense)	5,971	4,123	2,730	3,152	2,796	2,366
NOPLAT (capitalizing operating leases)	6,245	4,456	3,033	3,266	2,901	2,489
Invested capital						
Invested capital	37,403	30,689	28,778	21,300	23,422	25,086
Capitalized operating leases	9,141	7,878	8,298	3,034	3,528	3,913
Invested capital (with operating leases)	46,543	38,567	37,075	24,334	26,950	29,000
Return on average capital (percent)						
ROIC (using rental expenses)	17.3	12.1	9.2	14.3	12.5	9.8
ROIC (capitalizing operating leases)	14.5	10.5	8.0	14.0	11.3	8.9

[1] Implied interest equals each company's cost of debt times the prior year's value of operating leases. We normally prefer to use the secured cost of debt to compute an embedded interest expense, but instead use the company's cost of debt in order to tie enterprise DCF to equity cash flow valuation in Chapter 6.

For Home Depot, if we apply the 5.2 percent cost of secured debt (AA-rated debt) current at the time of writing and assume an asset life of 20 years, we can convert $846 million in rental expense to $8.3 billion in operating leases.[17] Exhibit 7.14 presents the resulting adjustment for operating leases for Home Depot and Lowe's. If operating leases are capitalized on the balance sheet, eliminate the interest cost embedded in rental expense from operating profits. In Exhibit 7.14, $486 million in embedded interest is added back to reported EBITA to compute adjusted EBITA. Also, operating taxes are adjusted to remove the associated tax shield. This raises both the numerator (NOPLAT) and the denominator (invested capital) of ROIC, but making these adjustments typically lowers a company's ROIC. For Home Depot, return on average invested capital drops from 9.2 percent to 8.0 percent upon the capitalization of leases.

The choice of accounting treatment for leases will not affect intrinsic value as long as it is incorporated correctly in free cash flow, the cost of capital,

[17] We use AA-rated debt in May 2009 to estimate lease interest cost because, unlike Home Depot's general obligation debt, leases are typically collateralized by physical assets. Rental expense is not typically disclosed in the financial statements. For Home Depot, rental expense of $846 million is reported in Note 9, Leases, in the company's 2008 annual report.

and debt equivalents. Chapter 27 describes the process for valuing leases in depth, and includes adjustments to free cash flow, cost of capital, and enterprise value.

Pensions and Other Postretirement Benefits

Following the passage of FASB Statement 158 under U.S. GAAP in 2006, companies now report the present value of pension shortfalls (and excess pension assets) directly on the balance sheet.[18] Since excess pension assets do not generate operating profits, nor do pension shortfalls fund operations, pension accounts should not be included in invested capital. Instead, pension assets should be treated as nonoperating, and pension shortfalls as a debt equivalent (and both should be valued separately from operations).[19] Reporting rules under IFRS (IAS 19) differ slightly in that companies can postpone recognition of their unfunded pension obligations resulting from changes in actuarial assumptions, but only as long as the cumulative unrecognized gain or loss does not exceed 10 percent of the obligations. This difference in accounting standards will not affect the treatment of excess pension assets or shortfalls when you are reorganizing the balance sheet, but will affect the valuation. For companies reporting under IFRS, search the notes for the current value of obligations.

FASB Statement 158 addressed deficiencies concerning pension obligations on U.S. balance sheets, but not on income statements. Pension expense, often embedded in cost of sales, aggregates the benefits given to employees for current work (known as the service cost) and the interest cost associated with pension liabilities, less the expected return on plan assets. The difference between expected return and interest cost will distort operating profit. Thus, to reflect the true economic expenses of pension benefits given to employees during the current period, remove the accounting pension expense from cost of sales, and replace it with service cost and amortization of prior service costs reported in the notes. For companies that use IFRS, extra care is required. The components of net pension cost can be included in different line items in the income statement (e.g., interest costs as part of interest expenses). Companies typically disclose the amounts for each component and the line on the income statement where the amount is included. Chapter 27 details how to use the pension note to create a clean measure of operating profit. The chapter also discusses how to analyze and value pensions.

---

[18] From December 2006, FASB Statement 158 eliminated pension smoothing on the balance sheet. Companies are now required to report excess pension assets and unfunded pension obligations on the balance sheet at their current values, not smoothed value as in the past.

[19] If pension accounts are not explicitly detailed on the company's balance sheet, search the pension footnote to determine where they are embedded. Often excess pension assets are embedded in other assets, and unfunded pension liabilities in other liabilities.

Capitalized Research and Development

In line with the conservative principles of accounting, accountants expense research and development (R&D), advertising, and certain other expenses in their entirety in the period they are incurred, even when economic benefits resulting from such expenses continue beyond the current reporting period. For companies that rely significantly on intangible assets, this practice will dramatically understate invested capital and overstate return on capital. If possible, therefore, R&D and other quasi investments should be capitalized and amortized in a manner similar to that used for capital expenditures. Equity should be adjusted correspondingly to balance the invested-capital equation.

If you decide to capitalize R&D, the R&D expense must *not* be deducted from revenue to calculate operating profit. Instead, deduct the amortization associated with past R&D investments, using a reasonable amortization schedule. Since amortization is based on past investments (versus expense, which is based on current outlays), this will prevent cuts in R&D from driving short-term improvements in ROIC.

Similar to the choice of accounting treatment for leasing, the choice of whether to capitalize certain expenses will not affect computed value; it will affect only perceptions of value creation. Chapter 28 analyzes the complete valuation process, including adjustments to free cash flow, and final value.

Nonoperating Charges and Restructuring Reserves

Provisions are noncash expenses that reflect future costs or expected losses. Companies record provisions by reducing current income and setting up a corresponding reserve as a liability (or deducting the amount from the relevant asset).

For the purpose of analyzing and valuing a company, we categorize provisions into one of four types: ongoing operating provisions, long-term operating provisions, nonoperating restructuring provisions, or provisions created for the purpose of smoothing income (transferring income from one period to another). Based on the characteristics of each provision, adjust the financial statements to reflect the company's true operating performance:

- *Ongoing operating provisions:* Operating provisions such as product warranties are part of operations. Therefore, deduct the provision from revenue to determine NOPLAT, and deduct the corresponding reserve from net operating assets to determine invested capital.

- *Long-term operating provisions:* For certain liabilities, such as expected plant decommissioning costs, deduct the operating portion from revenue to determine NOPLAT, and treat the interest portion as nonoperating. Treat the corresponding reserve as a debt equivalent.

- *Nonoperating provisions:* Restructuring charges, such as expected severance during a layoff, are nonoperating. Treat the expense as nonoperating and the corresponding reserve as a debt equivalent.

- *Income-smoothing provisions:* Provisions for the sole purpose of income smoothing should be treated as nonoperating, and their corresponding reserve as an equity equivalent. Since income-smoothing provisions are noncash, they do not affect value.

The process for classifying and properly adjusting for provisions and reserves is complex. Chapter 26 provides examples.

REVIEW QUESTIONS

1. Exhibit 7.15 presents the income statement and balance sheet for Companies A, B, and C. Compute each company's return on assets, return on equity, and return on invested capital. Based on the three ratios, which company has the best operating performance?

2. Why does the return on assets differ between Company A and Company B? Why do companies with equity investments tend to have a lower return on assets than companies with only core operations?

3. Why does the return on equity differ between Company A and Company C? Is this difference attributable to operating performance? Does return on assets best reflect operating performance? If not, which ratio does and why?

EXHIBIT 7.15 **Ratio Analysis: Consolidated Financial Statements**

$ million

	Company A	Company B	Company C
Operating profit	100	100	100
Interest	–	–	(20)
Earnings before taxes	100	100	80
Taxes	(25)	(25)	(20)
Net income	75	75	60
Balance sheet			
Inventory	125	125	125
Property and equipment	400	400	400
Equity investments	–	50	–
Total assets	525	575	525
Accounts payable	50	50	50
Debt	–	–	200
Equity	475	525	275
Liabilities and equity	525	575	525

EXHIBIT 7.16 **HealthCo: Income Statement and Balance Sheet**

$ million

Income statement			Balance sheet		
	Prior year	Current year		Prior year	Current year
Revenues	605	665	Working cash	5	5
Cost of sales	(200)	(210)	Accounts receivable	45	55
Selling costs	(300)	(320)	Inventories	15	20
Depreciation	(40)	(45)	Current assets	65	80
Operating profit	65	90			
			Property, plant, and equipment	250	260
Interest expense	(5)	(15)	Prepaid pension assets	10	50
Gain on sale	–	25	Total assets	325	390
Earnings before taxes	60	100			
			Accounts payable	10	15
Taxes	(16)	(40)	Short-term debt	20	40
Net income	44	60	Restructuring reserves	20	–
			Current liabilities	50	55
			Long-term debt	70	70
			Shareholders' equity	205	265
			Liabilities and equity	325	390

4. Exhibit 7.16 presents the income statement and balance sheet for HealthCo, a $665 million health care company. Compute NOPLAT, average invested capital, and ROIC. Assume an operating tax rate of 25 percent and a marginal tax rate of 35 percent.[20] If the weighted average cost of capital is 9 percent, is the company creating value?

5. Using the reorganized financial statements created in Question 4, what is the free cash flow for HealthCo in the current year?

6. You decide to look closer at HealthCo's current-year tax reconciliation footnote. The table reports $35 million in statutory taxes, a $5 million credit for manufacturing investments, and a one-time tax expense of $10 million related to a past-year audit. Reported taxes are therefore $40 million. What is HealthCo's statutory tax rate, operating tax rate, and effective rate? Why does computing the operating tax rate require judgment?

7. Many companies hold significant amounts of excess cash, that is, cash above the amount required for day-to-day operations. Does including excess cash as part of invested capital distort the ROIC upward or downward? Why?

[20] If you choose to reconcile NOPLAT with net income, nonoperating taxes are $1.5 million and $14.0 million in the prior and current year respectively. This will not match the in-depth tax analysis in Question 6.

8

Analyzing Performance
and Competitive Position

Understanding a company's past is essential to forecasting its future. For that reason, a critical component of valuation is the robust analysis of historical performance. Always start with the key drivers of value: return on invested capital (ROIC) and revenue growth. Examine trends in the company's long-run performance and its performance relative to that of its peers, so you can base your forecasts of future cash flows on reasonable assumptions about the company's key value drivers.

Start by analyzing ROIC, both with and without goodwill. ROIC with goodwill measures the company's ability to create value over and above premiums paid for acquisitions. ROIC without goodwill is a better measure of the company's performance compared with that of its peers. Then drill down into the components of ROIC to build an integrated view of the company's operating performance, and understand which aspects of the business are responsible for its overall performance. Next, examine the drivers of revenue growth. Is revenue growth driven, for instance, more by organic growth (critical to value creation, as discussed in Chapter 5) or by currency effects, which are largely beyond management control and probably not sustainable? Finally, assess the company's financial health to determine whether it has the financial resources to conduct business and make short- and long-term investments.

The first three sections of this chapter go through the steps involved in analyzing ROIC, revenue growth, and financial health, respectively. The final section of this chapter covers an alternative measure of financial performance: cash flow return on investment (CFROI).

ANALYZING RETURNS ON INVESTED CAPITAL

In Chapter 7, we reorganized the income statement into net operating profit less adjusted taxes (NOPLAT) and the balance sheet into invested capital. ROIC measures the ratio of NOPLAT to invested capital:

$$ROIC = \frac{NOPLAT}{Invested\ Capital}$$

Since profit is measured over an entire year, whereas capital is measured only at one point in time, we recommend that you average starting and ending invested capital. Companies that report ROIC in their annual reports often use starting capital. If new assets acquired during the year generate additional income, however, using starting capital alone will overestimate ROIC.

ROIC is a better analytical tool for understanding the company's performance than return on equity (ROE) or return on assets (ROA) because it focuses solely on a company's operations. Return on equity mixes operating performance with capital structure, making peer group analysis and trend analysis less meaningful. Return on assets (even when calculated on a preinterest basis) is an inadequate measure of performance because it not only includes non-operating assets but also ignores the benefits of accounts payable and other operating liabilities that together reduce the amount of capital required from investors.

Exhibit 8.1 plots ROIC for Home Depot and Lowe's from 2000 to 2008 based on invested capital and NOPLAT calculations (presented in Exhibits 7.5 and 7.10). The ROIC at Home Depot outpaced Lowe's by approximately five percentage points during the early 2000s. This gap disappeared in 2005, when Home Depot began acquiring other companies.[1] Although core operating profit improved in 2005, the premiums paid for acquisitions lowered ROIC. In 2007, the U.S. housing market collapsed, and ROIC fell dramatically for both companies. By 2008, Home Depot's ROIC trailed Lowe's by approximately one percentage point, with both companies earning roughly their cost of capital.

Analyzing ROIC with and without Goodwill and Acquired Intangibles

ROIC should be computed both with and without goodwill and acquired intangibles,[2] because each ratio analyzes different things. For instance, a company

---

[1] In 2005, Home Depot completed 21 acquisitions, including National Waterworks and Williams Bros. Lumber Company. According to the company's 2005 10-K, the total cash paid for businesses acquired in fiscal 2005 was $2.5 billion.

[2] Goodwill and acquired intangibles are intangible assets purchased in an acquisition. To be classified as an acquired intangible, the asset must be separable and identifiable, such as patents. Goodwill describes assets that are not separable or identifiable. In our analysis, we treat goodwill identically to acquired intangibles. Therefore, we will often shorten the expression *goodwill and acquired intangibles* to *goodwill*.

EXHIBIT 8.1 **Home Depot and Lowe's: Return on Invested Capital**[1]

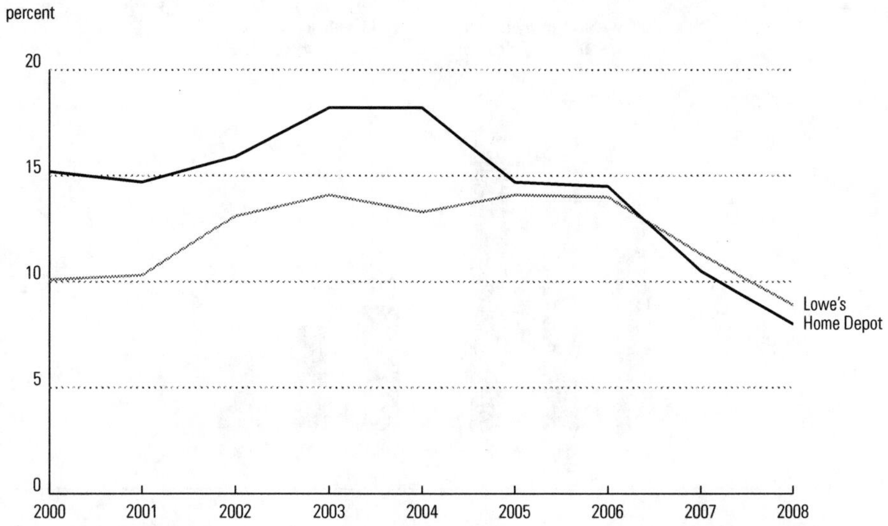

percent

¹ ROIC measured with goodwill and acquired intangibles. Goodwill and acquired intangibles do not meaningfully affect ROIC for either company.

that purchases another at a premium to book must spend real resources to acquire valuable economic assets. If the company does not properly compensate investors for the funds spent (or shares given away), it will destroy value. Thus, when you measure aggregate value creation for the company's shareholders, measure ROIC with goodwill. Conversely, ROIC excluding goodwill measures the underlying operating performance of the company and its businesses and is used to compare performance against peers and to analyze trends. It is not distorted by the price premiums paid for acquisitions.

For both Home Depot and Lowe's, goodwill is a relatively small part of invested capital, but for companies that make significant acquisitions, the difference between ROIC with and without goodwill can be large. Exhibit 8.2 presents ROIC with and without goodwill for the U.S. pharmacy CVS Caremark and a leading competitor. In 2006, CVS, as it was then known, earned an 18.4 percent ROIC without goodwill, compared with 17.9 percent for its leading competitor. In 2007, CVS purchased Caremark, a pharmaceutical benefits manager (PBM). PBMs have little working capital or fixed assets, so they have high ROICs. Consequently, CVS's aggregate ROIC without goodwill rose to 33.6 percent by 2008, reflecting the addition of a high-ROIC business. This aggregate ROIC cannot be used for benchmarking against peers, however. To understand the company's future value-creating potential, you need to examine the company's performance at the business unit level, because its two major businesses have such different underlying economics.

531

EXHIBIT 8.2 **CVS Caremark: Return on Invested Capital**

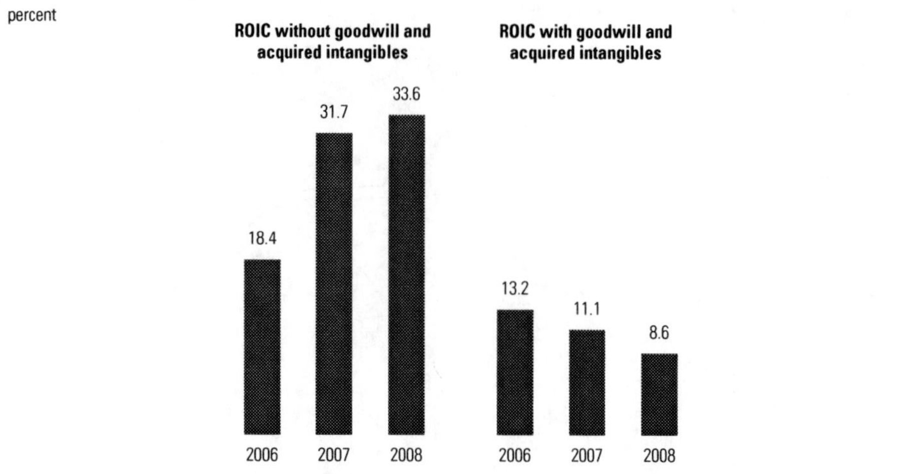

percent

Whereas CVS Caremark's ROIC without goodwill exceeds that of its competitor, the converse is true when ROIC is measured with goodwill. The premiums paid for acquisitions drop CVS Caremark's ROIC from 18.4 percent to 13.2 percent in 2006, below that of its leading competitor. Since the 2007 Caremark acquisition required a premium as well, the combined company's ROIC with goodwill fell to just 8.6 percent by 2008. Does the significant difference in ROIC when measured with and without goodwill imply the acquisition destroys value? It is too early to judge: since cost savings and cross selling opportunities take time to realize, it may take several years for the acquisition's return on capital to exceed its cost of capital.

Analyzing ROIC Using Market versus Book Invested Capital

The traditional measure of ROIC divides NOPLAT by invested capital stated at book value. Thus, ROIC represents the rate of return on capital at its original cost (less depreciation). Although this provides a good ex post measure of financial performance, it should not be used to make entry and exit decisions. Consider a company that built a facility for $1 billion five years ago. The facility is currently generating just $10 million in NOPLAT. Because the facility's 1 percent ROIC is well below its 10 percent cost of capital, the CEO recommends selling the facility. But what if the facility can be sold for only $50 million because the facility has little value to another owner? In this case, the rate of return (based on market-based opportunity costs, not book value) is 20 percent. At $50 million, the CEO would be better off keeping the facility than selling it, assuming current profits can be maintained.

Decomposing ROIC to Build an Integrated Perspective of Company Economics

Between 2006 and 2008, ROICs at both Home Depot and Lowe's fell dramatically. But what is causing this drop in performance? To understand which elements of a company's business are driving the company's ROIC, split apart the ratio as follows:

$$ROIC = (1 - \text{Operating Cash Tax Rate}) \times \frac{EBITA}{Revenues} \times \frac{Revenues}{Invested\ Capital}$$

The preceding equation is one of the most powerful equations in financial analysis. It demonstrates the extent to which a company's ROIC is driven by its ability to maximize profitability (EBITA divided by revenues, or the operating margin), optimize capital turnover (measured by revenues over invested capital), or minimize operating taxes.

Each of these components can be further disaggregated, so that each expense and capital item can be analyzed, line item by line item. Exhibit 8.3 shows how the components can be organized into a tree. On the right side of the tree are operational financial ratios, the drivers of value over which the manager has control. As we read from right to left, each subsequent box is a function

EXHIBIT 8.3 **Home Depot and Lowe's: ROIC Tree, 2008**

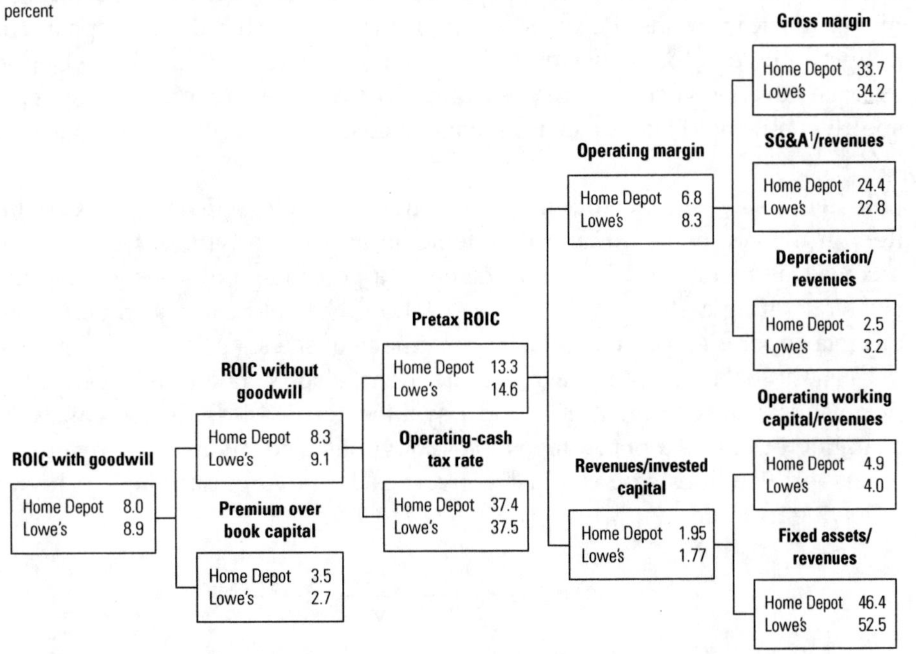

percent

	Gross margin	
	Home Depot	33.7
	Lowe's	34.2

Operating margin

| Home Depot | 6.8 |
| Lowe's | 8.3 |

SG&A[1]/revenues

| Home Depot | 24.4 |
| Lowe's | 22.8 |

Depreciation/ revenues

| Home Depot | 2.5 |
| Lowe's | 3.2 |

Pretax ROIC

| Home Depot | 13.3 |
| Lowe's | 14.6 |

ROIC without goodwill

| Home Depot | 8.3 |
| Lowe's | 9.1 |

Operating-cash tax rate

| Home Depot | 37.4 |
| Lowe's | 37.5 |

ROIC with goodwill

| Home Depot | 8.0 |
| Lowe's | 8.9 |

Premium over book capital

| Home Depot | 3.5 |
| Lowe's | 2.7 |

Revenues/invested capital

| Home Depot | 1.95 |
| Lowe's | 1.77 |

Operating working capital/revenues

| Home Depot | 4.9 |
| Lowe's | 4.0 |

Fixed assets/ revenues

| Home Depot | 46.4 |
| Lowe's | 52.5 |

[1] Implicit interest expense related to capitalized operating leases has been removed from selling, general, and administrative (SG&A) expense.

of the boxes to its right. For example, operating margin equals gross margin less SG&A/revenues less depreciation/revenues, and pretax ROIC equals operating margin times capital turnover. (SG&A refers to selling, general, and administrative expense.)

Once you have calculated the historical drivers of ROIC, compare them with the ROIC drivers of other companies in the same industry. You can then weigh this perspective against your analysis of the industry structure (opportunities for differentiation, barriers to entry or exit, etc.) and a qualitative assessment of the company's strengths and weaknesses.

To illustrate, in 2008 Home Depot's ROIC (8.0 percent) lagged Lowe's ROIC (8.9 percent) by approximately one percentage point. Using the ROIC tree in Exhibit 8.3, we can examine which drivers were responsible for the difference. From a margin perspective, Home Depot's operating margin was 6.8 percent versus 8.3 percent for Lowe's. The lower operating margin is primarily attributable to higher SG&A expense. According to press reports, the rise in SG&A reflects the cost of additional floor personnel to improve the customer experience. Whether this translates to higher sales through better service in the future is a key to the company's valuation.

Analyzing capital efficiency, we see that Home Depot averages 1.95 times revenue to average invested capital, compared with only 1.77 times for Lowe's. For these two companies, capital efficiency derives primarily from the efficiency of fixed assets, which in turn results from more revenues per dollar of store investment. So are Home Depot's stores more efficient or operating at higher-traffic locations? Perhaps, but after further investigation, it appears that a typical Lowe's store is newer and thus more expensive than Home Depot's average store. Newer stores may be a burden today (from a capital turnover perspective) but could lead to an advantage in customer retention going forward.

Line item analysis A comprehensive valuation model will convert every line item in the company's financial statements into some type of ratio. For the income statement, most items are taken as a percentage of sales. (Exceptions exist; operating cash taxes, for instance, should be calculated as a percentage of pretax operating profits, not as a percentage of sales.)

For the balance sheet, each line item can also be taken as a percentage of revenues (or for inventories and payables, to avoid distortion caused by changing prices, as a percentage of cost of goods sold). For operating current assets and liabilities, you can also convert each line item into days, using the following formula:[3]

$$\text{Days} = 365 \times \frac{\text{Balance Sheet Item}}{\text{Revenues}}$$

[3] If the business is seasonal, operating ratios such as inventories should be calculated using quarterly data.

EXHIBIT 8.4 **Home Depot and Lowe's: Operating Current Assets in Days**

Number of days in revenues

	Home Depot			Lowe's		
	2006	2007	2008	2006	2007	2008
Operating cash	2.5	2.2	2.7	6.2	4.0	5.0
Receivables, net	13.0	5.9	5.0	–	–	–
Merchandise inventories[1]	76.7	83.4	82.4	84.9	88.0	94.4
Other current assets	3.1	3.3	3.6	1.7	2.3	1.6
Operating current assets	95.2	94.7	93.6	92.7	94.3	101.1

[1] Merchandise inventories computed using cost of merchandise sold, rather than revenues.

The use of days lends itself to a simple operational interpretation. As can be seen in Exhibit 8.4, Home Depot's average inventory holding time (using cost of merchandise sold as a base) has risen from 77 to 82 days. For Lowe's, the inventory time is slightly higher, rising from 85 days to 94 days. The increase in inventory holding periods is not surprising, given the sharp decline in revenues for both companies.

Nonfinancial analysis In an external analysis, ratios are often confined to financial performance. If you are working from inside a company, however, or if the company releases operating data, link operating drivers directly to return on invested capital. By evaluating the operating drivers, you can better assess whether any differences in financial performance between competitors are sustainable.

Consider airlines, which are required for safety reasons to release a tremendous amount of operating data. Exhibit 8.5 details financial and operating data from three U.S. network carriers and three U.S. discount carriers for 2008.[4] Financial data include revenues, fuel costs, salaries, and other operating expenses. Operating data include the number of employees, measured using full-time equivalents, and available seat-miles (ASMs), the common measurement of capacity for U.S. airlines.

Exhibit 8.6 transforms the data presented in Exhibit 8.5 into a branch on the ROIC tree. Each box in the tree compares the average statistics for the three network carriers versus the three discount carriers. Because of losses at United and JetBlue, both types of carriers have negative operating margins (operating loss divided by total revenues, averaged across three carriers).

For airlines, operating margin is driven by three accounts: aircraft fuel, labor expenses, and other expenses. At first glance, it appears that the three network carriers match the three discount carriers in labor costs. Labor expenses as a percentage of revenues average 23.5 percent for the three network

[4] Network carriers have extensive networks, relying primarily on the hub-and-spoke system. Discount carriers typically fly point to point. In return for a lower price, they fly to fewer locations, use less-traveled airports, and offer fewer services.

EXHIBIT 8.5 **Financial and Operating Statistics across U.S. Airlines, 2008**

$ million

	Network carriers			Discount carriers		
	American	Delta[1]	United	AirTran	JetBlue	Southwest
Revenues	23,766	22,697	20,194	2,552	3,388	11,023
Aircraft fuel and related taxes	9,014	7,346	7,722	1,195	1,352	3,713
Salaries and related costs	6,655	4,802	4,311	475	694	3,340
Other operating expenses	8,773	10,436	9,983	969	1,656	3,521
Operating profit (loss)	(676)	113	(1,822)	(87)	(314)	449
Operating statistics						
Full-time equivalents	84,100	57,706	50,000	7,600	9,895	35,499
Available seat-miles (millions)	163,532	165,639	135,861	23,809	32,442	103,271

[1] Delta numbers adjusted for the acquisition of Northwest Airlines on October 29, 2008.

carriers and 23.1 percent for the network carriers. But this statistic is misleading. To see why, disaggregate the ratio of labor expenses to revenue using available seat-miles (ASMs):

$$\frac{\text{Labor Expenses}}{\text{Revenues}} = \left(\frac{\text{Labor Expenses}}{\text{ASMs}}\right) \Big/ \left(\frac{\text{Revenues}}{\text{ASMs}}\right)$$

The ratio of labor expenses to revenues is a function of labor expenses per ASM and revenues per ASM. Labor expenses per ASM are the labor costs required to fly one mile, and revenues per ASM represent average price per mile. Although labor expenses to revenues are similar for both carrier types, how they get there differs greatly. The discount carriers have a 38 percent advantage in labor cost per mile (2.5 cents per mile versus 3.4 cents for the

EXHIBIT 8.6 **Operational Drivers of Labor Expenses to Revenues**

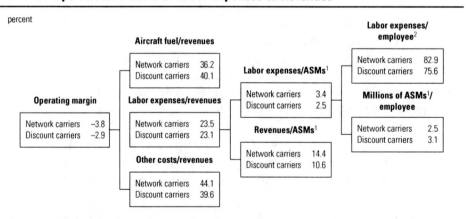

[1] Available seat-miles (ASMs) are the standard unit of capacity for the U.S. airline industry. Labor expense and revenue ratios measured in cents per mile.
[2] Labor expenses per employee measured in $ thousands.

network carrier). But what the network carriers lose in labor costs, they recover with higher prices. Because of their locations and reach, network carriers can charge an average price 35 percent higher than the discount carriers (14.4 cents per mile versus 10.6 cents per mile).

But what is driving this differential in labor expenses per ASM? Are the discounter's employees more productive? Or are they paid less? To answer these questions, disaggregate labor expenses to ASMs, using the following equation:

$$\frac{\text{Labor Expenses}}{\text{ASM}} = \left(\frac{\text{Labor Expenses}}{\text{Employees}}\right) \bigg/ \left(\frac{\text{ASMs}}{\text{Employees}}\right)$$

There are two drivers of labor expenses per ASM: the first term represents the average salary per full-time employee; the second measures the productivity of each full-time employee (millions of ASMs flown per employee). The boxes on the right side of Exhibit 8.6 report the calculations for this equation. The average salary is 9 percent higher for the three network carriers, and productivity per mile is 19.2 percent lower. Although the salary differential appears significant, it is quite small compared with earlier in the decade, when average salaries differed by a factor of almost two.

Analyzing performance using operating drivers gives additional insight into the competitive differences among airlines. But the analysis is far from done. In fact, a thoughtful analysis will often raise more questions than answers. For instance, can the salary difference between network and discount carriers be explained by the mix of employees (pilots are more expensive than gate personnel), the location of the employees (New York is more expensive than Texas), or poor contract negotiations? Each of these analyses will provide additional insight into the each carrier type's ability to survive and prosper.

ANALYZING REVENUE GROWTH

In Chapter 2, we determined that the value of a company is driven by ROIC, cost of capital, and growth in cash flows. But what drives long-term growth in cash flows? Assuming profits and reinvestment stabilize at steady rates over the long term, any long-term growth in cash flows will be directly tied to long-term growth in revenues. And by analyzing historical revenue growth, you can assess the potential for growth in the future.

The calculation of year-to-year revenue growth is straightforward, but the results can be misleading. The three prime culprits distorting revenue growth are the effects of changes in currency values, mergers and acquisitions, and changes in accounting policies. Strip out from revenues any distortions created by these effects in order to base forecast revenues for valuation on sustainable precedents.

EXHIBIT 8.7 **Compass and Sodexo: Revenue Growth Analysis**

percent

	Compass			Sodexo		
	2006	**2007**	**2008**	**2006**	**2007**	**2008**
Organic revenue growth	7.0	5.0	5.9	6.4	8.4	7.7
Currency effects	1.0	(5.1)	5.1	2.8	(3.7)	(6.7)
Portfolio changes	(22.9)	(5.0)	0.4	0.4	(0.1)	0.7
Reported revenue growth	(14.9)	(5.1)	11.4	9.6	4.6	1.7

Exhibit 8.7 demonstrates how misleading raw year-to-year revenue growth figures can be. Compass (based in the United Kingdom) and Sodexo (based in France) are global providers of canteen services in businesses, schools, and sporting venues. In 2008, total revenues at Compass grew by 11.4 percent, and revenues at Sodexo grew by 1.7 percent. The difference in growth rates appears dramatic but is driven primarily by changes in currency values (pounds sterling versus euros), not by organic revenue growth. Stripping out currency effects, acquisitions, and divestitures, organic revenue growth at Sodexo (7.7 percent) actually outpaced that of Compass (5.9 percent) by nearly two percentage points.

Given recent swings in currency values and large portfolio changes effected through restructurings by many companies, historical revenue growth for large multinationals can be extremely volatile, making benchmarking difficult. For Compass, revenue growth varied between negative 14.9 percent in 2006 and positive 11.4 percent in 2008. Sodexo exhibited similar volatility. In contrast, organic growth is more stable. Compass's organic revenue growth averaged 6.0 percent, and Sodexho's averaged 7.6 percent over the same period, but neither varied more than one percentage point from their average value.

In the next three sections, we examine drivers of revenue growth and discuss their effect on performance measurement, forecasting, and ultimately valuation.

Currency Effects

Multinational companies conduct business in many currencies. At the end of each reporting period, these revenues are converted to the currency of the reporting company. If foreign currencies are rising in value relative to the company's home currency, this translation, at better rates, will lead to higher revenue numbers. Thus, a rise in revenue may not reflect increased pricing power or greater quantities sold, but simply depreciation in the company's home currency.

Exhibit 8.8 reports revenue by geography for Compass and Sodexo. The companies have similar geographic mixes, with roughly 40 percent of

EXHIBIT 8.8 **Compass and Sodexo: Effect of Currencies on Revenue Growth**

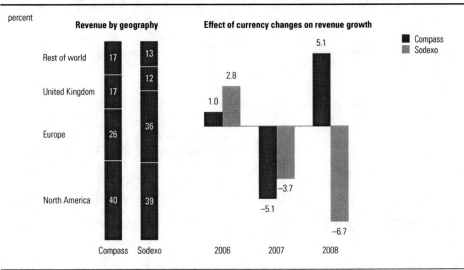

revenues coming from North America. Since each company translates U.S. dollars into a different currency, exchange rates will affect each company quite differently.

Compass translates U.S. dollars from its North American business into British pounds. Given the weakening of the pound against the U.S. dollar ($2.04 per pound in 2007 versus $1.78 per pound in 2008), Compass reported an increase in revenues of 5.1 percent attributable to the weakening pound. For Sodexo, exchange rates had the opposite effect. As the euro strengthened against the dollar, Sodexho translated revenue from North America into fewer euros, leading to a 6.7 percent drop in euro-denominated revenue.

The right side of Exhibit 8.8 demonstrates the dramatic effects of volatility in exchange rates. Movements that hurt Compass in 2007 reversed themselves in 2008. Failing to acknowledge these currency movements can lead to a critical misunderstanding of a global company's ability to grow organically.

Mergers and Acquisitions

Growth through acquisition may have very different effects on ROIC from internal growth because of the sizable premiums a company must pay to acquire another company. Therefore, it is important to understand how companies have been generating historical revenue growth: through acquisition or internally.

Stripping the effect of acquisitions from reported revenues is difficult. Unless an acquisition is deemed material by the company's accountants, company filings do not need to detail or even report the acquisition. For larger acquisitions, a company will report pro forma statements that recast historical

EXHIBIT 8.9 **Effect of Acquisitions on Revenue Growth**

$ million

	Year 1	Year 2	Year 3	Year 4	Year 5
Revenue by company					
Parent company	100.0	110.0	121.0	133.1	146.4
Target company	20.0	22.0	24.2	26.6	29.3
Consolidated revenues					
Revenue from parent	100.0	110.0	121.0	133.1	146.4
Revenue from target	–	–	14.1	26.6	29.3
Consolidated revenues[1]	100.0	110.0	135.1	159.7	175.7
Growth rates (percent)					
Consolidated revenue growth	–	10.0	22.8	18.2	10.0
Organic growth	–	10.0	10.0	10.0	10.0

[1] Only consolidated revenues are reported in a company's annual report.

financials as though the acquisition were completed at the beginning of the fiscal year. Revenue growth, then, should be calculated using the pro forma revenue numbers.[5] If the target company publicly reports its own financial data, you can construct pro forma statements manually by combining revenue of the acquirer and target for the prior year. But beware: The bidder will include partial-year revenues from the target for the period after the acquisition is completed. To remain consistent year to year, reconstructed prior years also must include only partial-year revenue.

Exhibit 8.9 presents the hypothetical purchase of a target company in the seventh month of year 3. Both the parent company and the target are growing organically at 10 percent per year. Consolidated revenues, however, spike during the two years surrounding the acquisition. Whereas the individual companies are growing at 10 percent each and every year, consolidated revenue growth is reported at 22.8 percent in year 3 and 18.2 percent in year 4.

To create an internally consistent comparison for years 3 and 4, adjust the prior year's consolidated revenues to match the current year's composition. To do this, add seven months of the target's year 2 revenue (7/12 × $22 million = $12.8 million) to the parent's year 2 revenue ($110.0 million). This leads to adjusted year 2 revenues of $122.8 million, which matches the composition of year 3. To compute an organic growth rate, compare year 3 revenues ($135.1 million) to adjusted year 2 revenues ($122.8 million). The resulting organic revenue growth rate equals 10 percent, which matches the underlying organic revenue growth of the individual companies.

[5] For example, Cablevision Systems purchased *Newsday* in July 2008. Consolidated revenue for Cablevision Systems in 2008 includes revenue generated by *Newsday*, but only subsequent to July 29, 2008. Since 2008 includes five months of *Newsday* revenue and 2007 does not, the company's consolidated revenue cannot be compared with the prior year's revenue without adjustment.

Even though the acquisition occurs in year 3, the revenue growth rate for year 4 also will be affected by the acquisition. Year 4 contains a full year of revenues from the target. Therefore, year 3 revenue must also contain a full year of target revenue. Consequently, year 3 should be increased by five months of target revenue (5/12 × $24.2 million = $10.1 million).

Accounting Changes and Irregularities

Each year, the Financial Accounting Standards Board (FASB) in the United States and the International Accounting Standards Board (IASB) make recommendations concerning the financial treatment of certain business transactions. Most changes in revenue recognition policies do not come as formal pronouncements from the boards themselves, but from task forces that issue topic notes. Companies then have a set amount of time to implement the required changes. Changes in a company's revenue recognition policy can significantly affect revenues during the year of adoption, distorting the one-year growth rate.[6] You therefore need to eliminate their effects in order to understand real historical revenue trends.

Consider Emerging Issues Task Force (EITF) 09-3 from the FASB, which changes the way revenue is recognized for companies that package computer hardware and software. Before 2010, companies were required to follow Statement of Position (SOP) 97-2, which states that revenue should be recognized using "contract accounting." For example, Apple recognizes the revenue from the sale of an iPhone over 24 months because the company provides free software upgrades for two years. Under EITF 09-3, companies will be able to recognize hardware revenue and profit at the point of sale. When Apple adjusts to the new rule, it will recognize the majority of iPhone revenue immediately versus gradually over two years. This will cause an artificial rise in Apple's revenue during the year of the accounting change.

If an accounting change is material, a company will document the change in its section on management discussion and analysis (MD&A). The company will also recast its historical financial statements. Some companies do not fully document changes in accounting policy, and this can lead to distorted views of performance.

Decomposing Revenue Growth to Build an Integrated Perspective of Company Economics

Once the effects of mergers and acquisitions, currency translations, and accounting changes have been removed from the year-to-year revenue growth

---

[6] Revenue recognition changes can also affect margins and capital turnover ratios. They will not, however, affect free cash flow.

numbers, analyze organic revenue growth from an operational perspective. The most standard breakdown is:

$$\text{Revenues} = \frac{\text{Revenues}}{\text{Units}} \times \text{Units}$$

Using this formula, determine whether prices or quantities are driving growth. Do not, however, confuse revenue per unit with price; they can be different. If revenue per unit is rising, the change could be due to rising prices, or the company could be shifting its product mix from low-priced to high-priced items.

The operating statistics that companies choose to report (if any) depend on the norms of the industry and the practices of competitors. For instance, most retailers provide information on the number of stores they operate, the number of square feet in those stores, and the number of transactions they conduct annually. By relating different operating statistics to total revenues, we can build a deeper understanding of the business. Consider this retailing standard:

$$\text{Revenues} = \frac{\text{Revenues}}{\text{Stores}} \times \text{Stores}$$

Using the operating statistics reported in Exhibit 8.10, we discover that Home Depot not only has more stores than Lowe's, but also generates more revenue per store ($31.1 million per store for Home Depot versus $29.2 million for Lowe's). Using the three operating statistics, we can build ratios on revenues per store, transactions per store, square feet per store, dollars per transaction, and number of transactions per square foot.

Although operating ratios are powerful in their own right, what can really change one's thinking about performance is how the ratios are changing over time. Exhibit 8.11 organizes each ratio into a tree. Rather than report a calculated ratio, such as revenues per store, however, we report the growth in the ratio and relate this back to the growth in revenue. At Home Depot, store-based revenues declined by 7.9 percent in 2008, while Lowe's held revenues flat in the same year. How did Lowe's avoid the growth problems of Home Depot? Actually, it did not. Lowe's kept aggregate revenues flat by opening 115 stores,

EXHIBIT 8.10 **Home Depot and Lowe's: Operating Data**

	Home Depot			Lowe's		
	2006	2007	2008	2006	2007	2008
Store revenues[1] ($ million)	78,337	76,793	70,736	46,906	48,276	48,211
Number of stores	2,147	2,234	2,274	1,385	1,534	1,649
Number of transactions (million)	1,330	1,336	1,272	680	720	740
Square footage at fiscal year-end (million)	224	235	238	157	174	187

[1] Store revenues are revenues generated by customer transactions. They do not include other revenues.

EXHIBIT 8.11 **Home Depot and Lowe's: Revenue Growth Analysis, 2008**

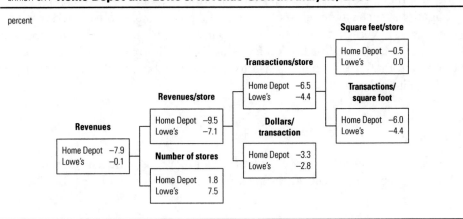

but same-store sales fell by 7.1 percent. Since Home Depot opened just 40 new stores, its decline in aggregate revenue was more dramatic. But remember: growth is a powerful valuation driver, but only when combined with an ROIC greater than the cost of capital. If Lowe's cannot earn its cost of capital on the new stores, the growth will destroy value, and the company's stock price will suffer as a result.

Stripping out the growth in stores, we can focus on the within-store growth. The implications of this analysis are extremely important, to the point that financial analysts have a special name for growth in revenue per store: *comps*, shorthand for comparables, or year-to-year same-store sales. Why is this revenue growth important? First, how many stores to open is an investment choice, whereas same-store sales growth reflects each store's ability to compete effectively in its local market. Second, new stores require large capital investments, whereas comps growth requires little incremental capital. Higher revenues and less capital lead to higher capital turnover, which leads to higher ROIC.

CREDIT HEALTH AND CAPITAL STRUCTURE

To this point, we have focused on the operating performance of the company and its ability to create value. We have examined the primary drivers of value: a company's return on invested capital and organic revenue growth. In the final step of historical analysis, we focus on how the company has financed its operations. What proportion of invested capital comes from creditors instead of from equity investors? Is this capital structure sustainable? Can the company survive an industry downturn? (See Chapter 23 for a detailed explanation of capital structure choices.)

To determine how robust a company's capital structure is, we examine two related but distinct concepts: liquidity (via the interest coverage ratio) and leverage. Liquidity measures the company's ability to meet short-term obligations, such as interest expenses, rental payments, and required principal payments. Leverage measures the company's ability to meet obligations over the long term. Since this book's focus is not credit analysis, we detail only a few ratios that credit analysts use to evaluate a company's capital structure and credit health.

Coverage

The company's ability to meet short-term obligations is measured with ratios that incorporate three measures of earnings:

1. Earnings before interest, taxes, and amortization (EBITA).
2. Earnings before interest, taxes, depreciation, and amortization (EBITDA).
3. Earnings before interest, taxes, depreciation, amortization, and rental expense (EBITDAR).

The ratios used to measure ability to meet short-term obligations are the traditional interest coverage ratio and a more advanced measure, the ratio of EBITDAR to the sum of interest expense and rental expense.

Interest coverage is calculated by dividing either EBITA or EBITDA by interest. The first coverage ratio, EBITA to interest, measures the company's ability to pay interest using profits without cutting capital expenditures intended to replace depreciating equipment. The second ratio, EBITDA to interest, measures the company's ability to meet short-term financial commitments using both current profits and the depreciation dollars earmarked for replacement capital. Although EBITDA provides a good measure of the short-term ability to meet interest payments, most companies cannot compete effectively without replacing worn assets.

Like the interest coverage ratio, the ratio of EBITDAR to interest expense plus rental expense measures the company's ability to meet its known future obligations, including the effect of operating leases. For many companies, especially retailers, including rental expenses is a critical part of understanding the financial health of the business.

Exhibit 8.12 presents financial data and coverage ratios for Home Depot and Lowe's. For 2008, Home Depot's EBITA/interest coverage ratio equals 7.0 times, whereas Lowe's has an interest coverage ratio of 11.8 times. Using regression results from Exhibit 23.5, we can translate each company's interest coverage ratio into a credit rating. Home Depot's Standard & Poor's credit rating as of May 2009 was BBB+. Lowe's was rated A+. These ratings match the model's prediction based on each company's interest coverage ratio.

EXHIBIT 8.12 **Home Depot and Lowe's: Measuring Coverage**

$ million

	Home Depot			Lowe's		
	2006	**2007**	**2008**	**2006**	**2007**	**2008**
EBITA	9,790	7,251	4,359	5,152	4,705	3,786
EBITDA	11,435	8,944	6,144	6,314	6,071	5,325
EBITDAR[1]	12,393	9,768	6,990	6,632	6,440	5,724
Interest	392	696	624	206	239	320
Rental expense	958	824	846	318	369	399
Interest plus rental expense	1,350	1,520	1,470	524	608	719
Coverage ratios						
EBITA/interest	25.0	10.4	7.0	25.0	19.7	11.8
EBITDA/interest	29.2	12.9	9.8	30.7	25.4	16.6
EBITDAR/interest plus rental expense	9.2	6.4	4.8	12.7	10.6	8.0

[1] Earnings before interest, taxes, depreciation, amortization, and rental expense.

Since both companies maintain investment-grade ratings, the likelihood of default is quite small.

Leverage

To better understand the power (and danger) of leverage, consider the relationship between return on equity (ROE) and return on invested capital (ROIC):

$$ROE = ROIC + [ROIC - (1 - T)k_d] \frac{D}{E}$$

As the formula demonstrates, a company's ROE is a direct function of its ROIC, its spread of ROIC over its after-tax cost of debt (k_d), and its book-based debt-to-equity ratio (D/E). Consider a company that is earning an ROIC of 10 percent and has an after-tax cost of debt of 5 percent. To raise its ROE, the company can either increase its ROIC (through operating improvements) or increase its debt-to-equity ratio (by swapping debt for equity). Although each strategy can lead to an identical change in ROE, increasing the debt-to-equity ratio makes the company's ROE more sensitive to changes in operating performance (ROIC). Thus, while increasing the debt-to-equity ratio can increase ROE, it does so by increasing the risks faced by shareholders.

To assess leverage, measure the company's (market) debt-to-equity ratio over time and against peers. Does the leverage ratio compare favorably with the industry? How much risk is the company taking? We answer these and other questions related to leverage in depth in Chapter 23.

Payout Ratio

The dividend payout ratio equals total common dividends divided by net income available to common shareholders. We can better understand the company's financial situation by analyzing the payout ratio in relation to its cash flow reinvestment ratio (examined earlier):

- If the company has a high dividend payout ratio and a reinvestment ratio greater than 1, then it must be borrowing money to fund negative free cash flow, to pay interest, or to pay dividends. But is this sustainable?

- A company with positive free cash flow and low dividend payout is probably paying down debt (or aggregating excess cash). In this situation, is the company passing up the valuable tax benefits of debt or hoarding cash unnecessarily?

Valuation Metrics

To conclude your assessment of capital structure, measure the shareholders' perception of future performance by calculating a market multiple. To build a market multiple, divide core operating value[7] by a normalizing factor, such as revenue, EBITA, or the book value of invested capital. By comparing the multiple of one company versus another, you can examine how the market perceives the company's future relative to other companies.

Exhibit 8.13 presents the core-operating-value-to-EBITA multiple for Home Depot and Lowe's between 2000 and 2009. In the early 2000s, both companies traded at extremely high multiples. By 2004, both companies stabilized at roughly 10 times EBITA. In Chapter 14, we describe how to build and analyze a robust set of market comparables.

ALTERNATIVES TO ROIC

For companies with large, uneven capital expenditures, ROIC may vary significantly over the asset's life, and this can give a distorted picture of when value is created. In this case, it may be helpful to convert ROIC into a measure similar to internal rate of return (IRR). One common measure based on the principles of IRR is cash flow return on investment (CFROI).[8]

Consider a livery company that plans to purchase a luxury sedan for $40,000. The vehicle will operate for four years. Since revenues are independent of the sedan's age, the vehicle will earn relatively constant profits over the four

[7] In Chapter 6, core operating value is defined as enterprise value less the market value of nonoperating assets, such as excess cash and nonconsolidated subsidiaries.

[8] For more information, see B. Madden, *CFROI Valuation: A Total System Approach to Valuing the Firm* (Oxford, UK: Butterworth-Heinemann, 1999).

EXHIBIT 8.13 **Home Depot and Lowe's: Core Operating Value[1] to EBITA**

Multiple of EBITA

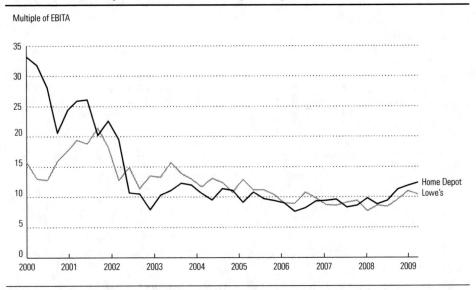

[1] Core operating values equals enterprise values less the market value of nonoperating assets.

years. In Exhibit 8.14, we present the NOPLAT, invested capital, and return on invested capital for the livery company. Note how the vehicle's ROIC rises from 8.9 percent to 26.7 percent over its life. If the company's cost of capital is 15 percent, it appears that the investment destroys value during its first two years but creates value during the last two years.

Alternatively, you could calculate the internal rate of return for each sedan. Using the classic IRR formula, you would find that the sedan earns an IRR of 12.7 percent over its life. Calculating IRR, however, requires

EXHIBIT 8.14 **Project-Based Return on Invested Capital**

$ thousand

	Year 0	Year 1	Year 2	Year 3	Year 4
Revenues	–	100	100	100	100
Operating costs	–	(86)	(86)	(86)	(86)
Depreciation	–	(10)	(10)	(10)	(10)
NOPLAT	–	4	4	4	4
Working capital	5	5	5	5	–
Fixed assets	40	30	20	10	–
Invested capital	45	35	25	15	–
ROIC[1] (percent)	–	8.9	11.4	16.0	26.7

[1] ROIC measured on beginning-of-year capital.

EXHIBIT 8.15 **Home Depot: CFROI, 2008**

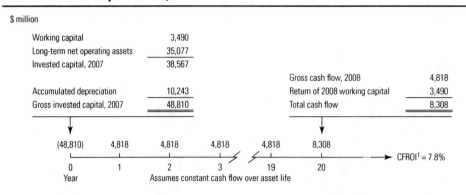

$ million

Working capital	3,490
Long-term net operating assets	35,077
Invested capital, 2007	38,567
Accumulated depreciation	10,243
Gross invested capital, 2007	48,810

Gross cash flow, 2008	4,818
Return of 2008 working capital	3,490
Total cash flow	8,308

(48,810) 4,818 4,818 4,818 4,818 8,308

0   1   2   3   19   20   CFROI[1] = 7.8%
Year   Assumes constant cash flow over asset life

[1] Results of internal rate of return (IRR) calculation on the cash flow stream.

making subjective forecasts, so it does not offer a consistent measure of historical performance.

Cash flow return on investment (CFROI) removes the subjectivity of year-by-year forecasting yet provides a smoothed measure. To calculate CFROI in a given year, use the traditional IRR methodology of setting the net present value to 0 and then solving for the discount rate. To avoid the subjectivity of forecasting, CFROI assumes a fixed cash flow for a fixed number of periods (the company's estimated asset life). To calculate CFROI, we need three components: the initial investment, the annual cash flow, and residual value. The initial investment equals the gross invested capital measured in the prior period (gross invested capital equals invested capital plus accumulated depreciation). The annual cash flow equals NOPLAT plus depreciation. The residual value equals NOPLAT plus depreciation, plus the return of the original working capital.

Exhibit 8.15 calculates the CFROI in 2008 for Home Depot. To measure initial investment, we add 2007's invested capital ($38,567 million) to 2007's accumulated depreciation ($10,243 million).[9] The annual gross cash flow over 20 years is $4,818 million (as measured by 2008 gross cash flow), and the return of working capital equals $3,490 million in year 20. Using a spreadsheet IRR function, we arrive at a CFROI of 7.8 percent.

CFROI captures the lumpiness of an investment better than ROIC. But it is complex to calculate and requires assumptions about the investment's estimated asset life. Weighing the simplicity of ROIC versus the smoothness

[9] Operating working capital, invested capital, and gross cash flow are defined in Chapter 7. Accumulated depreciation is found between gross property, plant, and equipment (PP&E) and net PP&E on the balance sheet. If only net PP&E appears on the balance sheet, check the notes for accumulated depreciation.

of CFROI, we suggest using CFROI only when companies have the following characteristics:

- Lumpy capital expenditure patterns.
- Fixed assets with long lives (over 15 years).
- Large ratio of fixed assets to working capital.

GENERAL CONSIDERATIONS

Although it is impossible to provide a comprehensive checklist for analyzing a company's historical financial performance, here are some guidelines to keep in mind:

- Look back as far as possible (at least 10 years). Long time horizons will allow you to determine whether the company and industry tend to revert to some normal level of performance, and whether short-term trends are likely to be permanent.
- Disaggregate value drivers—both ROIC and revenue growth—as far as possible. If possible, link operational performance measures with each key value driver.
- If there are any radical changes in performance, identify the source. Determine whether the change is temporary or permanent, or merely an accounting effect.

REVIEW QUESTIONS

1. JetCo is a manufacturer of high-speed aircraft. The company generates $100 million in operating profit on $600 million of revenue and $800 million of invested capital. JetCo's primary competitor, Gulf Aviation, generates $100 million in NOPLAT on $800 million in revenue. Gulf Aviation has $600 million in invested capital. Based on the preceding data, which company is creating more value? Assume an operating tax rate of 25 percent and cost of capital of 8 percent.

2. Using the data presented in Question 1, decompose ROIC into operating margin and capital turnover for each company. Which ratio is the key determinant of ROIC: operating margin or capital turnover?

3. DefenseCo announces a purchase of Gulf Aviation for $1.1 billion in cash. Consequently, Gulf Aviation's invested capital with goodwill and acquired intangibles rises from $600 million to $1.1 billion. The following year, while conducting its annual review of Gulf Aviation, senior management at

DefenseCo asks you the following questions: Based on the profitability figures presented in Question 1, is Gulf Aviation creating value for DefenseCo? Which company, JetCo or Gulf Aviation, has the best financial performance in the industry?

4. Gulf Aviation generates $800 million in revenue per year, with no material growth. The consolidated revenues for DefenseCo are $1.5 billion in year 1, $1.8 billion in year 2 (the year of the acquisition), and $2.5 billion in year 3. If DefenseCo closed the acquisition of Gulf Aviation on October 1 of year 2, what is the apples-to-apples organic growth for DefenseCo in year 2 and year 3? How does organic growth differ from the growth in reported revenues? Assume Gulf Aviation revenues are consolidated into DefenseCo only after the acquisition close date and that the fiscal year closes for both companies on December 31 of each year.

5. Using an Internet search tool, locate Procter & Gamble's investor relations web site. Under "Financial Reporting," you will find the company's 2009 annual report. In the annual report's section titled "Management's Discussion and Analysis," you will find a discussion on revenue growth. How fast did the company grow (or shrink) revenues in 2009? How much growth is attributable to price, number of units sold, foreign exchange impacts, and shifts in the mix of products sold? How does this compare to 2008 (which can also be found in the 2009 annual report)? What would the growth have been on a constant currency basis? Is the difference with and without foreign exchange impacts meaningful?

6. Which interest coverage ratio, EBITDA to interest or EBITA to interest, will lead to a higher number? When is the EBITDA interest ratio more appropriate than the EBITA ratio? When is the EBITA interest coverage ratio more appropriate than the EBITDA ratio?

10

Estimating
Continuing Value

As described in Chapter 6, continuing value (CV) provides a useful method for simplifying company valuations. To estimate a company's value, separate a company's expected cash flow into two periods, and define the company's value as follows:

$$\text{Value} = \frac{\text{Present Value of Cash Flow}}{during \text{ Explicit Forecast Period}} + \frac{\text{Present Value of Cash Flow}}{after \text{ Explicit Forecast Period}}$$

The second term is the continuing value: the value of the company's expected cash flow beyond the explicit forecast period. Making simplifying assumptions about the company's performance during this period (e.g., assuming a constant rate of growth and return on capital) allows you to estimate continuing value by using formulas instead of explicitly forecasting and discounting cash flows over an extended period.

A thoughtful estimate of continuing value is essential to any valuation, because continuing value often accounts for a large percentage of a company's total value. Exhibit 10.1 shows continuing value as a percentage of total value for companies in four industries, given an eight-year explicit forecast. In these examples, continuing value accounts for 56 percent to 125 percent of total value. These large percentages do not necessarily mean that most of a company's value will be created in the continuing-value period. Often continuing value is large because profits and other inflows in the early years are offset by outflows for capital spending and working-capital investment—investments that should generate higher cash flow in later years. We discuss the interpretation of continuing value in more detail later in this chapter.

This chapter begins with the recommended continuing-value formulas for discounted cash flow (DCF) and economic-profit valuation. We then discuss

EXHIBIT 10.1 **Continuing Value as a Percentage of Total Value**

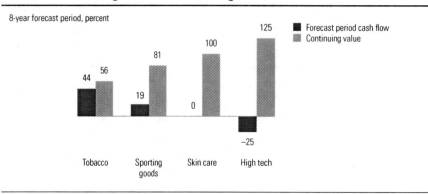

issues commonly raised about how to interpret continuing value and suggest some best practices in estimating continuing-value parameters such as growth and return on invested capital. Finally, we compare the recommended formulas with other continuing-value techniques and discuss more advanced formulas.

The continuing-value formulas developed over the next few pages are consistent with the DCF and economic profit. This is important because continuing value is sometimes treated as though it differs from the DCF of the explicit forecast period. For example, some acquirers estimate continuing value for a target company by applying the same price-to-earnings multiple five years in the future as the multiple they are currently paying for the target. By doing this, they are assuming that someone would be willing to pay the same multiple for the target company five years from now, regardless of changes in growth and return prospects over that period. This type of circular reasoning leads to inaccurate (and often overly optimistic) valuations. Instead, acquirers should try to estimate what the multiple should be at the end of the forecast period, given the industry conditions at that time.

RECOMMENDED FORMULA FOR DCF VALUATION

If you are using the enterprise DCF model, you should estimate continuing value by using the value driver formula derived in Chapter 2:

$$\text{Continuing Value}_t = \frac{\text{NOPLAT}_{t+1}\left(1 - \dfrac{g}{\text{RONIC}}\right)}{\text{WACC} - g}$$

where NOPLAT_{t+1} = net operating profit less adjusted taxes in the first year after the explicit forecast period
  g = expected growth rate in NOPLAT in perpetuity
  RONIC = expected rate of return on new invested capital
  WACC = weighted average cost of capital

A simple example demonstrates that the value driver formula does, in fact, replicate the process of projecting the cash flows and discounting them to the present. Begin with the following cash flow projections:

	YEAR				
	1	2	3	4	5
NOPLAT	$100	$106	$112	$119	$126
Net investment	50	53	56	60	63
Free cash flow	$ 50	$ 53	$ 56	$ 60	$ 63

The same pattern continues after the first five years presented. In this example, the growth rate in net operating profit less adjusted taxes (NOPLAT) and free cash flow each period is 6 percent. The rate of return on net new investment is 12 percent, calculated as the increase in NOPLAT from one year to the next, divided by the net investment in the prior year. The weighted average cost of capital (WACC) is assumed to be 11 percent.

To compare the methods of computing continuing value, first discount a long forecast—say, 150 years:

$$CV = \frac{50}{1.11} + \frac{53}{(1.11)^2} + \frac{56}{(1.11)^3} + \cdots + \frac{50(1.06)^{149}}{(1.11)^{150}}$$
$$CV = 999$$

Next, use the growing free cash flow (FCF) perpetuity formula:

$$CV = \frac{50}{11\% - 6\%}$$
$$CV = 1,000$$

Finally, use the value driver formula:

$$CV = \frac{100\left(1 - \dfrac{6\%}{12\%}\right)}{11\% - 6\%}$$
$$CV = 1,000$$

All three approaches yield virtually the same result. (If we had carried out the discounted cash flow beyond 150 years, the result would have been the same.)

Although the value driver formula and the growing FCF perpetuity formula are technically equivalent, applying the FCF perpetuity is tricky, and it is easy to make a common conceptual error. The typical error is to estimate incorrectly the level of free cash flow that is consistent with the growth rate being forecast. If growth in the continuing-value period is forecast to be less than the growth in the explicit forecast period (as is normally the case), then the proportion of NOPLAT that must be invested to generate growth also is likely to be less. In the continuing-value period, more of each dollar of NOPLAT becomes free cash flow available for the investors. If this transition is not explicitly taken into consideration, the continuing value could be significantly underestimated. Later in this chapter, we provide an example that illustrates what can go wrong when using the cash flow perpetuity formula.

Because perpetuity-based formulas rely on parameters that never change, use a continuing-value formula only when the company has reached a steady state, with low revenue growth and stable operating margins. Chapters 4 and 5 provide guidance for thinking about return on capital and long-term growth. In addition, when estimating the continuing-value parameters, keep in mind the following technical considerations:

- *NOPLAT:* The level of NOPLAT should be based on a normalized level of revenues and sustainable margin and return on invested capital (ROIC). The normalized level of revenues should reflect the midpoint of the company's business cycle and cycle average profit margins.

- *RONIC:* The expected rate of return on new invested capital (RONIC) should be consistent with expected competitive conditions. Economic theory suggests that competition will eventually eliminate abnormal returns, so for many companies, set RONIC equal to WACC. However, for companies with sustainable competitive advantages (e.g., brands and patents), you might set RONIC equal to the return the company is forecast to earn during later years of the explicit forecast period. Chapter 4 contains data on the long-term returns on capital for companies in different industries.

- *Growth rate:* Few companies can be expected to grow faster than the economy for long periods. The best estimate is probably the expected long-term rate of consumption growth for the industry's products, plus inflation. Sensitivity analyses also are useful for understanding how the growth rate affects continuing-value estimates. Chapter 5 provides empirical evidence on historical corporate growth rates.

- *WACC:* The weighted average cost of capital should incorporate a sustainable capital structure and an underlying estimate of business risk consistent with expected industry conditions.

The key value driver formula is highly sensitive to the formula's parameters. Exhibit 10.2 shows how continuing value, calculated using the value driver formula, is affected by various combinations of growth rate and RONIC. The example assumes a $100 million base level of NOPLAT and a 10 percent WACC. At an expected RONIC of 14 percent, changing the growth rate from

EXHIBIT 10.2 **Impact of Continuing-Value Assumptions**

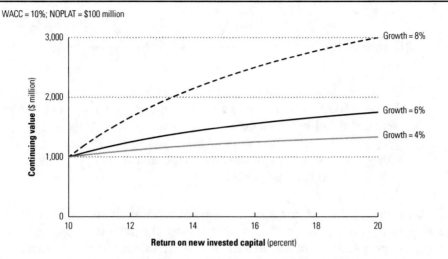

WACC = 10%; NOPLAT = $100 million

6 percent to 8 percent increases the continuing value by 50 percent, from about $1.4 billion to about $2.1 billion.

RECOMMENDED FORMULA FOR ECONOMIC-PROFIT VALUATION

With the economic-profit approach, the continuing value does not equal the value of the company following the explicit forecast period, as it does for discounted free cash flow. Instead, it is the incremental value over the company's invested capital at the end of the explicit forecast period. The total value of the company is as follows:

$$
\text{Value} = \begin{array}{c} \text{Invested Capital} \\ \text{at Beginning} \\ \text{of Forecast} \end{array} + \begin{array}{c} \text{Present Value of Forecast} \\ \text{Economic Profit during} \\ \text{Explicit Forecast Period} \end{array} + \begin{array}{c} \text{Present Value of Forecast} \\ \text{Economic Profit after} \\ \text{Explicit Forecast Period} \end{array}
$$

The economic-profit continuing value is the last term in the preceding equation. Although this continuing value differs from the DCF continuing value, today's value of the company will be the same, given the same projected financial performance.

The economic-profit formula for continuing value is:

$$
CV_t = \text{Economic Profits in Year } t+1 + \text{Economic Profits beyond Year } t+1
$$
$$
= \frac{IC_t (ROIC_t - WACC)}{WACC} + \frac{PV (\text{Economic Profit}_{t+2})}{WACC - g}
$$

such that

$$PV(\text{Economic Profit}_{t+2}) = \frac{NOPLAT_{t+1}\left(\dfrac{g}{RONIC}\right)(RONIC - WACC)}{WACC}$$

where IC_t = invested capital at the end of the explicit forecast period
    $ROIC_t$ = ROIC on existing capital after the explicit forecast period
    WACC = weighted average cost of capital
    g = expected growth rate in NOPLAT in perpetuity
    RONIC = expected rate of return on new invested capital after the explicit forecast period

According to the formula, total economic profit following the explicit forecast equals the present value of economic profit in the first year after the explicit forecast in perpetuity, plus any incremental economic profit after that year. Incremental economic profit is created by additional growth at returns exceeding the cost of capital. If expected RONIC equals WACC, the third term (economic profits beyond year 1) equals zero, and the continuing economic-profit value is the value of the first year's economic profit in perpetuity.

DCF-based and economic-profit-based continuing values are directly related but not identical. The continuing value using a DCF will equal the sum of the economic-profit continuing value plus the amount of invested capital in place at the end of the explicit forecast period.

SUBTLETIES OF CONTINUING VALUE

Three misunderstandings about continuing value are common. First is the misperception that the length of the explicit forecast affects the company's value. Second, people confuse return on new invested capital (RONIC) with return on invested capital (ROIC). Setting RONIC equal to WACC in the continuing-value formula does not imply the company will not create value beyond the explicit forecast period. Since return on capital from existing capital will remain at original levels, ROIC will only gradually approach the cost of capital. Finally, some analysts incorrectly infer that a large continuing value relative to the company's total value means value creation occurs primarily after the explicit forecast period.

Does Length of Forecast Affect a Company's Value?

While the length of the explicit forecast period you choose is important, it does not affect the value of the company; it only affects the distribution of the company's value between the explicit forecast period and the years that follow.

EXHIBIT 10.3 **Comparison of Total-Value Estimates Using Different Forecast Horizons**

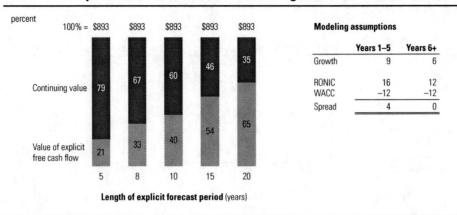

In Exhibit 10.3, value is $893, regardless of how long the forecast period is. With a forecast horizon of five years, the continuing value accounts for 79 percent of total value. With an eight-year horizon, the continuing value accounts for only 67 percent of total value. As the explicit forecast horizon grows longer, value shifts from the continuing value to the explicit forecast period, but the total value always remains the same. To see how the value shift works, compare Exhibits 10.4 and 10.5. Exhibit 10.4 details the calculations for the valuation model using a five-year explicit forecast period, whereas Exhibit 10.5 repeats the analysis with an eight-year period.

EXHIBIT 10.4 **Valuation Using Five-Year Explicit Forecast Period**

$ million

	Year 1	Year 2	Year 3	Year 4	Year 5	Base for CV
NOPLAT	100.0	109.0	118.8	129.5	141.2	149.6
Depreciation	20.0	21.8	23.8	25.9	28.2	
Gross cash flow	120.0	130.8	142.6	155.4	169.4	
Gross investment	(76.3)	(83.1)	(90.6)	(98.7)	(107.6)	
Free cash flow (FCF)	43.8	47.7	52.0	56.7	61.8	
Discount factor	0.893	0.797	0.712	0.636	0.567	
Present value of FCF	39.1	38.0	37.0	36.0	35.0	

Present value of FCF_{1-5}	185.1
Continuing value	707.5
Total value	892.6

Calculation of continuing value (CV)

$$CV_5 = \frac{NOPLAT_{CV}\left(1 - \frac{g}{RONIC}\right)}{WACC - g} = \frac{149.6\left(1 - \frac{6\%}{12\%}\right)}{12\% - 6\%} = \$1,246.9$$

$$CV_0 = \frac{CV_5}{(1 + WACC)^5} = \frac{1,246.9}{(1.12)^5} = \$707.5$$

EXHIBIT 10.5 **Valuation Using Eight-Year Explicit Forecast Period**

$ million

	Year 1	Year 2	Year 3	Year 4	Year 5	Year 6	Year 7	Year 8	Base for CV
NOPLAT	100.0	109.0	118.8	129.5	141.2	149.6	158.6	168.1	178.2
Depreciation	20.0	21.8	23.8	25.9	28.2	29.9	31.7	33.6	
Gross cash flow	120.0	130.8	142.6	155.4	169.4	179.6	190.3	201.7	
Gross investment	(76.3)	(83.1)	(90.6)	(98.7)	(107.6)	(104.7)	(111.0)	(117.7)	
Free cash flow (FCF)	43.8	47.7	52.0	56.7	61.8	74.8	79.3	84.1	
Discount factor	0.893	0.797	0.712	0.636	0.567	0.507	0.452	0.404	
Present value of FCF	39.1	38.0	37.0	36.0	35.0	37.9	35.9	34.0	

Present value of FCF_{1-8}	292.9	**Calculation of continuing value (CV)**
Continuing value	599.8	
Total value	892.6	

$$CV_8 = \frac{NOPLAT_{cv}\left(1 - \frac{g}{RONIC}\right)}{WACC - g} = \frac{178.2\left(1 - \frac{6\%}{12\%}\right)}{12\% - 6\%} = \$1,485.1$$

$$CV_0 = \frac{CV_8}{(1 + WACC)^8} = \frac{1,485.1}{(1.12)^8} = \$599.8$$

In Exhibit 10.4, NOPLAT starts at $100 million. During the first five years, NOPLAT grows at 9 percent per year. Following year 5, NOPLAT growth slows to 6 percent. To compute gross cash flow, add depreciation to NOPLAT. Free cash flow equals gross cash flow minus gross investment. To compute the company's gross investment, multiply NOPLAT by the reinvestment rate, where the reinvestment rate equals the ratio of growth to ROIC (9 percent divided by 16 percent), plus depreciation. To determine the present value of the company, sum the present value of the explicit forecast period cash flows plus the present value of continuing value. (Since the continuing value is measured as of year 5, the continuing value of $1,246.9 million is discounted by five years, not by six, a common mistake.) The total value equals $892.6 million.

Exhibit 10.5 details the calculations for a valuation model that uses an eight-year explicit forecast period and a continuing value that starts in year 9. The structure and forecast inputs of the model are identical to those of Exhibit 10.4. In the first five years, growth is 9 percent, and ROIC equals 16 percent. After five years, growth drops to 6 percent, and ROIC drops to 12 percent. As can be seen by comparing Exhibits 10.4 and 10.5, total value under each valuation method is identical. Since the underlying value drivers are the same in both valuations, the results will be the same. The length of your forecast horizon should affect only the proportion of total value allocated between the explicit forecast period and continuing value, not the total value.

The choice of forecast horizon will indirectly affect value if it is associated with changes in the economic assumptions underlying the continuing-value estimate. You can unknowingly change your performance forecasts when you change your forecast horizon. Many forecasters assume that the rate of return on new invested capital will equal the cost of capital in the continuing-value period but that the company will earn returns exceeding the cost of capital during the explicit forecast period. By extending the explicit forecast period, you also implicitly extend the time period during which returns on new capital are expected to exceed the cost of capital. Therefore, extending the forecast period indirectly raises the value.

So how do you choose the appropriate length of the explicit forecast period? The explicit forecast should be long enough that the business will have reached a steady state by the end of the period. Suppose you expect the company's margins to decline as its customers consolidate. Margins are currently 12 percent, and you forecast they will fall to 9 percent over the next seven years. In this case, the explicit forecast period must be at least seven years, because continuing-value approaches cannot account for the declining margin (at least not without complex computations). The business must be operating at an equilibrium level for the continuing-value approaches to be useful. If the explicit forecast is more than seven years, there will be no effect on the total value of the company.

Confusion about Competitive-Advantage Period

A related issue is the concept of a company's competitive-advantage period, or period of supernormal returns. This is the notion that companies will earn returns above the cost of capital for a period of time, followed by a decline to the cost of capital. While this concept is useful, linking it to the length of the forecast is dangerous. One reason is simply that, as we just showed, there is no direct connection between the length of the forecast and the value of a company.

More important is that the length of competitive advantage is sometimes inappropriately linked to the explicit forecast period. Remember, the key value driver formula is based on incremental returns on capital, not company-wide average returns. If you set incremental returns on new invested capital (RONIC) in the continuing-value period equal to the cost of capital, you are *not* assuming that the return on total capital (old and new) will equal the cost of capital. The original capital (prior to the continuing-value period) will continue to earn the returns projected in the last forecast period. In other words, the company's competitive-advantage period has not come to an end once the continuing-value period is reached. For example, imagine a retailer whose early stores are located in high-traffic, high-growth areas. The company's early stores earn a superior rate of return and fund ongoing expansion. But as the company grows, new locations become difficult to find, and the ROIC related to expansion starts to drop. Eventually, the ROIC on the newest store will approach the cost of capital. But does this imply ROIC on early stores will

EXHIBIT 10.6 **Gradual Decline in Average ROIC According to Continuing-Value Formula**

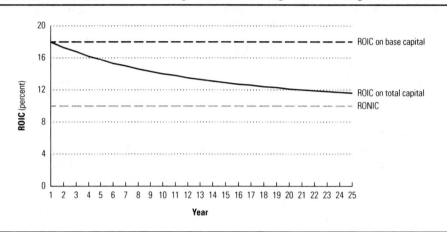

drop to the cost of capital as well? Probably not. A great location is hard to beat.

Exhibit 10.6 shows the implied average ROIC, assuming that projected continuing-value growth is 4.5 percent, the return on base capital is 18 percent, RONIC is 10 percent, and WACC is 10 percent. The average return on all capital declines only gradually. From its starting point at 18 percent, it declines to 14 percent (the halfway point to RONIC) after 10 years in the continuing-value period. It reaches 12 percent after 21 years, and 11 percent after 37 years.

When Is Value Created?

Executives often state uncomfortably that "all the value is in the continuing value." Exhibit 10.7 illustrates the problem for a hypothetical company, Innovation, Inc. Based on discounted free cash flow, it appears that 85 percent of Innovation's value comes from the continuing value. But there are other interesting ways to interpret the source of value.

Exhibit 10.8 suggests an alternative: a business components approach. Innovation, Inc. has a base business that earns a steady 12 percent return on capital and is growing at 4 percent per year. It also has developed a new product line that will require several years of negative cash flow for development of a new sales channel, which management hopes will lead to organic growth. As shown in Exhibit 10.8, the base business has a value of $877 million, or 71 percent of Innovation's total value. So 71 percent of the company's value comes from operations that are currently generating strong, stable cash flow. Only 29 percent of total value is attributable to the unpredictable growth business. When the situation is viewed this way, uncertainty plays only a small role in the total value.

EXHIBIT 10.7 **Innovation, Inc.: Free Cash Flow Forecast and Valuation**

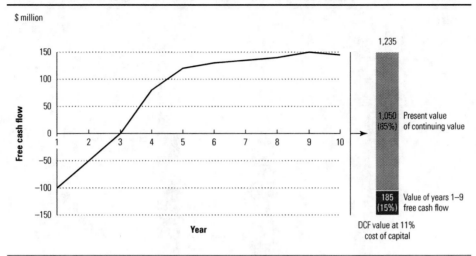

We can use the economic-profit model to generate another interpretation of continuing value. Exhibit 10.9 compares the components of value for Innovation, Inc., using the discounted free cash flow approach, the business components approach, and an economic-profit model. Under the economic-profit model, 62 percent of Innovation's value is simply the book value of invested capital. The rest of the value, $468 million, is the present value of projected economic profit, and of that, only 30 percent of total value is generated during the continuing-value period—a much smaller share than under the discounted FCF model.

EXHIBIT 10.8 **Innovation, Inc.: Valuation by Components**

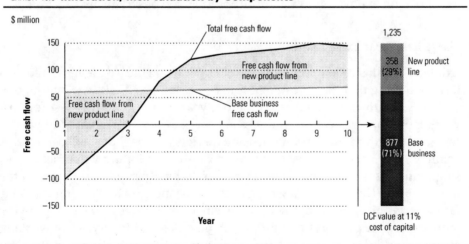

EXHIBIT 10.9 **Innovation, Inc.: Comparison of Continuing-Value Approaches**

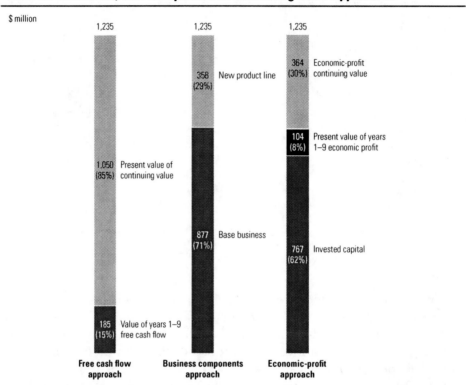

COMMON PITFALLS

Estimating a company's performance 10 to 15 years out is not a precise process. Common mistakes in estimating continuing value include naive base year extrapolation and both naive and purposeful overconservatism.

Naive Base Year Extrapolation

Exhibit 10.10 illustrates a common error in forecasting the base level of free cash flow: assuming that the investment rate is constant, so NOPLAT, investment, and FCF all grow at the same rate. From year 9 to year 10 (the last forecast year), the company's earnings and cash flow grow by 10 percent. You believe revenue growth in the continuing-value period will be 5 percent per year. A common, yet incorrect, forecast for year 11 (the continuing-value base year) simply increases every line item from year 10 by 5 percent, as shown in the third column. This forecast is wrong because the increase in working capital is far too large, given the projected increase in sales. Since revenues are growing more slowly, the proportion of gross cash flow devoted to increasing working capital should decline significantly, as shown in the last column. In the final column, the increase in working capital should be the amount necessary to

562

EXHIBIT 10.10 **Correct and Incorrect Methods of Forecasting Base FCF**

$ million

	Year 9	Year 10	Year 11 (5% growth)	
			Incorrect	Correct
Revenues	1,000	1,100	1,155	1,155
Operating expenses	(850)	(935)	(982)	(982)
EBITA	150	165	173	173
Operating taxes	(60)	(66)	(69)	(69)
NOPLAT	90	99	104	104
Depreciation	27	30	32	32
Gross cash flow	117	129	136	136
Capital expenditures	(30)	(33)	(35)	(35)
Increase in working capital	(27)	(30)	(32)	(17)
Gross investment	(57)	(63)	(67)	(52)
Free cash flow	60	66	69	84
Supplemental calculations				
Working capital, year-end	300	330	362	347
Working capital/revenues (percent)	30.0	30.0	31.3	30.0

maintain the year-end working capital at a constant percentage of revenues. The naive approach continually increases working capital as a percentage of revenues and will significantly understate the value of the company. Note that in the third column, free cash flow is 18 percent lower than it should be. The same problem applies to capital expenditures, though we limited the example to working capital to keep it simple. Using the value driver formula, instead of a cash flow perpetuity, automatically avoids the problem of naive base year extrapolation.

Naive Overconservatism

Many financial analysts routinely assume that the incremental return on capital during the continuing-value period will equal the cost of capital. This practice relieves them of having to forecast a growth rate, since growth in this case neither adds nor destroys value. For some businesses, this assumption is too conservative. For example, both Coca-Cola's and PepsiCo's soft-drink businesses earn high returns on invested capital, and their returns are unlikely to fall substantially as they continue to grow, due to the strength of their brands. An assumption that RONIC equals WACC for these businesses would understate their values. Even when RONIC remains high, growth will eventually drop as the market matures. Therefore, any assumption that RONIC is greater than WACC should be coupled with an economically reasonable growth rate.

EXHIBIT 10.11 **Continuing-Value Estimates for a Sporting Goods Company**

Technique	Assumptions	Continuing value ($ million)
Book value	Per accounting records	268
Liquidation value	80% of working capital	186
	70% of net fixed assets	
Price-to-earnings ratio	Industry average of 15 ×	624
Market-to-book ratio	Industry average of 1.4 ×	375
Replacement cost	Book value adjusted for inflation	275
Perpetuity based on final year's cash flow	Normalized FCF growing at inflation rate	428

This problem applies equally to almost any business selling a product or service that is unlikely to be duplicated, including many pharmaceutical companies, numerous consumer products companies, and some software companies.

Purposeful Overconservatism

Analysts sometimes are overly conservative because of the uncertainty and size of the continuing value. But if continuing value is to be estimated properly, the uncertainty should cut both ways: The results are just as likely to be higher than an unbiased estimate as they are to be lower. So conservatism overcompensates for uncertainty. Uncertainty matters, but it should be modeled using scenarios, not through conservatism.

EVALUATING OTHER APPROACHES TO CONTINUING VALUE

Several alternative approaches to continuing value are used in practice, often with misleading results. A few approaches are acceptable if used carefully, but we prefer the methods recommended earlier because they explicitly rely on the underlying economic assumptions embodied in the company analysis. Other approaches tend to obscure the underlying economic assumptions. Exhibit 10.11 illustrates, for a sporting goods company, the wide dispersion of continuing-value estimates arrived at by different techniques. This section explains why we prefer the recommended approaches. We classify the most common techniques into two categories: (1) other DCF approaches, and (2) non-cash-flow approaches.

Other DCF Approaches

The recommended DCF formulas can be modified to derive additional continuing-value formulas with more restrictive (and sometimes unreasonable) assumptions.

One variation is the *convergence* formula. For many companies in competitive industries, we expect that the return on net new investment will eventually converge to the cost of capital as all the excess profits are competed away. This assumption allows a simpler version of the value driver formula, as follows:

$$CV = \frac{NOPLAT_{t+1}}{WACC}$$

The derivation begins with the value driver formula:

$$CV = \frac{NOPLAT_{t+1}\left(1 - \dfrac{g}{RONIC}\right)}{WACC - g}$$

Assume that RONIC = WACC (that is, the return on incremental invested capital equals the cost of capital):

$$CV = \frac{NOPLAT_{t+1}\left(1 - \dfrac{g}{WACC}\right)}{WACC - g}$$

$$= \frac{NOPLAT_{t+1}\left(\dfrac{WACC - g}{WACC}\right)}{WACC - g}$$

Canceling the term WACC − g leaves a simple formula:

$$CV = \frac{NOPLAT_{t+1}}{WACC}$$

The fact that the growth term has disappeared from the equation does *not* mean that the nominal growth in NOPLAT will be zero. The growth term drops out because new growth adds nothing to value, as the return associated with growth equals the cost of capital. This formula is sometimes interpreted as implying zero growth (not even with inflation), but this is not the case.

Misinterpretation of the convergence formula has led to another variant: the *aggressive-growth* formula. This formula assumes that earnings in the continuing-value period will grow at some rate, most often the inflation rate. The conclusion is then drawn that earnings should be discounted at the real WACC rather than the nominal WACC. The resulting formula is:

$$CV = \frac{NOPLAT_{t+1}}{WACC - g}$$

Here, g is the inflation rate. This formula can substantially overstate continuing value because it assumes that NOPLAT can grow without any incremental capital investment. This is unlikely (or impossible), because any growth will probably require additional working capital and fixed assets.

EXHIBIT 10.12 **Rates of Return Implied by Alternative Continuing-Value Formulas**

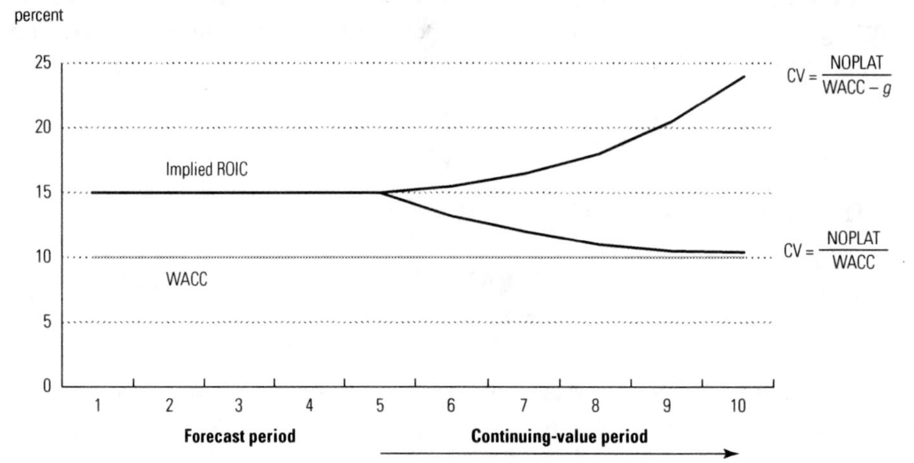

To see the critical assumption hidden in the preceding formula, we analyze the key value driver formula as RONIC approaches infinity:

$$CV = \frac{NOPLAT_{t+1}\left(1 - \dfrac{g}{RONIC}\right)}{WACC - g}$$

$$RONIC \rightarrow \infty, \text{ therefore } \frac{g}{RONIC} \rightarrow 0$$

$$CV = \frac{NOPLAT_{t+1}(1 - 0)}{WACC - g}$$

$$= \frac{NOPLAT_{t+1}}{WACC - g}$$

Exhibit 10.12 compares the two variations of the key value driver formula, showing how the average return on invested capital (both existing and new investment) behaves under the two assumptions. In the aggressive-growth case, NOPLAT grows without any new investment, so the return on invested capital eventually approaches infinity. In the convergence case, the average return on invested capital moves toward the weighted average cost of capital as new capital becomes a larger portion of the total capital base.

Non-Cash-Flow Approaches

In addition to DCF techniques, non-cash-flow approaches to continuing value are sometimes used. Three common approaches are multiples, liquidation value, and replacement cost.

Multiples Multiples approaches assume that a company will be worth some multiple of future earnings or book value in the continuing period. But how do you estimate an appropriate future multiple?

A common approach is to assume that the company will be worth a multiple of earnings or book value based on the multiple for the company today. Suppose we choose today's current industry average price-to-earnings (P/E) ratio. This ratio reflects the economic prospects of the industry during the explicit forecast period as well as the continuing-value period. In maturing industries, however, prospects at the end of the explicit forecast period are likely to be very different from today's. Therefore, we need a different P/E that reflects the company's prospects at the end of the forecast period. What factors will determine that ratio? As discussed in Chapter 3, the primary determinants are the company's expected growth, the rate of return on new capital, and the cost of capital. The same factors are in the key value driver formula. Unless you are comfortable using an arbitrary P/E, you are much better off with the value driver formula.

When valuing an acquisition, companies sometimes fall into the circular reasoning that the P/E for the continuing value should equal the P/E paid for the acquisition. In other words, if I pay 18 times earnings today, I should be able to sell the business for 18 times earnings at the end of the explicit forecast period. In most cases, the reason a company is willing to pay a particular P/E for an acquisition is that it plans to improve the target's earnings. So the effective P/E it is paying on the improved level of earnings will be much less than 18. Once the improvements are in place and earnings are higher, buyers will not be willing to pay the same P/E unless they can make additional improvements. Chapter 14 describes other common mistakes made when using multiples.

Liquidation value The liquidation value approach sets the continuing value equal to the estimated proceeds from the sale of the assets, after paying off liabilities at the end of the explicit forecast period. Liquidation value is often far different from the value of the company as a going concern. In a growing, profitable industry, a company's liquidation value is probably well below the going-concern value. In a dying industry, liquidation value may exceed going-concern value. Do not use this approach unless liquidation is likely at the end of the forecast period.

Replacement cost The replacement cost approach sets the continuing value equal to the expected cost to replace the company's assets. This approach has at least two drawbacks. First, not all tangible assets are replaceable. The company's organizational capital can be valued only on the basis of the cash flow the company generates. The replacement cost of just the company's tangible assets may greatly understate the value of the company.

Second, not all the company's assets will ever be replaced. Consider a machine used only by this particular industry. As long as it generates a positive cash flow, the asset is valuable to the ongoing business of the company. But the replacement cost of the asset may be so high that replacing it is not economical. Here, the replacement cost may exceed the value of the business as an ongoing entity.

ADVANCED FORMULAS FOR CONTINUING VALUE

In certain situations, you may want to break up the continuing-value (CV) period into two periods with different growth and ROIC assumptions. You might assume that during the first eight years after the explicit forecast period, the company will grow at 8 percent per year and earn an incremental ROIC of 15 percent. After those eight years, the company's growth rate will slow to 5 percent, and incremental ROIC will drop to 11 percent. In a situation such as this, you can use a two-stage variation of the value driver formula for DCF valuations:

$$
CV = \left[\frac{NOPLAT_{t+1}\left(1 - \dfrac{g_A}{RONIC_A}\right)}{WACC - g_A} \right] \left[1 - \left(\frac{1 + g_A}{1 + WACC}\right)^N \right]
$$

$$
+ \left[\frac{NOPLAT_{t+1}(1 + g_A)^N \left(1 - \dfrac{g_B}{RONIC_B}\right)}{(WACC - g_B)(1 + WACC)^N} \right]
$$

where N = number of years in the first stage of the CV period
          g_A = expected growth rate in the first stage of the CV period
          g_B = expected growth rate in the second stage of the CV period
   $RONIC_A$ = expected incremental ROIC during the first stage of the CV period
   $RONIC_B$ = expected incremental ROIC during the second stage of the CV period

Note that g_A can take any value; it does not have to be less than the weighted average cost of capital. Conversely, g_B must be less than WACC for this formula to be valid. (Otherwise the formula goes to infinity, and the company takes over the entire world economy.)

A two-stage variation can also be used for the economic-profit continuing-value formula:[1]

$$CV = \frac{\text{Economic Profit}_{t+1}}{\text{WACC}}$$

$$+ \left[\frac{\text{NOPLAT}_{t+1} \left(\frac{g_A}{\text{RONIC}_A} \right) (\text{RONIC}_A - \text{WACC})}{\text{WACC}(\text{WACC} - g_A)} \right] \left[1 - \left(\frac{1 + g_A}{1 + \text{WACC}} \right)^N \right]$$

$$+ \frac{\text{NOPLAT}(1 + g_A)^N \left(\frac{g_B}{\text{RONIC}_B} \right) (\text{RONIC}_B - \text{WACC})}{\text{WACC}(\text{WACC} - g_B)(1 + \text{WACC})^N}$$

These formulas always assume that the return on the base level of capital remains constant at the level of the last year of the explicit forecast.

If you want to model a decline in ROIC for all capital, including the base level of capital, it is best to model this into the explicit forecast. It is difficult to model changes in average ROIC with formulas, because the growth rate in revenues and NOPLAT will not equal the growth rate in FCF, and there are multiple ways for the ROIC to decline. You could model declining ROIC by setting the growth rate for capital and reducing NOPLAT over time (in which case NOPLAT will grow much slower than capital). Or you could set the growth rate for NOPLAT and adjust FCF each period (so FCF growth again will be slower than NOPLAT growth). The dynamics of these relationships are complex, and we do not recommend embedding the dynamics in continuing-value formulas, especially when the key value drivers become less transparent.

REVIEW QUESTIONS

1. Exhibit 10.13 presents free cash flow and economic profit forecasts for ApparelCo, a $250 million company that produces men's clothing. ApparelCo is expected to grow revenues, operating profits, and free cash flow at 6 percent per year indefinitely. The company earns a return on new capital of 15 percent. The company's cost of capital is 10 percent. Using the key value driver formula, what is the continuing value as of year 5? Using discounted cash flow, what is the value of operations for ApparelCo? What percentage of ApparelCo's total value is attributable to the continuing value?

2. Since growth is stable for ApparelCo, you decide to start the continuing value with year 3 cash flows (i.e., cash flows in year 3 and beyond are

[1] Thanks to Peter de Wit and David Krieger for deriving this formula.

EXHIBIT 10.13 **ApparelCo: Free Cash Flow and Economic Profit Forecasts**

$ million

	Today	Year 1	Year 2	Year 3	Year 4	Year 5	Continuing value[1]
Revenues	250.0	265.0	280.9	297.8	315.6	334.6	354.6
Operating costs	(225.0)	(238.5)	(252.8)	(268.0)	(284.1)	(301.1)	(319.2)
Operating profit	25.0	26.5	28.1	29.8	31.6	33.5	35.5
Operating taxes	(6.3)	(6.6)	(7.0)	(7.4)	(7.9)	(8.4)	(8.9)
NOPLAT	18.8	19.9	21.1	22.3	23.7	25.1	26.6
Net investment	–	(8.0)	(8.4)	(8.9)	(9.5)	(10.0)	–
Free cash flow	–	11.9	12.6	13.4	14.2	15.1	–
Economic profit							
NOPLAT	–	19.9	21.1	22.3	23.7	25.1	26.6
Invested capital$_{t-1}$	–	132.5	140.5	148.9	157.8	167.3	177.3
× Cost of capital (percent)	–	10.0	10.0	10.0	10.0	10.0	10.0
Capital charge	–	13.3	14.0	14.9	15.8	16.7	17.7
Economic profit	–	6.6	7.0	7.4	7.9	8.4	8.9

[1] Rounding error will cause small distortions in valuation.

part of the continuing value). Using the key value driver formula (and data provided in Question 1), what is the continuing value as of year 2? Using discounted cash flow, what is the value of operations for ApparelCo? What percentage of ApparelCo's total value is attributable to the continuing value? How do these percentages compare to Question 1?

3. Using the economic profit formula, what is the continuing value for ApparelCo as of year 5? Using discounted economic profit, what is the value of operations for ApparelCo? What percentage of ApparelCo's total value is attributable to current invested capital, to interim economic profits, and to economic profits in the continuing value period?

4. Since growth is stable for ApparelCo, you decide to start the continuing value with year 3 economic profits (i.e., economic profits in year 3 and beyond are part of the continuing value). Using the economic profit formula (and data provided in Question 1), what is the continuing value as of year 2? Using discounted economic profit, what is the value of operations for ApparelCo? What percentage of ApparelCo's total value is attributable to the continuing value? How do these compare to Question 3?

5. A colleague suggests that a 6 percent growth rate is too low for revenue, profit, and cash flow growth beyond year 5. He suggests raising growth to 12 percent in the continuing value. If NOPLAT equals $26.6 million, return on new capital equals 15 percent, and the cost of capital equals 10 percent, what is the continuing value as of year 5? Is there an alternative model that is more appropriate?

6. SuperiorCo earns a return on invested capital of 20 percent on its existing stores. Given intense competition for new stores sites, you believe new stores will only earn their cost of capital. Consequently, you set return on new capital (8 percent) equal to the cost of capital (8 percent) in the continuing value formula. A colleague argues that this is too conservative, as SuperiorCo will create value well beyond the forecast period. What is the flaw in your colleague's argument?

11

Estimating the Cost of Capital

To value a company using enterprise discounted cash flow (DCF), discount your forecast of free cash flow (FCF) by the weighted average cost of capital (WACC). The WACC represents the opportunity cost that investors face for investing their funds in one particular business instead of others with similar risk.

The most important principle underlying successful implementation of the cost of capital is consistency between the components of the WACC and free cash flow. Since free cash flow is the cash flow available to all financial investors, the company's WACC must also include the required return for each investor. To assure consistency among these elements, the cost of capital must meet the following criteria:

- It must include the opportunity costs of all investors—debt, equity, and so on—since free cash flow is available to all investors, who expect compensation for the risks they take.

- It must weight each security's required return by its target market-based weight, not by its historical book value.

- Any financing-related benefits or costs, such as interest tax shields, not included in free cash flow must be incorporated into the cost of capital or valued separately using adjusted present value.[1]

[1] For most companies, discounting forecast free cash flow at a constant WACC is a simple, accurate, and robust method of arriving at a corporate valuation. If, however, the company's target capital structure is expected to change significantly—for instance, in a leveraged buyout, WACC can overstate (or understate) the impact of interest tax shields. In this situation, you should discount free cash flow at the unlevered cost of equity and value tax shields and other financing effects separately (as described in Chapter 6).

- It must be computed after corporate taxes (since free cash flow is calculated in after-tax terms).

- It must be based on the same expectations of inflation as those embedded in forecasts of free cash flow.

- The duration of the securities used to estimate the cost of capital must match the duration of the cash flows.

Bearing these criteria in mind, to determine the weighted average cost of capital for a particular enterprise, you need to estimate the WACC's three components: the cost of equity, the after-tax cost of debt, and the company's target capital structure. Since *none* of the variables are directly observable, we employ various models, assumptions, and approximations to estimate each component. These models estimate the expected return on alternative investments with similar risk using market prices. This is why the term *expected return* is used interchangeably with cost of capital. Since the cost of capital is also used for allocating capital within the firm, it can also be referred to as a required return or hurdle rate.

In this chapter, we begin by defining the components of WACC and introducing the assumptions underlying their estimation. The next three sections detail how to estimate the cost of equity, cost of debt, and target capital structure, respectively. The chapter concludes with a discussion of WACC estimation when the company employs a complex capital structure.

WEIGHTED AVERAGE COST OF CAPITAL

In its simplest form, the weighted average cost of capital equals the weighted average of the after-tax cost of debt and cost of equity:

$$\text{WACC} = \frac{D}{V} k_d (1 - T_m) + \frac{E}{V} k_e$$

where D/V = target level of debt to enterprise value using market-based (not book) values

E/V = target level of equity to enterprise value using market-based values

k_d = cost of debt

k_e = cost of equity

T_m = company's marginal income tax rate

The equation shows the three critical components of the WACC: the cost of equity, the after-tax cost of debt, and the target mix between the two securities.[2]

---

[2] For companies with other securities, such as preferred stock, additional terms must be added to the cost of capital, representing each security's expected rate of return and percentage of total enterprise value.

EXHIBIT 11.1 **Weighted Average Cost of Capital**

Component	Methodology	Data requirements	Considerations
Cost of equity	Capital asset pricing model (CAPM)	• Risk-free rate	Use a long-term government rate denominated in same currency as cash flows.
		• Market risk premium	The market risk premium is difficult to measure. Various models point to a risk premium between 4.5% and 5.5%.
		• Company beta	To estimate beta, lever the company's industry beta to company's target debt-to-equity ratio.
After-tax cost of debt	Expected return proxied by yield to maturity on long-term debt	• Risk-free rate	Use a long-term government rate denominated in same currency as cash flows.
		• Default spread	Default spread is determined by company's bond rating and amount of physical collateral.
		• Marginal tax rate	In most situations, use company's statutory tax rate. The marginal tax rate should match marginal tax rate used to forecast net operating profit less adjusted taxes (NOPLAT).
Capital structure	Proportion of debt and equity to enterprise value		Measure debt and equity on a market, not book, basis. Use a forward-looking target capital structure.

Exhibit 11.1 identifies the methodology and data required for estimating each component.

The cost of equity is determined by three factors: the risk-free rate of return, the market-wide risk premium (the expected return of the market portfolio less the return of risk-free bonds), and a risk adjustment that reflects each company's riskiness relative to the average company. In this book, we use the capital asset pricing model (CAPM) to estimate a company's risk adjustment factor. The CAPM adjusts for company-specific risk through the use of beta, which measures a stock's co-movement with the market and represents the extent to which a stock may diversify the investor's portfolio. Stocks with high betas must have excess returns that exceed the market risk premium; the converse is true for low-beta stocks.

To approximate the after-tax cost of debt for an investment-grade firm, use the company's after-tax yield to maturity (YTM) on its long-term debt. For companies with publicly traded debt, calculate yield to maturity directly from the bond's price and promised cash flows. For companies whose debt trades infrequently, use the company's debt rating to estimate the yield to maturity. Since free cash flow is measured without interest tax shields, measure the cost of debt on an after-tax basis using the company's marginal tax rate.

Finally, the after-tax cost of debt and cost of equity should be weighted using target levels of debt to value and equity to value. For mature companies,

The cost of capital does not include expected returns of operating liabilities, such as accounts payable. Required compensation for capital provided by customers, suppliers, and employees is included in operating expenses, so it is already incorporated in free cash flow. Including operating liabilities in the WACC would incorrectly double-count their cost of financing.

EXHIBIT 11.2 **Home Depot: Weighted Average Cost of Capital**

percent

Source of capital	Proportion of total capital	Cost of capital	Marginal tax rate	After-tax opportunity cost	Contribution to weighted average[1]
Debt	31.5	6.8	37.6	4.2	1.3
Equity	68.5	10.4		10.4	7.1
WACC	100.0				8.5

[1] Total does not sum due to rounding error.

the target capital structure is often approximated by the company's current debt-to-value ratio, using market values of debt and equity. As will be explained later in this chapter, you should not use book values.

In Exhibit 11.2, we present the WACC calculation for Home Depot. The company's cost of equity was estimated using the CAPM, which led to a cost of equity of 10.4 percent. To apply the CAPM, we used the May 2009 10-year U.S. government zero-coupon STRIPS[3] rate of 3.9 percent, a market risk premium of 5.4 percent, and an industry beta of 1.21. To estimate Home Depot's pretax cost of debt, we used the May 2009 yield to maturity on BBB+ rated debt, which led to a cost of debt of 6.8 percent. In Chapter 7, we estimated Home Depot's marginal tax rate at 37.6 percent,[4] so its after-tax cost of debt equals 4.2 percent. Finally, we assume Home Depot will maintain a current debt-to-value ratio of 31.5 percent going forward.[5] Adding the weighted contributions from debt and equity, we arrive at a WACC equal to 8.5 percent.

We discuss each component of the weighted average cost of capital in the following sections.

ESTIMATING THE COST OF EQUITY

The cost of equity is built on the three factors: the risk-free rate, the market risk premium, and a company-specific risk adjustment. The most commonly used model to estimate the cost of equity is the capital asset pricing model (CAPM). Other models include the Fama-French three-factor model and the arbitrage pricing theory model (APT). The three models differ primarily in

[3] Introduced by the U.S. Treasury in 1985, STRIPS stands for "separate trading of registered interest and principal of securities." The STRIPS program enables investors to hold and trade the individual components of Treasury notes and bonds as separate securities.

[4] The marginal tax rate used to determine the after-tax cost of debt must match the marginal tax rate used to determine free cash flow. For Home Depot, the marginal tax rate equals the summation of federal (35 percent) and state (2.6 percent) income taxes, presented in Exhibit 7.11.

[5] Net debt equals reported debt plus the present value of operating leases, less excess cash. Since we last examined Home Depot in 2004, the debt-to-value ratio has risen substantially, from 8.3 percent to 31.5 percent, following the acquisition of Hughes Supply in 2006. Given the company's recent focus on core operations and the challenging economy, the company will probably reduce its debt-to-value ratio. For simplicity, we assume the company will maintain its current capital structure.

how they define risk. The CAPM defines a stock's risk as its sensitivity to the stock market,[6] whereas the Fama-French three-factor model defines risk as a stock's sensitivity to three portfolios: the stock market, a portfolio based on firm size, and a portfolio based on book-to-market ratios.

Despite recent criticism, we believe that the CAPM remains the best model for estimating the cost of equity if you are developing a WACC to use in a company valuation. We analyze these three models next, starting with a detailed examination of the CAPM.

Capital Asset Pricing Model

Because the CAPM is discussed at length in modern finance textbooks,[7] we will not delve into the theory here. Instead, we focus on best practices for implementation.

The CAPM postulates that the expected rate of return on any security equals the risk-free rate plus the security's beta times the market risk premium:

$$E(R_i) = r_f + \beta_i \left[E(R_m) - r_f \right]$$

where $E(R_i)$ = expected return of security i

r_f = risk-free rate

β_i = stock's sensitivity to the market

$E(R_m)$ = expected return of the market

In the CAPM, the risk-free rate and market risk premium, defined as the difference between $E(R_m)$ and r_f, are common to all companies; only beta varies across companies. Beta represents a stock's incremental risk to a diversified investor, where risk is defined as the extent to which the stock covaries with the aggregate stock market.

Consider HJ Heinz, a manufacturer of ketchup and frozen foods, and Motorola, a maker of cellular phones and set-top boxes. Basic consumer foods purchases are relatively independent of the stock market's value, so the beta for Heinz is low; we estimated it at 0.60. Based on a risk-free rate of 3.9 percent and a market risk premium of 5.4 percent, the cost of equity for Heinz is estimated at 7.1 percent (see Exhibit 11.3). In contrast, technology companies tend to have high betas. When the economy struggles, the stock market drops, and companies stop purchasing new technology. Thus, Motorola's value is highly correlated with the market's value, and its beta is high. Based on a beta of 1.5, Motorola's expected rate of return is 12.0 percent. Since Heinz offers greater

---

[6] In theory, the market portfolio represents the value-weighted portfolio of all assets, both traded (such as stocks) and untraded (such as a person's skill set). Throughout this chapter, we use a well-diversified stock portfolio, such as the Morgan Stanley Capital International (MSCI) World Index, as a proxy for the market portfolio.

[7] For example, Richard Brealey, Stewart Myers, and Franklin Allen, *Principles of Corporate Finance*, 9th ed. (New York: McGraw-Hill, 2008); and Thomas Copeland, Fred Weston, and Kuldeep Shastri, *Financial Theory and Corporate Policy* (Boston: Addison-Wesley, 2005).

EXHIBIT 11.3 **Capital Asset Pricing Model (CAPM)**

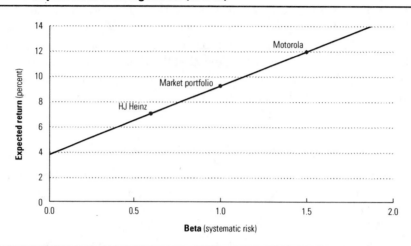

protection against market downturns than Motorola does, investors are willing to pay a premium for the stock, driving down the stock's expected return. Conversely, since Motorola offers little diversification in relation to the market portfolio, the company must earn a higher return to entice investors.

Although the CAPM is based on solid theory (the 1990 Nobel Prize in economics was awarded to the model's primary author, William Sharpe), the model provides little guidance for its use in valuation. For instance, when valuing a company, which risk-free rate should you use? How do you estimate the market risk premium and beta? In the following section, we address these issues. Our general conclusions are the following:

- To estimate the risk-free rate in developed economies, use highly liquid, long-term government securities, such as the 10-year zero-coupon STRIPS.

- Based on historical averages and forward-looking estimates, the appropriate market risk premium is between 4.5 and 5.5 percent.

- To estimate a company's beta, use an industry-derived unlevered beta relevered to the company's target capital structure. Company-specific betas vary too widely over time to be used reliably.

Estimating the risk-free rate   To estimate the risk-free rate, we look to government default-free bonds.[8] Government bonds come in many maturities.

---

[8] In its most general form, the risk-free rate is defined as the return on a portfolio (or security) that has no covariance with the market (represented by a CAPM beta of 0). Hypothetically, one could construct a zero-beta portfolio, but given the cost and complexity of designing such a portfolio, we recommend focusing on long-term government *default-free* bonds. Although not necessarily *risk free*, long-term government bonds in the United States and Western Europe have extremely low betas.

EXHIBIT 11.4 **Government Zero-Coupon Yields, May 2009**

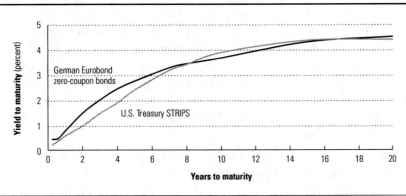

Source: Bloomberg.

For instance, the U.S. Treasury issues bonds with maturities ranging from one month to 30 years. However, different maturities can generate different yields to maturity. Which maturity should you use?

Ideally, each cash flow should be discounted using a government bond with the same maturity. For instance, a cash flow generated 10 years from today should be discounted by a cost of capital derived from a 10-year zero-coupon government bond (known as STRIPS). We prefer government STRIPS because long-term government bonds make interim interest payments, causing their effective maturity to be shorter than their stated maturity.

In reality, few practitioners discount each cash flow using a matched maturity. For simplicity, most choose a single yield to maturity from the government STRIPS that best matches the entire cash flow stream being valued. For U.S.-based corporate valuation, the most common proxy is 10-year government STRIPS (longer-dated bonds such as the 30-year Treasury bond might match the cash flow stream better, but their illiquidity means their prices and yield premiums may not reflect their current value). When valuing European companies, we prefer the 10-year German Eurobond. German bonds have higher liquidity and lower credit risk than bonds of other European countries. Always use government bond yields denominated in the same currency as the company's cash flow to estimate the risk-free rate. This way inflation will be modeled consistently between cash flow and the discount rate.

In Exhibit 11.4, we plot the yield to maturity for various U.S. and German zero-coupon STRIPS versus their years to maturity (a relationship commonly known as the yield curve or term structure of interest rates). As of May 2009, 10-year U.S. Treasury STRIPS were trading at 3.9 percent, and German zero-coupon bonds were trading at 3.7 percent.

If you are valuing a company or long-term project, do *not* use a short-term Treasury bill to determine the risk-free rate. When introductory finance textbooks calculate the CAPM, they typically use a short-term Treasury rate because they are estimating expected returns for the next *month*. As can be seen in Exhibit 11.4, short-term Treasury bills (near the *y*-axis) traded well below 10-year bonds in May 2009. Investors typically demand higher interest rates from long-term bonds when they believe short-term interest rates will rise over time. Using the yield from a short-term bond as the risk-free rate in a valuation fails to recognize that a bondholder can probably reinvest at higher rates when the short-term bond matures. Thus, the short-term bond rate misestimates the opportunity cost of investment for longer-term projects.

Estimating the market risk premium   Sizing the market risk premium—the difference between the market's expected return and the risk-free rate—is arguably the most debated issue in finance. The ability of stocks to outperform bonds over the long run has implications for corporate valuation, portfolio composition, and retirement savings. But similar to a stock's expected return, the expected return on the market is unobservable. And since no single model for estimating the market risk premium has gained universal acceptance, we present the results of various models.

Methods to estimate the market risk premium fall into three general categories:

1. Estimating the future risk premium by measuring and extrapolating historical returns.
2. Using regression analysis to link current market variables, such as the aggregate dividend-to-price ratio, to project the expected market risk premium.
3. Using DCF valuation, along with estimates of return on investment and growth, to reverse engineer the market's cost of capital.

None of today's models precisely estimate the market risk premium. Still, based on evidence from each of these models, we believe the market risk premium varies continually between 4.5 and 5.5 percent and as of May 2009 equaled 5.4 percent. We step through the three models next.

Historical market risk premium   Investors, being risk averse, demand a premium for holding stocks rather than bonds. If the level of risk aversion hasn't changed over the past 100 years, then historical excess returns should be a reasonable proxy for future premiums. For the best measurement of the risk premium using historical data, follow these guidelines:

- *Calculate the premium relative to long-term government bonds.* When calculating the market risk premium, compare historical market returns with the return on 10-year government bonds. As discussed in the previous section, long-term government bonds better match the duration of a company's cash flows than do short-term bonds.

- *Use the longest period possible.* When using historical observations to predict future results, how far back should you look? If the market risk premium is stable, a longer history will reduce estimation error. Alternatively, if the premium changes and estimation error is small, a shorter period is better. To determine the appropriate historical period, consider any trends in the market risk premium compared with the noise associated with short-term estimates.

  To test for the presence of a long-term trend, we regress the U.S. market risk premium against time. Over the past 108 years, no statistically significant trend is observable.[9] Based on regression results, the average excess return has fallen by 4.2 basis points a year, but this result cannot be statistically distinguished from zero. In addition, premiums calculated over shorter periods are extremely noisy. For instance, U.S. stocks outperformed bonds by 18 percent in the 1950s but offered no premium in the 1970s. Given the lack of any discernible trend and the significant volatility of shorter periods, you should use the longest time series possible.

- *Use an arithmetic average of longer-dated intervals (such as 10 years).* When reporting market risk premiums, most data providers report an annual number, such as 6.1 percent per year. But how do they convert a century of data into an annual number? And is the annualized number even relevant?

Annual returns can be calculated using either an arithmetic average or a geometric average. An arithmetic (simple) average sums each year's observed premium and divides by the number of observations (T):

$$\text{Arithmetic Average} = \frac{1}{T} \sum_{t=1}^{T} \frac{1 + R_m(t)}{1 + r_f(t)} - 1$$

A geometric average compounds each year's excess return and takes the root of the resulting product:

$$\text{Geometric Average} = \left(\prod_{t=1}^{T} \frac{1 + R_m(t)}{1 + r_f(t)} \right)^{1/T} - 1$$

[9] Some authors, such as Jonathan Lewellen, argue that the market risk premium does change over time—and can be measured using financial ratios, such as the dividend yield. We address these models separately. J. Lewellen, "Predicting Returns with Financial Ratios," *Journal of Financial Economics* 74, no. 2 (2004): 209–235.

The choice of averaging methodology will affect the results. For instance, between 1900 and 2009, U.S. stocks outperformed long-term government bonds by 6.1 percent per year when averaged arithmetically. Using a geometric average, the number drops to 4.0 percent. This difference is not random; arithmetic averages always exceed geometric averages when returns are volatile.

So which averaging method on historical data best estimates the *expected* future rate of return? To estimate the mean (expectation) for any random variable, well-accepted statistical principles dictate that the arithmetic average is the best unbiased estimator. Therefore, to determine a security's expected return for *one period*, the best unbiased predictor is the arithmetic average of many one-period returns. A one-period risk premium, however, can't value a company with many years of cash flow. Instead, long-dated cash flows must be discounted using a compounded rate of return. But when compounded, the arithmetic average will generate a discount factor that is biased upward (too high). The cause of the bias is quite technical, so we provide only a summary here.

There are two reasons why compounding the historical arithmetic average leads to a biased discount factor. First, the arithmetic average is measured with error. Although this estimation error will not affect a one-period forecast (the error has an expectation of zero), squaring the estimate (as you do in compounding) in effect squares the measurement error, causing the error to be positive. This positive error leads to a multiyear expected return that is too high. Second, a number of researchers have argued that stock market returns are negatively autocorrelated over time. If positive returns are typically followed by negative returns (and vice versa), then squaring the average will lead to a discount factor that overestimates the actual two-period return, again causing an upward bias.

To correct for the bias caused by estimation error and negative autocorrelation in returns, we have two choices. First, we can calculate multiyear returns directly from the data, rather than compound single-year averages. Using this method, a cash flow received in 10 years will be discounted by the average 10-year market risk premium, not by the annual market risk premium compounded 10 times.[10] In Exhibit 11.5, we present arithmetic averages for holding periods of 1, 2, 4, 5, and 10 years.[11] From 1900 through 2009, the average one-year excess return equaled 6.1 percent. The average 10-year cumulative excess

[10] Jay Ritter writes, "There is no theoretical reason why one year is the appropriate holding period. People are used to thinking of interest rates as a rate per year, so reporting annualized numbers makes it easy for people to focus on the numbers. But I can think of no reason other than convenience for the use of annual returns." J. Ritter, "The Biggest Mistakes We Teach," *Journal of Financial Research* 25 (2002): 159–168.

[11] To compute the average 10-year cumulative return, we use overlapping 10-year periods. To avoid underweighting early and late observations (for instance, the first observation would be included only once, whereas a middle observation would be included in 10 separate samples), we create a synthetic 10-year period by combining the most recent observations with the oldest observations. Nonoverlapping windows lead to similar results but are highly dependent on the starting year.

EXHIBIT 11.5 **Cumulative Returns for Various Intervals, 1900–2009**

percent

	Average cumulative returns			Annualized returns	
Arithmetic mean of	U.S. stocks	U.S. government bonds	U.S. excess returns	U.S. excess returns	Blume estimator
1-year holding periods	11.2	5.4	6.1	6.1	6.1
2-year holding periods	23.7	11.1	12.3	6.0	6.1
4-year holding periods	50.8	23.7	24.4	5.6	6.0
5-year holding periods	66.5	30.7	31.0	5.5	6.0
10-year holding periods	170.7	73.7	69.1	5.4	5.9

Source: Morningstar SBBI data, Morningstar Dimson, Marsh, Staunton Global Returns data.

return equaled 69.1 percent. This translates to an annual rate of 5.4 percent. The range of excess returns falls between 5.4 percent and 6.1 percent.

Alternatively, researchers have used simulation to show that an estimator proposed by Marshall Blume best adjusts for problems caused by estimation error and autocorrelation of returns:[12]

$$R = \left(\frac{T-N}{T-1}\right) R_A + \left(\frac{N-1}{T-1}\right) R_G$$

where $T =$ number of historical observations in the sample
$N =$ forecast period being discounted
$R_A =$ arithmetic average of the historical sample
$R_G =$ geometric average of the historical sample

Blume's estimator depends on the length of time for which you plan to discount. The first year's cash flow should be discounted using the arithmetic average ($T = 110, N = 1$), whereas the 10th year's cash flow should discounted based on a return constructed with a 91.7 percent weighting on the arithmetic average and an 8.3 percent weighting on the long-term geometric average ($T = 110, N = 10$). In the last column of Exhibit 11.5, we report Blume's estimate for the market risk premium by the length of the forecast window.

The bottom line? No matter how we annualize excess returns, group the aggregation windows, or simulate estimators, the excess return on U.S. stocks over government bonds generally falls between 5 and 6 percent.

Adjust the result for econometric issues, such as survivorship bias Other statistical difficulties exist with historical risk premiums. According to one argument,[13]

[12] D. C. Indro and W. Y. Lee, "Biases in Arithmetic and Geometric Averages Premia," *Financial Management* 26, no. 4 (Winter 1997); and M. E. Blume, "Unbiased Estimators of Long Run Expected Rates of Return," *Journal of the American Statistical Association* 69, no. 347 (September 1974).

[13] S. Brown, W. Goetzmann, and S. Ross, "Survivorship Bias," *Journal of Finance* (July 1995): 853–873.

even properly measured historical premiums can't predict future premiums, because the observable sample includes only countries with strong historical returns. Statisticians refer to this phenomenon as survivorship bias. Zvi Bodie writes, "There were 36 active stock markets in 1900, so why do we only look at two, [the UK and U.S. markets]? I can tell you—because many of the others don't have a 100-year history, for a variety of reasons."[14]

Since it is unlikely that the U.S. stock market will replicate its performance over the next century, we adjust downward the historical market risk premium. Elroy Dimson, Paul Marsh, and Mike Staunton find that between 1900 and 2005, the U.S. arithmetic annual return exceeded a 17-country composite return by 0.8 percent in real terms.[15] If we subtract a 0.8 percent survivorship premium from the U.S. excess returns reported in Exhibit 11.5, the difference implies that the U.S. market risk premium falls between 4.6 and 5.3 percent.

Estimating the market risk premium with current financial ratios Although we find no long-term trend in the historical risk premium, many argue that the market risk premium is predictable using observable variables, such as current financial ratios, or forward-looking estimation models. Different forms of measurement converge on an appropriate range of market risk premium of 4.5 to 5.5 percent, which has held even during the financial crisis of 2008.

The use of current financial ratios, such as the aggregate dividend-to-price ratio, the aggregate book-to-market ratio, or the aggregate ratio of earnings to price, to estimate the expected return on stocks is well documented and dates back to Charles Dow in the 1920s. The concept has been tested by many authors.[16] To predict the market risk premium using financial ratios, regress excess market returns against a financial ratio, such as the market's aggregate dividend-to-price ratio:

$$R_m - r_f = \alpha + \beta \ln \left(\frac{\text{Dividend}}{\text{Price}} \right) + \varepsilon$$

where α = the regression intercept, β = the regression slope, and ε represents noise in the regression.

Using advanced regression techniques unavailable to earlier authors, Jonathan Lewellen found that dividend yields *do* predict future market returns. However, the model has a major drawback: the risk premium prediction

---

[14] Z. Bodie, "Longer Time Horizon 'Does Not Reduce Risk,'" *Financial Times*, January 26, 2002.

[15] E. Dimson, P. Marsh, and M. Staunton, "The Worldwide Equity Premium: A Smaller Puzzle," in *Handbook of Investments: Equity Risk Premium*, ed. R. Mehra (Amsterdam: Elsevier Science, 2007).

[16] E. Fama and K. French, "Dividend Yields and Expected Stock Returns," *Journal of Financial Economics* 22, no. 1 (1988): 3–25; R. F. Stambaugh, "Predictive Regressions," *Journal of Financial Economics* 54, no. 3 (1999): 375–421; and J. Lewellen, "Predicting Returns with Financial Ratios," *Journal of Financial Economics* 74, no. 2 (2004): 209–235.

can be negative (as it was in the late 1990s). A negative risk premium is inconsistent with risk-averse investors who demand a premium for holding volatile securities. Other authors question the explanatory power of financial ratios, arguing that a financial analyst relying solely on data available at the time would have done better using unconditional historical averages (as we did in the last section) in place of more sophisticated regression techniques.[17]

Estimating the market risk premium with forward-looking models   A stock's price equals the present value of its dividends. Assuming dividends are expected to grow at a constant rate, we can rearrange the growing perpetuity to solve for the market's expected return:

$$\text{Price} = \frac{\text{Dividend}}{k_e - g} \quad \text{converts to} \quad k_e = \frac{\text{Dividend}}{\text{Price}} + g$$

where k_e = cost of equity
  g = expected growth in dividends

In the previous section, Lewellen and others regressed market returns on the dividend-to-price ratio. Using a simple regression, however, ignores valuable information and oversimplifies a few market realities. First, the dividend-to-price yield itself depends on the expected growth in dividends, which simple regressions ignore (the regression's intercept is determined by the data). Second, dividends are only one form of corporate payout. Companies can use free cash flow to repurchase shares or hold excess cash for significant periods of time; consider Microsoft, which accumulated more than $50 billion in liquid securities before paying its first dividend.

Using the principles of discounted cash flow and estimates of growth, various authors have attempted to reverse engineer the market risk premium. Two studies used analyst forecasts to estimate growth,[18] but many argue that analyst forecasts focus on the short term and are severely upward-biased. In a 2001 working paper, Fama and French use long-term dividend growth rates as a proxy for future growth, but they focus on dividend yields, not on available cash flow.[19] Alternatively, our own research has focused on *all* cash

---

[17] A. Goyal and I. Welch, "Predicting the Equity Premium with Dividend Ratios," *Management Science* 49, no. 5 (2003): 639–654.

[18] J. Claus and J. Thomas, "Equity Premia as Low as Three Percent? Evidence from Analysts' Earnings Forecasts for Domestic and International Stocks," *Journal of Finance* 56, no. 5 (October 2001): 1629–1666; and W. R. Gebhardt, C. M. C. Lee, and B. Swaminathan, "Toward an Implied Cost of Capital," *Journal of Accounting Research* 39, no. 1 (2001): 135–176.

[19] Eugene F. Fama and Kenneth R. French, "The Equity Premium," Center for Research in Security Prices Working Paper 522 (April 2001).

EXHIBIT 11.6 **Real and Nominal Expected Market Returns**

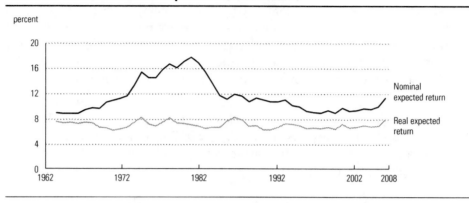

flow available to equity holders, as measured by a modified version of the key value driver formula (detailed in Chapter 2):[20]

$$k_e = \frac{\text{Earnings}\left(1 - \dfrac{g}{\text{ROE}}\right)}{\text{Price}} + g \quad \text{because} \quad CF_e = \text{Earnings}\left(1 - \frac{g}{\text{ROE}}\right)$$

where ROE = return on equity

CF_e = cash flow to equity holders

Based on this formula, we used the long-run return on equity (13.5 percent) and the long-run growth in real gross domestic product (GDP) (3.5 percent) to convert a given year's S&P 500 median earnings-to-price ratio into the cost of equity.[21]

Exhibit 11.6 plots the nominal and real expected market returns between 1962 and 2008. The results are striking. After inflation is stripped out, the expected market return (*not* excess return) is remarkably constant, averaging 7 percent. For the United Kingdom, the real market return is slightly more volatile, averaging 6 percent. Based on these results, we estimate the current market risk premium by subtracting the current real long-term risk-free rate from the real equity return of 7 percent (for U.S. markets). In May 2009, the yield on a U.S. Treasury inflation-protected securities (TIPS) equaled 1.6 percent. Subtracting 1.6 percent from 7.0 percent gives an estimate of the risk premium at 5.4 percent.

Appropriate range of market risk premium   Although many in the finance profession disagree about how to measure the market risk premium, we believe

[20] Marc H. Goedhart, Timothy M. Koller, and Zane D. Williams, "The Real Cost of Equity," *McKinsey on Finance*, no. 5 (Autumn 2002): 11–15.

[21] Using a two-stage model (i.e., short-term ROE and growth rate projections, followed by long-term estimates) did not change the results in a meaningful way. Estimated reinvestment rates (g/ROE) were capped at 70 percent of earnings.

4.5 to 5.5 percent is an appropriate range. Historical estimates found in most textbooks (and locked in the minds of many), which often report numbers near 8 percent, are too high for valuation purposes because they compare the market risk premium versus short-term bonds, use only 75 years of data, and are biased by the historical strength of the U.S. market.

Even the recent severe financial crisis has not caused a dramatic rise in the market risk premium. Between October 2007 and March 2009, the S&P 500 index dropped by more than 50 percent as the global financial crisis dominated the news. Many of our clients questioned whether a lower appetite for risk among investors caused the drop in value, implying a dramatic rise in the market risk premium and consequently the cost of capital. The data say no. Using the key value driver formula and the parameters outlined earlier, the real cost of equity rose only one percentage point during the crisis, from 6.8 percent in 2007 to 7.8 percent in 2008. This rise matches the increase in the risk premium reported by chief financial officers (CFOs) to the Duke CFO survey.[22] So why the large drop in equity prices? The global financial crisis leaked into the real economy, and corporate earnings suffered as a result. Based on these results, we do not believe companies should increase the risk premium embedded in their internal hurdle rates.

Estimating beta According to the CAPM, a stock's expected return is driven by beta, which measures how much the stock and entire market move together. Since beta cannot be observed directly, you must *estimate* its value. To do this, begin by measuring a raw beta using regression, and then improve the estimate by using industry comparables and smoothing techniques. Even with a robust estimation process, judgment is still required. When necessary, consider how the industry is likely to move with the economy, in order to bound your results.

Start with the empirical estimation of beta. The most common regression used to estimate a company's raw beta is the market model:

$$R_i = \alpha + \beta R_m + \varepsilon$$

In the market model, the stock's return (R_i), not price, is regressed against the market's return.

In Exhibit 11.7, we plot 60 months of Home Depot stock returns versus Morgan Stanley Capital International (MSCI) World Index returns between 2001 and 2006.[23] The solid line represents the "best fit" relationship between

---

[22] John Graham and Campbell Harvey, "The Equity Risk Premium amid a Global Financial Crisis," SSRN working paper (May 14, 2009).

[23] Even though Home Depot matched the market in aggregate losses during 2007 and 2008 (37 percent for Home Depot versus 35 percent for the MSCI World Index), a slight difference in timing caused the two measures to be uncorrelated. Prior to 2007, Home Depot's market beta was relatively stable. For this reason, we measure unlevered beta as of 2006.

EXHIBIT 11.7 **Home Depot: Stock Returns, 2001–2006**

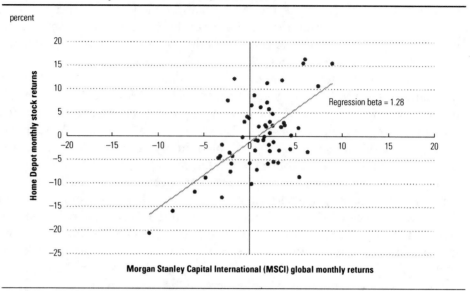

Morgan Stanley Capital International (MSCI) global monthly returns

Home Depot's stock returns and the stock market. The slope of this line is commonly denoted as beta. For Home Depot, the company's raw beta (slope) is 1.28. Since typical betas range between 0 and 2, with the value-weighted average beta equaling 1, this raw result implies Home Depot is riskier than the typical stock.

But why did we choose to measure Home Depot's returns in months? Why did we use five years of data? And how precise is this measurement? The CAPM is a one-period model and provides little guidance on how to use it for valuation. Yet following certain market characteristics and the results of a variety of empirical tests leads to several guiding conclusions:

- The measurement period for raw regressions should include at least 60 data points (e.g., five years of monthly returns). Rolling betas should be graphed to search for any patterns or systematic changes in a stock's risk.

- Raw regressions should be based on monthly returns. Using more frequent return periods, such as daily and weekly returns, leads to systematic biases.

- Company stock returns should be regressed against a value-weighted, well-diversified market portfolio, such as the MSCI World Index, bearing in mind that this portfolio's value may be distorted if measured during a market bubble.

Next, recalling that raw regressions provide only estimates of a company's true beta, improve the results from the regression by deriving an unlevered

EXHIBIT 11.8 **IBM: Market Beta, 1985–2008**

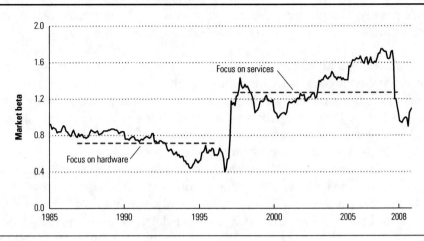

industry beta and then relevering the industry beta to the company's target capital structure. If no direct competitors exist, you should adjust raw company betas by using a smoothing technique. We describe the basis for our conclusions next.

Measurement period   Although there is no common standard for the appropriate measurement period, we follow the practice of data providers such as Morningstar Ibbotson, which use five years of monthly data to determine beta. Using five years of monthly data originated as a rule of thumb during early tests of the CAPM.[24] In subsequent tests of optimal measurement periods, researchers confirmed five years as appropriate.[25] Not every data provider uses five years. The data service Bloomberg, for instance, creates raw betas using two years of weekly data.

Because estimates of beta are imprecise, plot the company's rolling 60-month beta to *visually inspect* for structural changes or short-term deviations. For instance, changes in corporate strategy or capital structure often lead to changes in risk for stockholders. In this case, a long estimation period would place too much weight on irrelevant data.

In Exhibit 11.8, we graph IBM's raw beta between 1985 and 2008. As the exhibit shows, IBM's beta hovered near 0.7 in the 1980s and most of the 1990s but rose dramatically in the late 1990s to a peak above 1.6 in 2007. This rise in beta occurred during a period of great change for IBM, as the company

[24] F. Black, M. Jensen, and M. Scholes, "The Capital Asset Pricing Model: Some Empirical Tests," in *Studies in Theory of Capital Markets*, ed. M. Jensen (New York: Praeger, 1972).

[25] Alexander and Chervany tested the accuracy of estimation periods from one to nine years. They found four-year and six-year estimation periods performed best but were statistically indistinguishable. G. Alexander and N. Chervany, "On the Estimation and Stability of Beta," *Journal of Financial and Quantitative Analysis* 15 (1980): 123–137.

moved from hardware (such as mainframes) to services (such as consulting). Subsequently, using a long estimation period (for instance, 10 years) would underestimate the risk of the company's new business model.

Frequency of measurement In 1980, Nobel laureate Robert Merton argued that estimates of covariance, and subsequently beta, improve as returns are measured more frequently.[26] Implementing Merton's theory, however, has proven elusive. Empirical problems make high-frequency beta estimation unreliable. Therefore, we recommend using monthly data.

Using daily or even weekly returns is especially problematic when the stock is rarely traded. An illiquid stock will have many reported returns equal to zero, not because the stock's value is constant but because it hasn't traded (only the last trade is recorded). Consequently, estimates of beta on illiquid stocks are biased downward. Using longer-dated returns, such as monthly returns, lessens this effect. One proposal for stocks that trade infrequently even on a monthly basis is to sum lagged betas.[27] In lagged-beta models, a stock's return is simultaneously regressed on concurrent market returns and market returns from the prior period. The two betas from the regression are then summed.

A second problem with using high-frequency data is the bid-ask bounce. Periodic stock prices are recorded at the last trade, and the recorded price depends on whether the last trade was a purchase (using the ask price) or a sale (using the bid price). A stock whose intrinsic value remains unchanged will therefore bounce between the bid and ask prices, causing distortions in beta estimation. Using longer-period returns dampens this distortion.

Over the past few years, promising research on high-frequency beta estimation has emerged, spawned by improvements in computing power and data collection. One study applied a filter to daily data to extract information about beta while avoiding the microstructure issues just described.[28] Another used five-minute returns to measure beta, and the estimation method produced more accurate measurements than the standard 60-month rolling window.[29] Since that research was limited to highly liquid stocks, however, we continue to focus on longer-dated intervals in practice.

Market portfolio In the CAPM, the market portfolio equals the value-weighted portfolio of all assets, both traded (such as stocks and bonds) and

---

[26] R. Merton, "On Estimating the Expected Return on the Market," *Journal of Financial Economics* 8 (1980): 323–361.

[27] M. Scholes and J. T. Williams, "Estimating Betas from Nonsynchronous Data," *Journal of Financial Economics* 5 (1977): 309–327. See also E. Dimson, "Risk Measurement When Shares Are Subject to Infrequent Trading," *Journal of Financial Economics* 7 (1979): 197–226.

[28] B. Chen and J. Reeves, "Dynamic Asset Beta Measurement," University of New South Wales, School of Banking and Finance (May 31, 2009).

[29] T. Bollerslev and B. Y. B. Zhang, "Measuring and Modeling Systematic Risk in Factor Pricing Models Using High-Frequency Data," *Journal of Empirical Finance* 10 (2003): 533–558.

untraded (such as private companies and human capital). Since the true market portfolio is unobservable, a proxy is necessary. For U.S. stocks, the most common proxy is the S&P 500, a value-weighted index of large U.S. companies. Outside the United States, financial analysts rely on either a regional index like the MSCI Europe Index or the MSCI World Index, a value-weighted index comprising large stocks from 23 developed countries (including the United States).

Most well-diversified indexes, such as the S&P 500 and MSCI World Index, are highly correlated (the two indexes had a 95.8 percent correlation between 2000 and 2009). Thus, the choice of index will have only a small effect on beta. For instance, Home Depot's regression beta with respect to the MSCI World Index is 1.28, whereas the company's beta with respect to the S&P 500 is slightly higher at 1.41. Do *not*, however, use a local market index. Most countries are heavily weighted in only a few industries and, in some cases, a few companies. Consequently, when measuring beta versus a local index, you are not measuring market-wide systematic risk, but rather a company's sensitivity to a particular industry.

In the late 1990s, equity markets rose dramatically, but this increase was confined primarily to extremely large capitalization stocks and stocks in the telecommunications, media, and technology sectors (commonly known as TMT). Historically, TMT stocks contribute approximately 15 percent of the market value of the S&P 500. Between 1998 and 2000, this percentage rose to 40 percent. And as the market portfolio changed, so too did industry betas. Exhibit 11.9 presents the median beta over time for stocks outside TMT, such as food companies, airlines, and pharmaceuticals.[30] The median beta drops from 1.0 to 0.6 as TMT becomes a dominant part of the overall market portfolio.

With the collapse of the TMT sector in 2001, TMT stocks returned to their original proportion of the overall market. Since beta is computed using historical data, however, the median non-TMT beta still reflected the TMT-heavy market composition. Instead of using the 2001 beta to evaluate future cash flows as of 2001, a more appropriate beta would be from 1997, when the market composition last matched the 2001 composition. Remember, the end goal is not to measure beta historically, but rather to use the historical estimate as a predictor of future value. In this case, recent history isn't very useful and should not be overweighted.

Although it is too early to tell, we suspect a similar phenomenon occurred during 2007 and 2008 with financial institutions. During the late 2000s, financial institutions became a greater proportion of the market portfolio as interest rates dropped and lending was quite profitable. With their collapse in late 2008, betas

[30] André Annema and Marc Goedhart, "Better Betas," *McKinsey on Finance*, no. 6 (Winter 2003): 10–13; and André Annema and Marc Goedhart, "Betas: Back to Normal," *McKinsey on Finance*, no. 20 (Summer 2006): 14–16.

EXHIBIT 11.9 **Effect of the Dot-Com Bubble on Beta**

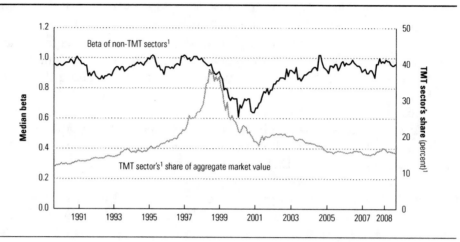

[1] TMT = telecommunications, media, and technology.

measured using 2008 data probably do not reflect future betas as well as betas measured prior to 2007.

Improving estimates of beta: Industry betas   Estimating beta is an imprecise process. Earlier, we used historical regression to estimate Home Depot's raw beta at 1.28. But the regression's R-squared was only 37 percent, and the standard error of the beta estimate was 0.216. Using two standard errors as a guide, we feel confident Home Depot's true beta lies between 0.85 and 1.71—hardly a tight range.

To improve the precision of beta estimation, use industry, rather than company-specific, betas.[31] Companies in the same industry face similar *operating* risks, so they should have similar operating betas. As long as estimation errors across companies are uncorrelated, overestimates and underestimates of individual betas will tend to cancel, and an industry median (or average) beta will produce a superior estimate.[32]

Simply using the median of an industry's raw regression betas, however, overlooks an important factor: leverage. A company's beta is a function of not only its operating risk, but also the financial risk it takes. Shareholders of a company with more debt face greater risks, and this increase is reflected in

[31] Consider two companies in the same industry competing for a large customer contract. Depending on which company wins the contract, one company's stock price will rise; the other company's stock price will fall. If the market rises during this period, the winning company will have a higher measured beta, and the losing company will have a lower measured beta, even though the decision had nothing to do with market performance. Using an industry beta to proxy for company risk lessens the effect of idiosyncratic shocks.

[32] Statistically speaking, the sample average will have the lowest mean squared error. However, because sample averages are heavily influenced by outliers, we recommend examining both the mean and median betas.

beta. Therefore, to compare companies with similar operating risks, you must first strip out the effect of leverage. Only then can you compare betas across an industry.

To undo the effect of leverage (and its tax shield), we rely on the theories of Franco Modigliani and Merton Miller, introduced in Chapter 6. According to Modigliani and Miller, the weighted average risk of a company's financial claims equals the weighted average risk of a company's economic assets. Using beta to represent risk, this relationship is as follows:

$$\underbrace{\frac{V_u}{V_u + V_{txa}}\beta_u}_{\text{Operating Assets}} + \underbrace{\frac{V_{txa}}{V_u + V_{txa}}\beta_{txa}}_{\text{Tax Assets}} = \underbrace{\frac{D}{D + E}\beta_d}_{\text{Debt}} + \underbrace{\frac{E}{D + E}\beta_e}_{\text{Equity}}$$

where V_u = value of the company's operating assets
V_{txa} = value of the company's interest tax shields
D = market value of the company's debt
E = market value of the company's equity

In Appendix D, we rearrange the equation to solve for the beta of equity (β_e). This leads to:

$$\beta_e = \beta_u + \frac{D}{E}(\beta_u - \beta_d) - \frac{V_{txa}}{E}(\beta_u - \beta_{txa})$$

To simplify the formula further, most practitioners impose two additional restrictions.[33] First, because debt claims have first priority, the beta of debt tends to be low. Thus, for simplicity, many assume the beta of debt is 0. Second, if the company maintains a constant capital structure, the value of tax shields will fluctuate with the value of operating assets, and beta of the tax shields (β_{txa}) will equal the beta of the unlevered company (β_u). Setting β_{txa} equal to β_u eliminates the final term:

$$\beta_e = \beta_u \left(1 + \frac{D}{E}\right) \tag{11.1}$$

Thus, a company's equity beta equals the company's operating beta (commonly known as the unlevered beta) times a leverage factor. As leverage rises, so will the company's equity beta. Using this relationship, we can convert

[33] In Chapter 6, we detail alternative restrictions that can be imposed to simplify the general equation regarding risk. Rather than repeat the analysis, we focus on the least restrictive assumption for mature companies: that debt remains proportional to value. For a full discussion of which restrictions to impose and how they affect the cost of capital, see the section on adjusted present value in Chapter 6.

EXHIBIT 11.10 **Determining Industry Beta**[1]

	Home Depot	Lowe's
Unlevering calculation		
Regression beta (step 1)	1.28	0.69
Debt-to-equity in 2006	0.26	0.16
Unlevered beta (step 2)	1.01	0.59
Relevering calculation		
Industry-average unlevered beta (step 3)	0.80	0.80
Debt-to-equity in 2008	0.51	0.32
Relevered beta (step 4)	1.21	1.06
Debt-to-equity ratio, 2006 ($ million)		
Short-term debt	18	111
Long-term debt	11,643	4,325
Operating leases	9,141	3,034
Less: Excess cash	0	0
Total net debt	20,802	7,470
Share price ($)	40	31
Shares outstanding (millions)	1,970	1,525
Market value of equity	79,115	47,504
Debt-to-equity ratio, 2006	0.26	0.16

[1] Even though Home Depot matched the market in aggregate losses during 2007 and 2008, a slight difference in timing caused the two measures to be uncorrelated. Prior to 2007, Home Depot's market beta was relatively stable. For this reason, we measure unlevered beta as of 2006. To determine the current cost of capital, we relever the 2006 industry beta at 2008 debt-to-equity levels.

equity betas into unlevered betas. Since unlevered betas focus solely on operating risk, they can be averaged across an industry (assuming industry competitors have similar operating characteristics).

To estimate an industry-adjusted company beta, use the following four-step process. First, regress each company's stock returns against the MSCI World Index to determine raw beta. In Exhibit 11.10, we report regression betas for Home Depot (1.28) and Lowe's (0.69). Second, to unlever each beta, calculate each company's market-debt-to-equity ratio, which equals 0.26 for Home Depot and 0.16 for Lowe's. Applying equation 11.1 leads to an unlevered beta of 1.01 for Home Depot and 0.59 for Lowe's. In step 3, determine the industry unlevered beta by calculating the median (in this case, the median and average betas are the same).[34] In the final step, relever the industry unlevered beta to each company's *target* debt-to-equity ratio (using current market values as proxies). Home Depot's relevered industry beta equals 1.21, which we use in Exhibit 11.2 to estimate the cost of capital. Note how the relevered beta differs across companies even though unlevered beta is the same for all companies within the industry.

[34] In most industries, more than two company betas are available. For Home Depot, Lowe's is the only publicly traded competitor. As a general rule, use as many direct comparables as possible.

Unlevered cost of equity   As just demonstrated, we can unlever an equity beta in order to improve beta estimation for use in the CAPM and WACC. We also can use unlevered industry betas to estimate a company's unlevered cost of equity for use in an adjusted present value (APV) valuation. To compute the unlevered cost of equity, simply apply the CAPM to the industry unlevered beta.

Improving estimates of beta: Smoothing   For well-defined industries, an industry beta will suffice. But if few direct comparables exist, an alternative is beta smoothing. Smoothing dampens extreme observations toward the overall average. Consider the simple smoothing process used by Bloomberg:

$$\text{Adjusted Beta} = 0.33 + 0.67(\text{Raw Beta})$$

Using this formula smooths raw regression estimates toward 1. For instance, a raw beta of 0.5 leads to an adjusted beta of 0.67, while a raw beta of 1.5 leads to an adjusted beta of 1.34.

Bloomberg's smoothing mechanism dates back to Marshall Blume's observation that betas revert to the mean.[35] Today, more advanced smoothing techniques exist.[36] Although the proof is beyond the scope of this book, the following adjustment will reduce beta estimation error:

$$\beta_{\text{adj}} = \frac{\sigma_\varepsilon^2}{\sigma_\varepsilon^2 + \sigma_b^2}(1) + \left(1 - \frac{\sigma_\varepsilon^2}{\sigma_\varepsilon^2 + \sigma_b^2}\right)\beta_{\text{raw}}$$

where σ_ε = standard error of the regression beta
        σ_b = cross-sectional standard deviation of all betas

The raw regression beta receives the most weight when the standard error of beta from the regression (σ_ε) is smallest. In fact, when beta is measured perfectly ($\sigma_\varepsilon = 0$), the raw beta receives all the weight. Conversely, if the regression provides no meaningful results (σ_ε is very large), you should set beta equal to 1.

Alternatives to the CAPM: Fama-French Three-Factor Model

In 1992, Eugene Fama and Kenneth French published a paper in the *Journal of Finance* that received a great deal of attention because they concluded: "In short, our tests do not support the most basic prediction of the SLB [Sharpe-Lintner-Black] Capital Asset Pricing Model that average stock returns are positively

[35] M. Blume, "Betas and Their Regression Tendencies," *Journal of Finance* 30 (1975): 1–10.
[36] For instance, see P. Jorion, "Bayes-Stein Estimation for Portfolio Analysis," *Journal of Financial and Quantitative Analysis* 21 (1986): 279–292.

related to market betas."[37] At the time, theirs was the most recent in a series of empirical studies that questioned the usefulness of estimated betas in explaining the risk premium on equities. Among the factors negatively or positively associated with equity returns were the size of the company, a seasonal (January) effect, the degree of financial leverage, and the firm's book-to-market ratio.[38] Based on prior research and their own comprehensive regressions, Fama and French concluded that equity returns are inversely related to the size of a company (as measured by market capitalization) and positively related to the ratio of a company's book value to its market value of equity.

Given the strength of Fama and French's empirical results, the academic community now measures risk with a model commonly known as the Fama-French three-factor model. With this model, a stock's excess returns are regressed on excess market returns (similar to the CAPM), the excess returns of small stocks over big stocks (SMB), and the excess returns of high book-to-market stocks over low book-to-market stocks (HML).[39] Because the risk premium is determined by a regression on the SMB and HML stock portfolios, a company does not receive a premium for being small. Instead, the company receives a risk premium if its stock returns are correlated with those of small stocks or high book-to-market companies. The SMB and HML portfolios are meant to replicate unobservable risk factors, factors that cause small companies with high book-to-market values to outperform their CAPM expected returns.

To run a Fama-French regression, regress the company's monthly stock returns on the returns for three portfolios: the market portfolio, the SMB portfolio, and the HML portfolio. Given the model's popularity, Fama-French portfolio returns are now available from professional data providers.

We use the Fama-French three-factor model to estimate Home Depot's cost of equity in Exhibit 11.11. To determine the company's three betas, regress Home Depot stock returns against the excess market portfolio, SMB, and HML. The regression in Exhibit 11.11 used monthly returns and was specified as follows:

$$R_i - r_f = \alpha + \beta_1(R_m - r_f) + \beta_2(R_s - R_b) + \beta_3(R_h - R_l) + \varepsilon$$

[37] E. Fama and K. French, "The Cross-Section of Expected Stock Returns," *Journal of Finance* (June 1992): 427–465.

[38] R. Blanz, "The Relationship between Return and the Market Value of Common Stocks," *Journal of Financial Economics* (March 1981): 3–18; M. Reinganum, "Misspecification of Capital Asset Pricing: Empirical Anomalies Based on Earnings Yields and Market Values," *Journal of Financial Economics* (March 1981): 19–46; S. Basu, "The Relationship between Earnings Yield, Market Value and Return for NYSE Common Stocks: Further Evidence," *Journal of Financial Economics* (June 1983): 129–156; L. Bhandari, "Debt/Equity Ratio and Expected Common Stock Returns: Empirical Evidence," *Journal of Finance* (April 1988): 507–528; D. Stattman, "Book Values and Stock Returns," *Chicago MBA: A Journal of Selected Papers* (1980): 25–45; and B. Rosenberg, K. Reid, and R. Lanstein, "Persuasive Evidence of Market Inefficiency," *Journal of Portfolio Management* (1985): 9–17.

[39] For a complete description of the factor returns, see E. Fama and K. French, "Common Risk Factors in the Returns on Stocks and Bonds," *Journal of Financial Economics* 33 (1993): 3–56.

EXHIBIT 11.11 **Home Depot's Fama-French Cost of Equity, 2006**

Factor	Average monthly premium[1] (percent)	Average annual premium (percent)	Regression coefficient[2]	Contribution to expected return (percent)
Market portfolio		5.4	1.39	7.5
SMB portfolio	0.23	2.8	(0.09)	(0.3)
HML portfolio	0.40	5.0	(0.14)	(0.7)
Premium over risk-free rate[3]				6.6
			Risk-free rate	3.9
			Cost of equity	10.5

[1] SMB and HML premiums based on average monthly returns data, 1926–2009.
[2] Based on monthly returns data, 2002–2006.
[3] Summation rounded to one decimal point.

As the exhibit indicates, Home Depot's market portfolio beta is slightly higher in the Fama-French regression than when measured in Exhibit 11.7, but its raw cost of equity is lower because Home Depot is negatively correlated with small companies (small companies outperform big companies) and companies with a high book-to-market ratio (high book-to-market companies outperform low book-to-market companies). Based on the historical annualized premiums for SMB (2.8 percent) and HML (5.0 percent), Home Depot's cost of equity equals 10.5 percent, versus 10.8 percent from the CAPM using a regression beta. (These values are not comparable to the cost of equity presented in Exhibit 11.2, which used relevered industry betas.)

The Fama-French model suffers from the same implementation issues as the CAPM. For instance, how much data should you use to determine each factor's risk premium? Since 1926, small companies have outperformed large companies, but since the premium's discovery in 1982, they have not.[40] Should returns be regressed using monthly data? Should regressions use five years of data? Given the model's recent development, many of these questions are still under investigation.

Alternatives to the CAPM: Arbitrage Pricing Theory

Another alternative to the CAPM, the arbitrage pricing theory (APT), resembles a generalized version of the Fama-French three-factor model. In the APT, a security's actual returns are generated by k factors and random noise:

$$R_i = \alpha + \beta_1 F_1 + \beta_2 F_2 + \cdots + \beta_k F_k + \varepsilon$$

where F_i = return on factor i

[40] Small stocks outperformed large stocks from 1926 to 2009, with significant separation occurring between 1975 and 1984. However, from 1963 to 1973 and from 1984 to 2000, large stocks outperformed small stocks.

By creating well-diversified factor portfolios, a security's expected return must equal the risk-free rate plus the cumulative sum of its exposure to each factor times the factor's risk premium (λ):[41]

$$E\left(R_t\right) = r_f + \beta_1\lambda + \beta_2\lambda + \cdots + \beta_k\lambda_k$$

Otherwise, arbitrage (positive return with zero risk) is possible.

On paper, the theory is extremely powerful. Any deviations from the model result in unlimited returns with no risk. In practice, implementation of the model has been tricky, as there is little agreement about how many factors there are, what the factors represent, or how to measure the factors. For this reason, use of the APT resides primarily in the classroom.

In Defense of Beta

Fama and French significantly damaged the credibility of the CAPM and beta. Today, most academics rely on three-factor models to measure *historical* risk. Even so, the three-factor model has its critics. To start, the CAPM is based on solid theory about risk and return (albeit with strong assumptions), whereas the Fama-French model is based purely on empirical evidence. Although the latter model has been loosely tied to risk factors such as illiquidity (size premium) and default risk (book-to-market premium), no theory has gained universal acceptance.

In addition, S. P. Kothari, Jay Shanken, and Richard Sloan argue that beta may work better than portrayed in Fama and French. They point out that Fama and French's statistical tests were of low enough power that the tests could not reject a nontrivial (beta-related) risk premium of 6 percent over the post-1940 period.[42] Second, when they used annual returns rather than monthly returns to estimate beta (to avoid seasonality in returns), they found a significant linear relationship between beta and returns. Finally, they argue that the economic magnitude of the size factor is quite small, and book-to-market premiums could be a result of survivorship bias.

Other research argues that the Fama-French three-factor model historically outperforms the CAPM because either beta or the market portfolio has been improperly measured. In a recent study, a one-factor model based on time-varying betas eliminated the book-to-market effect.[43] Betas conditioned on observable information, such as labor income, also perform better than

[41] For a thorough discussion of the arbitrage pricing theory, see Mark Grinblatt and Sheridan Titman, *Financial Markets & Corporate Strategy*, 2nd ed. (New York: McGraw-Hill, 2001).

[42] S. Kothari, J. Shanken, and R. Sloan, "Another Look at the Cross-Section of Expected Returns," *Journal of Finance* (December 1995).

[43] A. Ang and J. Chen, "CAPM over the Long Run: 1926–2001" (working paper, University of Southern California, 2004); C. Armstrong, S. Banerjee, and C. Corona, "Uncertainty about Betas and Expected Returns," McCombs Research Paper Series ACC-07-09 (August 6, 2009).

older models.[44] Another article argues that regressions based on equity-only portfolios, such as the S&P 500, lead to the incorrect measurement of beta.[45] This faulty measurement is correlated with leverage, which in turn is correlated with size and book-to-market ratio. When the researchers controlled for leverage, excess returns associated with HML and SMB disappeared.

The bottom line? It takes a better theory to kill an existing theory, and we have yet to see the better theory. Therefore, we continue to use the CAPM while keeping a watchful eye on new research in the area.

ESTIMATING THE AFTER-TAX COST OF DEBT

The weighted average cost of capital blends the cost of equity with the after-tax cost of debt. To estimate the cost of debt for investment-grade companies, use the yield to maturity of the company's long-term, option-free bonds. Multiply your estimate of the cost of debt by 1 minus the marginal tax rate to determine the cost of debt on an after-tax basis.

Technically speaking, yield to maturity is only a proxy for expected return, because the yield is actually a *promised* rate of return on a company's debt (it assumes all coupon payments are made on time and the debt is paid in full). An enterprise valuation based on the yield to maturity is therefore theoretically inconsistent, as expected free cash flows should be discounted by an expected return, not a promised yield. For companies with investment-grade debt, the probability of default is so low that this inconsistency is immaterial, especially when compared with the estimation error surrounding beta and the market risk premium. Thus, for estimating the cost of debt for a company with investment-grade debt (debt rated at BBB or better), yield to maturity is a suitable proxy. For companies with below-investment-grade debt, we recommend using adjusted present value (APV) based on the unlevered cost of equity rather than the WACC to value the company.

Bond Ratings and Yield to Maturity

To solve for yield to maturity (YTM), reverse engineer the discount rate required to set the present value of the bond's promised cash flows equal to its price:

$$\text{Price} = \frac{\text{Coupon}}{(1 + \text{YTM})} + \frac{\text{Coupon}}{(1 + \text{YTM})^2} + \cdots + \frac{\text{Face} + \text{Coupon}}{(1 + \text{YTM})^N}$$

[44] T. Santos and P. Veronesi, "Labor Income and Predictable Stock Returns," *Review of Financial Studies* 19 (2006): 1–44.

[45] M. Ferguson and R. Shockley, "Equilibrium 'Anomalies,'" *Journal of Finance* 58, no. 6 (2003): 2549–2580.

EXHIBIT 11.12 **Home Depot: Trading Data on Corporate Debt**

Bond: 5.875% due December 2036

Trade time	Trade volume ($ thousand)	Bond price (dollars)	Yield (percent)
16:15:51	29	78.75	7.75
16:15:51	29	78.75	7.75
14:48:00	5	78.00	7.83
14:03:19	110	81.85	7.43
12:08:43	2,000	80.06	7.62
12:08:00	2,000	80.06	7.62
12:08:00	2,000	80.00	7.62
12:08:00	2,000	80.06	7.62
12:06:22	2,000	80.25	7.60
	Home Depot bond yield		7.62
	30-year U.S. Treasury yield		(4.39)
	Home Depot default premium		3.23

Source: Financial Industry Regulatory Authority (FINRA) TRACE system, May 28, 2009.

Ideally, yield to maturity should be calculated on liquid, option-free, long-term debt. As discussed earlier in this chapter, short-term bonds do not match the duration of the company's free cash flow. If the bond is rarely traded, the bond price will be stale. Using stale prices will lead to an outdated yield to maturity. Yield to maturity will also be distorted when corporate bonds have attached options, such as callability or convertibility, as their value will affect the bond's price but not its promised cash flows.

In the United States, you can download the yield to maturity for corporate debt free of charge using the TRACE pricing database.[46] Exhibit 11.12 displays TRACE data for Home Depot's 5.875 percent bonds due in December 2036. TRACE reports four data items: when the trade occurred, the size of the trade, the bond price, and the implied yield to maturity. As can be seen in the exhibit, the 2036 bond trades infrequently—only nine times in four hours. Home Depot's short-maturity debt trades more frequently, but at only five years to maturity, its duration is a poor match for the company's long-term cash flows. When measuring the yield to maturity, use trades greater than $1 million, as smaller trades are unreliable. Large trades for Home Depot's 2036 bond were completed at 7.62 percent (3.23 percent above the 30-year U.S. Treasury bond).

For companies with only short-term bonds or bonds that rarely trade, determine yield to maturity by using an indirect method. First, determine the company's credit rating on unsecured long-term debt. Next, examine the average yield to maturity on a portfolio of long-term bonds with the same

[46] The Financial Industry Regulatory Authority (FINRA) introduced TRACE (Trade Reporting and Compliance Engine) in July 2002. The system captures and disseminates transactions in investment-grade, high-yield, and convertible corporate debt, representing all over-the-counter market activity in these bonds.

EXHIBIT 11.13 **Yield Spread over U.S. Treasuries by Bond Rating, May 2009**

Basis points

Rating	Maturity (years)						
	1	2	3	5	7	10	30
Aaa/AAA	36	59	55	69	82	58	139
Aa2/AA	154	140	150	160	168	139	179
A1/A+	159	153	166	169	168	139	182
A2/A	183	178	192	193	189	152	190
A3/A−	195	194	213	210	210	177	199
Baa1/BBB+	324	310	336	333	324	288	320
Baa2/BBB	332	315	340	338	328	292	324
Baa3/BBB−	402	408	425	433	421	380	416
Ba2/BB	559	583	586	590	578	545	577
B2/B	870	916	913	925	909	878	904

Source. Bloomberg.

credit rating. Use this yield as a proxy for the company's implied yield on long-term debt.

Since the probability of default is critical to bond pricing, professional rating agencies, such as Standard & Poor's (S&P) and Moody's, will rate a company's debt. To determine a company's bond rating, a rating agency will examine the company's most recent financial ratios, analyze the company's competitive environment, and interview senior management. Corporate bond ratings are freely available to the public and can be downloaded from rating agency web sites. For example, consider Home Depot. On July 5, 2007, S&P downgraded Home Depot long-term debt from A+ to BBB+. Moody's quickly followed, downgrading Home Depot to Baa1 on July 27, 2007. For a short period, the two agencies' ratings were different, but such splits in ratings occur relatively infrequently (if they do, use the most recent rating).

Once you have a rating, convert the rating into a yield to maturity. Exhibit 11.13 presents U.S. corporate yield spreads over U.S. government bonds. All quotes are presented in basis points, where 100 basis points equals 1 percent. Since Home Depot is rated BBB+ by S&P and Baa1 by Moody's, we estimate that the 10-year yield to maturity is 288 basis points over the 10-year U.S. Treasury bond. Adding 2.9 percent to the risk-free rate of 3.9 percent equals 6.8 percent.[47]

Using the company's bond ratings to determine the yield to maturity is a good alternative to calculating the yield to maturity directly. Never, however, approximate the yield to maturity using a bond's coupon rate. Coupon rates are set by the company at time of issuance and only approximate the yield if the

[47] In May 2009, the 30-year default spread for BBB+-rated corporate bonds equaled 3.2 percent. This matches the default spread for Home Depot's 2036 bonds. Individual bonds can trade at rates different from the average for a variety of reasons, including anticipation of a ratings change and different levels of recoverable collateral.

bond trades near its par value. When valuing a company, you must estimate expected returns relative to *today's* alternative investments. Thus, when you measure the cost of debt, estimate what a comparable investment would earn if bought or sold today.

Below-Investment-Grade Debt

In practice, few financial analysts distinguish between expected and promised returns. But for debt below investment grade, using the yield to maturity as a proxy for the cost of debt can cause significant error.

To understand the difference between expected returns and yield to maturity, consider the following example. You have been asked to value a one-year zero-coupon bond whose face value is $100. The bond is risky; there is a 25 percent chance the bond will default and you will recover only half the final payment. Finally, the cost of debt (not yield to maturity), estimated using the CAPM, equals 6 percent. Based on this information, you estimate the bond's price by discounting *expected* cash flows by the cost of debt:

$$\text{Price} = \frac{E\,(\text{CF})}{1 + k_d} = \frac{(.75)(\$100) + (.25)(\$50)}{1.06} = \$82.55$$

Next, to determine the bond's yield to maturity, place promised cash flows, rather than expected cash flows, into the numerator. Then solve for the yield to maturity:

$$\text{Price} = \frac{\text{Promised CF}}{1 + \text{YTM}} = \frac{\$100}{1 + \text{YTM}} = \$82.55$$

Solving for YTM, the $82.55 price leads to a 21.1 percent yield to maturity.

This yield to maturity is *much* higher than the cost of debt. So what drives the yield to maturity? Three factors: the cost of debt, the probability of default, and the recovery rate after default. When the probability of default is high and the recovery rate is low, the yield to maturity will deviate significantly from the cost of debt. Thus, for companies with high default risk and low ratings, the yield to maturity is a poor proxy for the cost of debt.

When a company is rated BB (non-investment-grade) or below, we do not recommend using the weighted average cost of capital to value the company. Instead, use adjusted present value (APV). The APV model discounts projected free cash flow at the company's industry-based unlevered cost of equity (see Exhibit 11.10) and adds the present value of tax shields. For more on APV valuation, see Chapter 6.

Incorporating the Interest Tax Shield

To calculate free cash flow (using techniques detailed in Chapter 7), we compute taxes as if the company were entirely financed by equity. By using all-equity taxes, we can make comparisons across companies and over time, without regard to capital structure. Yet since the tax shield has value, it must be accounted for. In an enterprise DCF using the WACC, the tax shield is valued as part of the cost of capital. To value the tax shield, reduce the cost of debt by the marginal tax rate:

$$\text{After-Tax Cost of Debt} = \text{Cost of Debt} \times (1 - T_m)$$

Chapter 7 details how to calculate the marginal tax rate for historical analysis. For use in the cost of capital, you should calculate the marginal tax rate in a consistent manner, with one potential modification to account for the timing of future tax payments. According to research by John Graham, the statutory marginal tax rate overstates the *future* marginal tax rate because of rules related to tax loss carry-forwards, tax loss carry-backs, investment tax credits, and alternative minimum taxes.[48] For instance, when a company loses money, it will receive a cash credit only if it has been profitable in the past three years; otherwise, it must carry the loss forward until it is once again profitable.

Graham uses simulation to estimate the realizable marginal tax rate on a company-by-company basis. For investment-grade companies, use the statutory rate. For instance, because Home Depot is highly profitable, Graham's model estimates the company's future marginal statutory tax rate at the full 35 percent. The typical company, however, does not always fully use its tax shields. Graham estimates that the marginal tax rate is on average 5 percentage points below the statutory rate.

USING TARGET WEIGHTS TO DETERMINE THE COST OF CAPITAL

With our estimates of the cost of equity and after-tax cost of debt, we can now blend the two expected returns into a single number. To do this, use the target weights of debt and equity to enterprise value, on a market (not book) basis:

$$\text{WACC} = \frac{D}{V} k_d (1 - T_m) + \frac{E}{V} k_e$$

[48] J. Graham and L. Mills, "Using Tax Return Data to Simulate Corporate Marginal Tax Rates," *Journal of Accounting and Economics* 46 (2009): 366–388; and J. Graham, "Proxies for the Corporate Marginal Tax Rate," *Journal of Financial Economics* 42 (1996): 187–221.

Using market values to weight expected returns in the cost of capital follows directly from the formula's derivation (see Appendix C for a derivation of free cash flow and WACC). But consider a more intuitive explanation: the WACC represents the expected return on an *alternative* investment with identical risk. Rather than reinvest in the company, management could return capital to investors, who could reinvest elsewhere. To return capital without changing the capital structure, management can repay debt and repurchase shares, but must do so at their *market* value. Conversely, book value represents a sunk cost, so it is no longer relevant.

The cost of capital should rely on target weights, rather than current weights, because at any point, a company's current capital structure may not reflect the level expected to prevail over the life of the business. The current capital structure may merely reflect a short-term swing in the company's stock price, a swing that has yet to be rebalanced by management. Thus, using today's capital structure may cause you to overestimate (or underestimate) the value of tax shields for companies whose leverage is expected to drop (or rise).

Many companies are already near their target capital structure. If the company you are valuing is not, decide how quickly the company will achieve the target. In the simplest scenario, the company will rebalance immediately and maintain the new capital structure. In this case, using the target weights and a constant WACC (for all future years) will lead to a reasonable valuation. If you expect the rebalancing to happen over a significant period of time, then use a different cost of capital each year, reflecting the capital structure at the time. In practice, this procedure is complex; you must correctly model the weights, as well as the changes in the cost of debt and equity (because of increased default risk and higher betas). For extreme changes in capital structure, modeling enterprise DCF using a constant WACC can lead to significant error. In this case, value the company with adjusted present value (APV).

To estimate the target capital structure for a company you are valuing from an external perspective, use a combination of three approaches:

1. Estimate the company's current market-value-based capital structure.
2. Review the capital structure of comparable companies.
3. Review management's implicit or explicit approach to financing the business and its implications for the target capital structure.

Estimating Current Capital Structure

To determine the company's current capital structure, measure the market value of all claims against enterprise value. For most companies, the claims will consist primarily of debt and equity (we address more complex securities in this chapter's final section). If a company's debt and equity are publicly traded, simply multiply the quantity of each security by its most recent price.

Most difficulties arise when securities are not traded such that prices can be readily observed.

Debt   In the United States, the current market value of a company's debt can be determined using the TRACE pricing database. Exhibit 11.12 shows that Home Depot's 2036 bond traded at $80.06, or 80.06 percent of par value at 12:08 on May 28, 2009. To determine the market value of the bond, multiply 80.06 percent by the bond's book value of $2,959 million, which equals $2,369 million.[49] Since a bond's price depends on its coupon rate versus its yield, not every Home Depot bond trades at the same price. The Home Depot bond maturing in 2016 recently closed at 98.53 percent of par over the same time period. Consequently, value each debt separately.

If an observable market value is not readily available, value debt securities at book value, or use discounted cash flow. In most cases, book value reasonably approximates the current market value. This will not be the case, however, if interest rates have changed since the time of issuance or the company is in financial distress. In these two situations, the current price will differ from book value because either expected cash flows have changed (increased probability of default lowers expected cash flow) or the discount rate has changed from its original level (interest rates drive discount rates).[50]

In these situations, value each bond separately by discounting promised cash flows at the appropriate yield to maturity. The size and timing of coupons will be disclosed in the notes of a company's annual report. Determine the appropriate yield to maturity by examining the yields from comparably rated debt with similar maturities.

Debt-equivalent claims   Next, value off-balance-sheet debt, such as operating leases and pension liabilities. As detailed in Chapter 27, operating leases can be valued using the following formula:

$$\text{Lease Value}_{t-1} = \frac{\text{Rental Expense}_t}{k_d + \dfrac{1}{\text{Asset Life}}}$$

Include operating leases in debt only if you plan to adjust free cash flow for operating leases as well. Consistency between free cash flow and the cost of capital is paramount.

Any pension adjustments made to free cash flow must be properly represented in the debt portion of the cost of capital. Specifically, if you add back any pension-related tax shields during adjustments to net operating profit less

---

[49] Home Depot reports the book value for each of its bonds in note 6 of its 2008 annual report.
[50] For floating-rate bonds, changes in Treasury rates won't affect value, since coupons float with Treasury yields. Changes in market-based default premiums, however, will affect the market value of floating-rate bonds, since bonds are priced at a fixed spread above Treasury yields.

adjusted taxes (NOPLAT), you must account for the tax shields in the present value of pension liabilities and the cost of debt.

Equity   If common stock is publicly traded, multiply the market price by the number of shares *outstanding*. The market value of equity should be based on shares outstanding in the capital market. Therefore, do not use shares issued, as they may include shares repurchased by the company.

At this point, you may be wondering why you are valuing the company if you are going to rely on the market's value of equity in the cost of capital. Shouldn't you be using the estimated equity value? The answer is no. Remember, you are only estimating today's market value to frame management's philosophy concerning capital structure. To value the company, use *target* weights.

For privately held companies, no market-based values are available. In this case, you must determine equity value (for the cost of capital) either using a multiples approach or through DCF iteratively. To perform an iterative valuation, assume a reasonable capital structure, and value the enterprise using DCF. Using the estimate of debt to enterprise value, repeat the valuation. Continue this process until the valuation no longer materially changes.

Reviewing Capital Structure of Comparable Companies

To place the company's current capital structure in the proper context, compare its capital structure with those of similar companies. Exhibit 11.14 presents the median debt-to-value levels for 10 industries. As the exhibit shows,

EXHIBIT 11.14 **Median Debt to Value by Industry**[1]

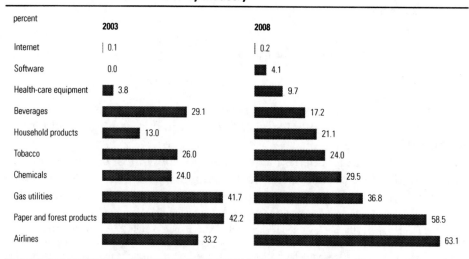

[1] S&P 1500 classified by Global Industry Classification System (GICS) industry. Debt to value measured using market values.

high-growth industries like software and health-care equipment, especially those with intangible investments, tend to use very little debt. Industries with heavy fixed investment in tangible assets, like utilities and airlines, tend to have higher debt levels. Economy-wide, the median debt-to-value ratio for S&P 1500 nonfinancials is 22.5 percent, and the median debt-to-equity ratio is 28.9 percent.

As Exhibit 11.14 demonstrates, industry debt-to-value ratios change over time. As share prices dropped during the financial crisis of 2008, the debt-to-value ratio rose for most industries, but by unequal proportions. Industries prone to the economic downturn, such as airlines, saw the largest rise in leverage, whereas staples like gas utilities experienced a decline in their relative leverage. Given the turmoil of 2008, a one-year view is probably misleading. For a proper perspective, examine the long-term trend for your company's particular industry.

For a company to have a different capital structure from that of its industry is perfectly acceptable, but you should understand why. For instance, is the company by philosophy more aggressive or innovative in the use of debt financing, or is the capital structure only a temporary deviation from a more conservative target? Often, companies finance acquisitions with debt they plan to retire quickly or refinance with a stock offering. Alternatively, is there anything different about the company's cash flow or asset intensity that can explain the difference? Always use comparables to help you assess the reasonableness of estimated debt-to-equity levels.

Reviewing Management's Financing Philosophy

As a final step, review management's historical financing philosophy (or question management outright). Has the current team been actively managing the company's capital structure? Is the management team aggressive in its use of debt? Or is it overly conservative? Consider Nike, the athletic shoe company. Although cash flow is strong and stable, the company rarely issues debt. From a financing perspective, it doesn't need to issue additional securities; investments can be funded with current profits.

Over the long run, one would expect most companies to aim toward a target capital structure that minimizes cost of capital. We address the choice of capital structure in Chapter 23.

COMPLEX CAPITAL STRUCTURES

The weighted average cost of capital is determined by weighting each security's expected return by its proportional contribution to total value. For a complex security, such as convertible debt, measuring expected return is challenging. Is a convertible bond like straight debt, enabling us to use the yield to maturity?

Is it like equity, enabling us to use the CAPM? In actuality, it is neither, so we recommend an alternative method.

If the treatment of hybrid securities will make a material difference in valuation results,[51] we recommend using adjusted present value (APV). In the APV, enterprise value is determined by discounting free cash flow at the industry-based unlevered cost of equity. The value of incremental cash flows related to financing, such as interest tax shields, is then computed separately. To determine the company's unlevered cost of equity, use the unlevered industry beta. This avoids the need to compute company-specific components, such as the debt-to-equity ratio, a required input in the unlevering equation.

In some situations, you may still desire an accurate representation of the cost of capital. In these cases, split hybrid securities into their individual components. For instance, you can replicate a convertible bond by combining a traditional bond with a call option on the company's stock. You can further disaggregate a call option into a portfolio consisting of a risk-free bond and the company's stock. By converting a complex security into a portfolio of debt and equity, you once again have the components required for the traditional cost of capital. The process of creating replicating portfolios to value options is discussed in Chapter 32.

REVIEW QUESTIONS

1. São Paolo Foods is a Brazilian producer of breads and other baked goods. Over the past year, profitability has been strong and the share price has risen from R$15 per share to R$25 per share. The company has 20 million shares outstanding. The company's borrowing is conservative; the company has only R$100 million in debt. The debt trades at a yield to maturity 50 basis points above Brazilian risk-free bonds. São Paolo Foods has a market beta of 0.7. If the Brazilian risk-free rate is 7 percent, the market risk premium is 5 percent, and the marginal tax rate is 30 percent, what is São Paolo's cost of capital?

2. São Paolo Foods (introduced in Question 1) is considering a leveraged recapitalization of the company. Upon announcement, management expects the share price to rise by 10 percent. If the company raises R$200 million in new debt to repurchase shares, how many shares can the company repurchase? Assuming management will actively manage to the new capital structure, estimate the company's new market beta. If the company's cost of

---

[51] If the hybrid security is unlikely to be converted, it can be treated as traditional debt. Conversely, if the hybrid security is well in the money, it should be treated as traditional equity. In these situations, errors are likely to be small, and a WACC-based valuation remains appropriate.

debt rises to 100 basis points above the Brazilian risk-free rate, what will its new cost of capital equal?

3. Your company, EuropeCo (a conglomerate of food, beverages, and consumer products), has announced its intention to purchase São Paolo Foods (introduced in Question 1). If the German risk-free rate is 5 percent and the beta of EuropeCo is 0.9, what is the cost of capital for São Paolo Foods once under EuropeCo control?

4. In 2009, the median price-to-earnings ratio for the S&P 500 was 11.1. If the long-run return on equity is 13.5 percent and the long-run growth in GDP is expected to be 6.7 percent (3.5 percent real growth and 3.2 percent inflation), what is the real cost of equity implied by the equity-denominated key value driver formula?

5. Market betas are typically computed with five years of monthly data or two weeks of yearly data. For computational simplicity, we present only 12 data points. Using a spreadsheet regression package or other software tool, compute a regression beta for the following data:

Returns, in percent

	1	2	3	4	5	6	7	8	9	10	11	12
Company	1.3	2.0	5.0	−1.0	−1.4	2.2	6.1	0.3	−4.0	3.8	−1.2	0.0
Market	1.0	1.2	3.4	0.3	−0.6	3.7	4.8	−2.3	−4.5	3.9	−1.3	1.8

6. You are analyzing a distressed bond with one year to maturity. The bond has a face value of $100 and pays a coupon rate of 5 percent per year. The bond is currently trading at $80. What is the yield to maturity on the bond? If the probability of default is 35 percent, what is the cost of debt? Assume that upon default only 50 percent of face value will be recovered and that remaining coupons will not be paid.

12

Moving from Enterprise Value to Value per Share

When you have completed the valuation of core operations, as described in Chapter 6, you are ready to estimate enterprise value, equity value, and value per share. Enterprise value represents the value of the entire company, while equity value represents the portion owned by shareholders. To determine enterprise value, add to the value of core operations the value of nonoperating assets, such as excess cash and nonconsolidated subsidiaries. To convert enterprise value to equity value, subtract short-term and long-term debt, debt equivalents (such as unfunded pension liabilities), and hybrid securities (such as employee stock options). Finally, to estimate value per share, divide the resulting equity value by the most recent number of undiluted shares outstanding.[1]

When converting core operations to enterprise value, be sure to follow these two guiding principles: (1) avoid double-counting, and (2) evaluate interdependencies between the value of core operations and the value of nonoperating assets. To avoid double-counting, take care not to value separately any asset or liability embedded in free cash flow. For instance, nonconsolidated subsidiaries are typically treated as nonoperating because any income generated by nonconsolidated subsidiaries appears in the parent company's nonoperating income, not in earnings before interest, taxes, and amortization (EBITA). That income must therefore be valued separately from EBITA. Conversely, if you choose to include nonoperating income as part of EBITA, do not value the nonconsolidated subsidiary separately.

Double-counting can also occur when moving from enterprise value to equity value. Any financing expense included in EBITA, such as rental expense

---

[1] Estimating the value per share completes the technical aspect of the valuation, yet the job is not complete. It is time to revisit the valuation with a comprehensive look at its implications. We examine this process in Chapter 13.

EXHIBIT 12.1 **Sample Comprehensive Valuation Buildup**

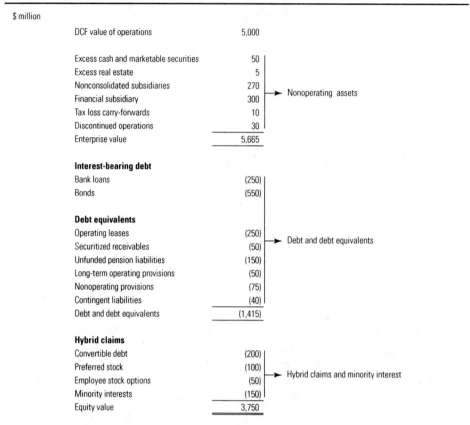

$ million		
DCF value of operations	5,000	
Excess cash and marketable securities	50	
Excess real estate	5	
Nonconsolidated subsidiaries	270	Nonoperating assets
Financial subsidiary	300	
Tax loss carry-forwards	10	
Discontinued operations	30	
Enterprise value	5,665	
Interest-bearing debt		
Bank loans	(250)	
Bonds	(550)	
Debt equivalents		
Operating leases	(250)	Debt and debt equivalents
Securitized receivables	(50)	
Unfunded pension liabilities	(150)	
Long-term operating provisions	(50)	
Nonoperating provisions	(75)	
Contingent liabilities	(40)	
Debt and debt equivalents	(1,415)	
Hybrid claims		
Convertible debt	(200)	
Preferred stock	(100)	Hybrid claims and minority interest
Employee stock options	(50)	
Minority interests	(150)	
Equity value	3,750	

from operating leases, should not be deducted again to determine equity value. Also, watch out for any interdependencies between enterprise value and financial claims against the company. For example, the value of debt for a company in financial distress will typically vary with enterprise value. Changes in operating performance will affect not just the value of the company, but also the likelihood of default. For that reason, and contrary to what is often assumed, the value of debt will not remain constant as enterprise value changes.

This chapter lays out the process for converting core operating value (via discounted cash flow) into enterprise value and subsequently into equity value. Exhibit 12.1 details the valuation buildup for a complex hypothetical company to demonstrate a comprehensive analysis of nonoperating items. For many companies, nonoperating assets comprise only excess cash, and financial claims comprise only traditional debt.

As noted already in this chapter, converting core operating value into enterprise value entails adding to the value of operations the value of nonoperating assets whose income is not included in EBITA and consequently excluded from free cash flow. The most common nonoperating assets are excess cash, nonconsolidated subsidiaries (also known as equity investments), and financial subsidiaries. To complete enterprise value, add the value of other nonoperating assets such as tax loss carry-forwards, excess pension assets, excess real estate, and discontinued operations. The resulting enterprise value represents the total value of the company that can be allocated among the various claim holders.

Converting enterprise value to equity value entails deducting nonequity claims. Similar to nonoperating assets, nonequity claims are financial claims against enterprise value whose expenses are not included in EBITA and consequently excluded from free cash flow. Double-counting an expense and its associated liability would bias your valuation downward. The most typical nonequity claims—bank loans and corporate bonds—are reported on the balance sheet; but off-balance-sheet debt, such as operating leases, securitized receivables, and contingent claims, are not and must be estimated separately. Hybrid securities, such as preferred stock, convertible debt, and employee options, have characteristics of both debt and equity. Such hybrids require special care, as their valuations are highly dependent on enterprise value, so you should value them using option-pricing models rather than book value. Finally, if minority shareholders have claims against certain consolidated subsidiaries, deduct the value of minority interest.

Using the valuation buildup as our framework, we will go step-by-step through how to value nonoperating assets, debt and debt equivalents, hybrid securities, and minority interests, ending with the final step in valuation, estimating the intrinsic value per share.

VALUING NONOPERATING ASSETS

Although not included in operations, nonoperating assets still represent value to the shareholder. Thus, you must estimate the market value of each nonoperating asset separately and add the resulting value to the DCF value of operations to arrive at enterprise value. If necessary, adjust for circumstances that could affect shareholders' ability to capture the full value of these assets. For example, if the company has announced it will sell off a nonoperating asset in the near term, deduct the estimated capital gains taxes (if any) on the asset from its market value. If ownership of the asset is shared with another company, include only your company's portion of the value.

In this section, we identify the most common nonoperating assets and describe how to handle these in the valuation.

Excess Cash and Marketable Securities

Nonoperating assets that can be converted into cash on short notice and at low cost are classified as excess cash and marketable securities. Under U.S.

Generally Accepted Accounting Principles (GAAP) and International Financial Reporting Standards (IFRS), companies must report such assets at their fair market value on the balance sheet. You can use the most recent book values as a proxy for the market value of these assets unless you have reason to believe they have significantly changed in value since the reporting date (as in the case of volatile equity holdings).

In general, we do not recommend valuing liquid nonoperating assets yourself if the market values are available. If you decide to perform a DCF valuation of liquid securities, estimate meaningful cash flow projections, and discount these at the appropriate cost of capital. In general, this will not equal the company's weighted average cost of capital (WACC). For example, discounting interest income from U.S. government bonds owned by the company at the company's WACC would lead to an undervaluation, because the appropriate opportunity cost of capital for U.S. government securities is the risk-free rate.

Nonconsolidated Subsidiaries and Equity Investments

Nonconsolidated subsidiaries and equity investments are companies in which the parent company holds a noncontrolling equity stake. Because the parent company does not have formal control over these subsidiaries, their financials are not consolidated, so these investments must be valued separately from operations. Under U.S. GAAP and IFRS, there are two ways in which nonconsolidated subsidiaries can appear in the parent company's accounts:

1. For equity stakes between 20 percent and 50 percent, the parent company is assumed to have influence but not control over the subsidiary. The equity holding in the subsidiary is reported in the parent balance sheet at the investment's historical cost plus any reinvested income. The parent company's portion of the subsidiary's profits is shown below operating profit on the parent company's income statement.

2. For equity stakes below 20 percent, the parent company is assumed to have no influence. The equity holdings are shown at historical cost on the parent's balance sheet. The parent's portion of the subsidiary's *dividends* is included below operating profit on the income statement.

Publicly traded subsidiaries If the subsidiary is publicly listed, use the market value for the company's equity stake. Verify that the market value is indeed a good indicator of intrinsic value. In some cases, these listed subsidiaries have very limited free float and/or very low liquidity, so the share price may not properly reflect current information.

Exhibit 12.2 presents a partial enterprise valuation of Philips, a Dutch consumer products, health care, and lighting company. As of October 2008, Philips

EXHIBIT 12.2 **Philips Enterprise Value, October 2008**

€ millions

	Holding (percent)				
Core operating value		21,630	**Valuation of LG Display stake**		
			Market capitalization (millions of won)		10,433,000
Associates			÷ Currency conversion (wons/euro)		1,680
LG Display	19.9	1,236 ◄	Market capitalization (millions of euros)		6,211
TPV Technologies	13.4	95			
NXP Semiconductors	19.9	598	× Percent ownership		19.9
Pace Micro Technologies	23.0	76	Ownership stake (millions of euros)		1,236
Excess cash		8,233			
Enterprise value		31,868			

Source: UBS Analyst Report, October 2008, Thomson First Call.

owned stakes in a few unconsolidated subsidiaries.[2] One significant investment was LG Display, a South Korean manufacturer of TFT-LCD panels for use in televisions, notebook computers, and other applications. Although LG Display is publicly traded, Philips used subsidiary accounting for LG Display because the company was "represented on the board of directors and continues to exercise influence." Under this accounting classification, the book value reported on the balance sheet will not represent the investment's current value.

To estimate Philips's stake in LG Display, start with LG Display's market capitalization (10,433 billion won), and divide by the exchange rate of South Korean won to euros (1,680). This converts LG Display's local market capitalization into euros. To determine the value of Philips's partial ownership, multiply the resulting market capitalization in euros by Philips's ownership stake (19.9 percent).

Repeat this process for each of Philips's holdings to find each subsidiary's contribution to Philips's enterprise value.

Privately held subsidiaries If the subsidiary is not listed but you have access to its financial statements, perform a separate DCF valuation of the equity stake. Discount the cash flows at the appropriate cost of capital (which, as before, is not necessarily the parent company's WACC). Also, when completing the parent valuation, include only the value of the parent's equity stake and not the subsidiary's entire enterprise value or equity value.

If the parent company's accounts are the only source of financial information for the subsidiary, we suggest the following alternatives to DCF:

- *Simplified cash-flow-to-equity valuation:* This is a feasible approach when the parent has a 20 to 50 percent equity stake, because the subsidiary's net income and book equity are disclosed in the parent's

---

[2] On March 11, 2009, Philips announced the sale of its remaining stake in LG Display.

accounts.[3] Build forecasts for how the equity-based key value drivers (net income growth and return on equity) will develop, so you can project cash flows to equity. Discount these cash flows at the *cost of equity* for the subsidiary in question and not at the parent company's cost of capital.

- *Multiples valuation:* As a second alternative, estimate the partial stake using a price-to-earnings and/or market-to-book multiple. If the company owns 20 to 50 percent of the subsidiary, apply an appropriate multiple to reported income.

- *Tracking portfolio:* For parent equity stakes below 20 percent, you may have no information beyond the investment's original cost—that is, the book value shown in the parent's balance sheet. Even applying a multiple is difficult because neither net income nor the current book value of equity is reported. If you know when the stake was acquired, you can approximate its current market value by applying the relative price change for a portfolio of comparable stocks over the same holding period.

You should triangulate your results as much as possible, given the lack of precision for these valuation approaches.

Loans to Other Companies

For loans to nonconsolidated subsidiaries and other companies, use the reported book value. This is a reasonable approximation of market value if the loans were given at fair market terms and if the borrower's credit risk and general interest rates have not changed significantly since issuance. If this is not the case, you should perform a separate DCF valuation of the promised interest and principal payments at the yield to maturity for corporate bonds with similar risk and maturity.

Finance Subsidiaries

To make their products more accessible, some companies operate customer financing businesses.[4] Because financial subsidiaries differ greatly from manufacturing and services businesses, it is critical to separate revenues, expenses, and balance sheet accounts associated with the subsidiary from core operations. Failing to do so will distort return on invested capital, free cash flow, and ultimately your perspective on the company's valuation.

To demonstrate the proper analysis of a company with a customer financing subsidiary—and analytical pitfalls—we have constructed a hypothetical

---

[3] The book value of the subsidiary equals the historical acquisition cost plus retained profits, which is a reasonable approximation of book equity. If any goodwill is included in the book value of the subsidiary, this should be deducted.

[4] Companies that sell expensive products typically offer financing of purchases. Significant customer financing subsidiaries exist at Caterpillar, IBM, and Textron, among others.

EXHIBIT 12.3 **FinanceCo: Income Statement and Balance Sheet**

$ million

Income statement		Balance sheet	
Sales of machinery	1,100	Operating assets	3,000
Revenues of financial products	300	Financial receivables	3,500
Total revenues	1,400	Total assets	6,500
Cost of goods sold	(800)		
Interest expense of financial products	(250)	Operating liabilities	500
Total operating costs	(1,050)	General obligation debt	700
		Debt related to financial products	3,200
Operating profit	350	Stockholders' equity	2,100
Interest expense, general obligation	(50)	Total liabilities and equity	6,500
Net income	300		

company, FinanceCo. Exhibit 12.3 presents FinanceCo's income statement and balance sheet. Last year, the company sold $1,100 million of machinery at a cost of $800 million. The company finances a significant percentage of its products for its customers, generating $300 million per year in lease revenue. The company currently holds $3,500 million in financial receivables. To finance its leasing business, FinanceCo raises securitized debt, collateralized by the financial receivables. The company also has general obligation debt to fund everyday operations.

To analyze FinanceCo, start by constructing separate income statements and balance sheets for the manufacturing and customer financing subsidiaries. Most companies will denote which line items are related to each group. For line items that consolidate expenses across both groups (such as selling and administrative expenses), search in the company's notes for financial statements by business segment.

Exhibit 12.4 presents the reorganized financial statements for the manufacturing group and the customer financing subsidiary. The manufacturing group's operating profit equals $300 million ($1,100 million in revenue less $800 million in cost of goods sold). Invested capital equals $2,500 million ($3,000 million in operating assets less $500 million in operating liabilities). Return on invested capital (ROIC) for the manufacturing group is 12.0 percent. For the customer financing subsidiary, return on equity is a better measure than ROIC, because capital structure is an integral part of a financial institution's operations. To compute return on equity, divide net income ($50 million) by allocated equity ($300 million).[5] This leads to a return on allocated equity of 16.7 percent.

---

[5] An allocation of equity is required because equity is not available by business segment. The simplest method to allocate equity is to net the group's liabilities against the group's assets. This can be misleading, however, because one group can borrow against the collective assets of the company, lowering the amount of allocated equity beyond what a stand-alone company can hold. As an alternative, use an industry benchmark for the debt-to-equity of stand-alone financing companies.

EXHIBIT 12.4 **FinanceCo: Reorganized Financial Statements**

$ million

Manufacturing subsidiary		Customer financing subsidiary	
Operating profit		**Net income**	
Sales of machinery	1,100	Revenues of financial products	300
Cost of goods sold	(800)	Interest expense of financial products	(250)
Operating profit	300	Net income	50
Reorganized balance sheet		**Reorganized balance sheet**	
Operating assets	3,000	Financial receivables	3,500
Operating liabilities	(500)		
Invested capital	2,500	Debt related to financial products	3,200
		Allocated equity	300
General obligation debt	700	Liabilities and allocated equity	3,500
Allocated equity	1,800		
Invested capital	2,500		
Return on invested capital (percent)	12.0	Return on allocated equity (percent)	16.7

Using the returns calculated in Exhibit 12.4, we can benchmark each of FinanceCo's subsidiaries against its peers. We cannot, however, aggregate the ratios to determine a combined return for FinanceCo as a whole. For instance, the ratio of FinanceCo's operating profit ($350 million) to FinanceCo's net assets ($2,500 million in net operating assets plus $3,500 in financial receivables) equals 5.8 percent, which is well below the 12.0 percent return on invested capital for the manufacturing group. This downward bias is caused by the small spread banks typically earn on loaned assets. A common alternative is to sum the manufacturing subsidiary's operating profit with the finance subsidiary's net income, divided by the invested capital of manufacturing plus the allocated equity from the financing business. This ratio blends the ROIC of manufacturing with the ROE of the financing business into a single ratio. Since blending different ratio types can cause systematic distortions, we recommend benchmarking each business separately.

To value a customer financing subsidiary, use the process and tools for valuing financial institutions (detailed in Chapter 36).

Discontinued Operations

Discontinued operations are businesses being sold or closed down. The earnings from discontinued operations are explicitly shown in the income statement, and the associated net asset position is disclosed on the balance sheet. Because discontinued operations are no longer part of a company's operations, their value should not be modeled as part of free cash flow or included in the DCF value of operations. Under U.S. GAAP and IFRS, the assets and liabilities associated with the discontinued operations are written down to their fair value and disclosed as a net asset on the balance sheet, so the most recent book value is usually a reasonable approximation.[6]

Excess Real Estate

Excess real estate and other unutilized assets are assets no longer required for the company's operations. As a result, any cash flows that the assets could generate are excluded from the free cash flow projection, and the assets are not included in the DCF value of operations. Identifying these assets in an outside-in valuation is nearly impossible unless they are specifically disclosed in the company's footnotes. For that reason, only internal valuations are likely to include their value separately as a nonoperating asset. For excess real estate, use the most recent appraisal value when it is available. Alternatively, estimate the real estate value either by using a multiple, such as value per square meter, or by discounting expected future cash flows from rentals at the appropriate cost of capital. Of course, be careful to exclude any operating real estate from these figures, because that value is implicitly included in the free cash flow projections and value of operations.

We do not recommend a separate valuation for unutilized operating assets unless they are expected to be sold in the near term. If the financial projections for the company reflect growth, the value of any underutilized assets should instead be captured in lower future capital expenditures.

Tax Loss Carry-Forwards

As detailed in Chapter 25, there are three types of deferred tax assets (DTAs): operating DTAs, nonoperating DTAs, and tax loss carry-forwards. Only tax loss carry-forwards should be valued separately.[7] Tax loss carry-forwards—or net operating losses (NOLs), as they are called in the United States—are the tax credits generated by past losses. They can be used to lower future taxes. To value tax loss carry-forwards, create a separate account for the accumulated tax loss carry-forwards, and forecast the development of this account by adding any future losses and subtracting any future taxable profits on a year-by-year basis. For each year in which the account is used to offset taxable profits,

---

[6] Any upward adjustment to the current book value of assets and liabilities is limited to the cumulative historical impairments on the assets. Thus, the fair market value of discontinued operations could be higher than the net asset value disclosed in the balance sheet.

[7] Operating deferred tax assets (DTAs), such as those corresponding to ongoing inventory write-downs, are incorporated directly into net operating profit less adjusted taxes (NOPLAT) and subsequently free cash flow. Therefore, operating DTAs should not be valued separately. Nonoperating DTAs, such as pension-related DTAs, should be ignored. Instead, value the future tax burden (or relief) associated with the nonoperating asset as part of the nonoperating asset. For instance, pension DTAs represent taxes that were paid when historical contributions exceeded recognized expenses. Since past taxes paid are unrelated to future cash savings, they are irrelevant to valuation. Future cash savings are based on the current level of pension underfunding.

discount the tax savings at the cost of debt. Some practitioners simply set the carry-forwards' value at the tax rate times the accumulated tax losses.

Excess Pension Assets

Surpluses in a company's pension funds show up as net pension assets on the balance sheet. (Small amounts are typically embedded within other assets.) Following recent changes to U.S. accounting standards, excess pension assets are typically reported at market value.[8] On an after-tax basis, the pension's value depends on management's plans going forward. If pensions are expected to be dissolved soon, subtract liquidation taxes (typically set higher than the marginal tax rate) from the market value of excess pension assets. Otherwise, subtract taxes at the marginal rate (which reflects lower future contributions). For details on pension accounting and valuation, see Chapter 27.

VALUING DEBT AND DEBT EQUIVALENTS

With enterprise value in hand, you are ready to determine equity value. You do this by subtracting from enterprise value the value of nonequity financial claims, which are typically found in the liabilities section of the balance sheet. Remember, deduct only those financial claims that are not incorporated as part of free cash flow. Also, be aware that not all financial claims have to be reported on the balance sheet, so make sure to search the footnotes carefully for undisclosed liabilities.

In this section, we go though the most typical financial claims and how to determine their value.

Debt

Corporate debt comes in many forms: commercial paper, notes payable, fixed and floating bank loans, corporate bonds, and capitalized leases. If the debt is relatively secure and actively traded, use its market value.[9] If the debt instrument is not traded, estimate current value by discounting the promised interest payments and the principal repayment at the yield to maturity. The book value of debt is a reasonable approximation for fixed-rate debt if interest rates and default risk have not significantly changed since the debt issuance. For floating-rate debt, market value is not sensitive to interest rates, and book

---

[8] Under IFRS, companies can still report excess pension assets at book value. If pensions are not marked to market, search the company's pension footnote for the value of excess pension assets.

[9] When a bond's yield is below its coupon rate, the bond will trade above its face value. Intuition dictates that, at most, the bond's face value should be deducted from enterprise value. Yet since enterprise value is computed using the cost of debt (via the weighted average of cost of capital), subtracting face value is inconsistent with how enterprise value is computed. In cases where bonds are callable at face value, market prices will rarely exceed face value.

EXHIBIT 12.5 **Valuation of Equity Using Scenario Analysis**

$ million

	Enterprise value	Face value of debt	Equity value[1]	Probability (percent)	Weighted equity value
Scenario A					
New owner successfully implements value improvements.	1,500	1,200	300	50	150
Scenario B					
Company maintains current performance.	900	1,200	–	50	–
				Equity value	150

[1] Equity value equals enterprise value less the face value of debt or zero, whichever is greater

value is a reasonable approximation if the company's default risk has been fairly stable.

If you are using your valuation model to test changes in operating performance (for instance, a new initiative that will improve operating margins), the value of debt may differ from its current market value. Always check interest coverage ratios to test whether the company's bond rating will change under the new forecasts—often they will not. A change in bond rating can be translated into a new yield to maturity for debt, which in turn will allow you to revalue the debt. For more on debt ratings and interest rates, see Chapter 23.

Highly levered companies For companies with significant debt or companies in financial distress, valuing debt requires careful analysis. For distressed companies, the value of the debt will be at a significant discount to its book value and will fluctuate with the value of the enterprise. Essentially, the debt has become similar to equity: its value will depend directly on your estimate for the enterprise value, and you should not simply deduct the current market value of the debt.

For distressed companies, apply an integrated-scenario approach to value operations as well as equity. Exhibit 12.5 presents a simple two-scenario example of equity valuation with significant debt. In scenario A, the company's new owner is able to implement improvements in operating margin, inventory turns, and so on. In scenario B, changes are unsuccessful, and performance remains at its current level. For each scenario, estimate the enterprise value conditional on your financial forecasts, deduct the *full value* of the debt[10] and other nonequity claims,[11] and calculate the equity value as the residual (which should be zero for any scenario where the conditional enterprise value is less than the value of debt plus other nonequity claims). Next, weight each

[10] That is, the market value of debt for a nondistressed company—typically close to book value.
[11] All nonequity claims need to be included in the scenario approach for distressed companies. The order in which nonequity claims are paid upon liquidation will make a difference for the value of nonequity claims, but not for the equity value.

scenario's conditional value of equity by its probability of occurrence to obtain an estimate for the value of equity. For the company in Exhibit 12.5, scenario A leads to an equity valuation of $300 million, whereas the equity value in scenario B is zero. If the probability of each scenario is 50 percent, the weighted average value of equity is $150 million.

The scenario valuation approach treats equity like a call option on enterprise value. A more comprehensive model would estimate the entire distribution of potential enterprise values and use an option-pricing model, such as the Black-Scholes model, to value equity.[12] Using an option-pricing model to value equity, however, has serious practical drawbacks. First, to model the distribution of enterprise values, you must forecast the expected change and volatility for each source of uncertainty, such as revenue growth and gross margin. This too easily becomes a mechanical exercise that replaces a thoughtful analysis of the underlying economics of potential scenarios. Second, most options models treat each source of uncertainty as independent of the others. This can lead to outcomes that are economically unrealistic. For these reasons, we believe a thoughtful scenario analysis will lead to a more accurate valuation than an options model will.

Operating Leases

Under certain restrictions, companies can avoid capitalizing leased assets on their balance sheets. Instead, they treat rental charges for so-called operating leases as an expense. In Chapter 6, we outlined a method for capitalizing leased assets. If NOPLAT, invested capital, and consequently free cash flow are adjusted for operating leases, you must deduct the present value of operating leases from enterprise value to determine equity value. Do *not* subtract the value of operating leases, however, if no adjustments are made. Chapter 27 details the valuation of leases.

Securitized Receivables

When companies sell accounts receivable to a third party, the discount on the sale is typically embedded in either selling, general, and administrative (SG&A) expense or interest expense. Deduct the value of securitized receivables from enterprise value when discounts are incorporated in interest expense *or* if you adjust SG&A to remove embedded discounts. Chapter 27 discusses the valuation of securitized receivables in detail.

Unfunded Pension and Other Postretirement Liabilities

Unfunded retirement liabilities should be treated as debt equivalents and deducted from enterprise value to determine equity value. Following recent

---

[12] Option-pricing models are described in Chapter 32.

changes to accounting standards, unfunded pension and other retirement liabilities are typically reported at market value. If pensions are not marked to market, search the company's pension footnote for the value of unfunded pension liabilities. Since the future contributions to fill unfunded liabilities are tax deductible at the marginal tax rate, multiply unfunded pension liabilities by 1 minus the marginal tax rate. For details on pension accounting and valuation, please see Chapter 27.

Provisions

Certain provisions other than retirement-related liabilities need to be deducted as nonequity financial claims. Following the guidelines in Chapter 7, we distinguish four types of provisions and value them as follows:

1. Ongoing operating provisions (e.g., for warranties and product returns) are already accounted for in the free cash flows and should therefore *not be deducted* from enterprise value.

2. Long-term operating provisions (e.g., for plant-decommissioning costs) *should be deducted* from enterprise value as debt equivalents. Because these provisions cover cash expenses that are payable in the long term, they are typically recorded at the discounted value in the balance sheet. In this case, there is no need to perform a separate DCF analysis, and you can *use the book value of the liability* in your valuation.

3. Nonoperating provisions (e.g., for restructuring charges resulting from layoffs) *should be deducted* from enterprise value as a debt equivalent. Although a discounted value would be ideal, the book value from the balance sheet is often a reasonable approximation. These provisions are recorded on the financial statements at a nondiscounted value, because outlays are usually in the near term.

4. Income-smoothing provisions do not represent actual future cash outlays, so they should *not be deducted* from enterprise value. These provisions are difficult to find and will disappear as companies around the world adopt IFRS.

For specifics on how to identify, analyze, and value provisions, see Chapter 26.

Contingent Liabilities

Certain liabilities are not disclosed in the balance sheet but are separately discussed in the notes to the balance sheet. Examples are possible liabilities from pending litigation and loan guarantees. When possible, estimate the associated expected after-tax cash flows (if the costs are tax deductible), and discount these at the cost of debt. Unfortunately, assessing the probability of such cash flows materializing is difficult, so the valuation should be interpreted with caution. To provide some boundaries on your final valuation, estimate the value of contingent liabilities for a range of probabilities.

VALUING HYBRID SECURITIES AND MINORITY INTERESTS

For stable companies, the current values of debt and debt equivalents are typically independent of enterprise value. For hybrid securities and minority interests, this is not the case. Each must be valued in conjunction with estimates of enterprise value. The most common hybrid securities are convertible debt, convertible preferred stock, and employee stock options.

Convertible Debt and Convertible Preferred Stock

Convertible bonds are corporate bonds that can be exchanged for common equity at a predetermined conversion ratio. A convertible bond is essentially a package of a straight corporate bond plus a call option on equity (the conversion option).[13] Because the conversion option can have significant value, this form of debt requires treatment different from that of regular corporate debt.

The value of convertibles depends on the enterprise value. In contrast to straight debt, neither the book value nor the simple DCF value of bond cash flows is a good proxy for the value of convertibles. Depending on the information available, there are three potential methods:

1. *Market value:* If your estimate of value per share is near the market price and the convertible bond is actively traded, use its market value. If you plan to modify enterprise value (via operating changes), the market value is no longer appropriate, as convertible debt value will change with enterprise value.

2. *Black-Scholes value:* When the market value is inappropriate, we recommend using an option-based valuation for convertible debt. In contrast to the treatment of employee stock options, annual reports do not provide any information on the value of convertible debt. Accurate valuation of convertible bonds with option-based models is not straightforward, but following methods outlined by John Ingersoll, you can apply an adjusted Black-Scholes option-pricing model for a reasonable approximation.[14]

---

[13] See R. Brealey, S. Myers, and F. Allen, *Principles of Corporate Finance,* 8th ed. (New York: McGraw-Hill, 2006), chap. 23. If you are doing a discounted-cash-flow-to-equity valuation, you subtract only the value of the conversion option from your DCF valuation. The straight-debt component of the convertible debt has already been included in the equity cash flows.

[14] For more on the valuation of employee stock options, see, for example, J. Hull and A. White, "How to Value Employee Stock Options," *Financial Analysts Journal* 60, no. 1 (January/February 2004): 114–119.

EXHIBIT 12.6 **Hasbro Convertible Debt, November 2008**

$ million

Capital structure	Market value	Black-Scholes value	Conversion value	Book value
Enterprise value	5,050.0	5,050.0	5,050.0	
Traditional debt	(556.3)	(556.3)	(556.3)	(605.2)
→ Convertible debt at 2.75% due 2021	(334.3)	(326.4)	–	(249.8)
Unfunded pensions	(38.3)	(38.3)	(38.3)	(38.3)
Employee options	(134.0)	(134.0)	(134.0)	
Equity value	3,987.1	3,994.9	4,321.4	
Number of shares (million)				
Number of nondiluted shares	142.6	142.6	142.6	
→ New shares issued	–	–	11.6	
Number of diluted shares	142.6	142.6	154.2	
Value per share (dollars)	28.0	28.0	28.0	

Source: Hasbro 2007 10-K, NASD TRACE system, Black-Scholes option-pricing model.

3. *Conversion value:* The conversion value approach assumes that all convertible bonds are immediately exchanged for equity and ignores the time value of the conversion option. It leads to reasonable results when the conversion option is deep in the money, meaning the bond is more valuable when converted into equity than held for future coupon and principal payments.

In Exhibit 12.6, we illustrate all three valuation methods for the toy manufacturer Hasbro. The first column values Hasbro's equity using the market price of each bond. Market prices for U.S. corporate debt are reported on the Financial Industry Regulatory Authority (FINRA) TRACE system. In November 2008, Hasbro's traditional debt traded at a small discount to its book value. Conversely, the company's convertible debt traded at a significant premium ($334.3 million versus $249.8 million in book value) because the bonds are convertible into equity at a discount. According to the debt contract, the bonds are convertible at $21.60 per share.[15] At this conversion price, $249.8 million in bonds are convertible into 11.56 million shares. With Hasbro's stock trading at $28, the bonds can be converted into the equivalent of $323.7 million (known as intrinsic value). The convertible bond's market price ($334.3 million) trades slightly higher than the bond's intrinsic value given the unlimited upside and downside protection the bonds offer.

To model the value of Hasbro's convertible debt, disaggregate the value of convertible debt into underlying straight debt and the option value to convert. The value of straight debt equals the net present value of a 2.75 percent coupon

[15] Reported in Hasbro's 2007 annual report, note 7.

bond yielding 7.81 percent (the yield on comparable bonds without conversion features), maturing in 12 years (the remaining life). Without conversion, Hasbro's debt is valued at 61.5 percent of face value, or $153.6 million.[16]

To determine an option's value, you need six inputs: the underlying asset value, the strike price, the dividend rate on the underlying asset, the volatility of the underlying asset, the risk-free rate, and the time to maturity. For the option embedded in Hasbro's convertible bond, the underlying asset is 11.56 million shares of Hasbro stock, whose current value equals $323.7 million (11.56 million shares times $28 per share). The strike price equals $153.6 million (the current value of straight debt). The expected dividend rate (1.97 percent) and volatility of Hasbro's shares (22.0 percent) are reported in the company's 10-K. The bond's time to maturity is 12 years, and the current risk-free rate is 4.79 percent.[17] Inputting the data into a Black-Scholes estimator leads to an option value of $172.8 million. Thus, the Black-Scholes value of the convertible debt equals $326.4 million ($153.6 in straight debt plus $172.8 in option value).

A simple alternative to option pricing is the conversion value approach. Under the conversion value approach, convertible bonds are converted immediately into equity. Since Hasbro's bonds are convertible into 11.6 million shares, nondiluted shares are increased from 142.6 million to 154.2 million. The third column of Exhibit 12.6 zeros out convertible debt and divides by diluted shares. In this case, each approach leads to a similar value because the value of conversion is much higher than the value of traditional debt (known as being in the money). For bonds out of the money, the conversion approach will lead to an underestimation of the bonds' value. Therefore, we recommend using an option valuation model, such as Black-Scholes.

Employee Stock Options

Many companies offer their employees stock options as part of their compensation. Options give the holder the right, but not the obligation, to buy company stock at a specified price, known as the exercise price. Since employee stock options have long maturities and the company's stock price could eventually rise above the exercise price, options can have great value.

Employee stock options affect a company valuation in two ways. First, the value of options that will be *granted in the future* needs to be captured in the free cash flow projections or in a separate DCF valuation, following the guidelines in Chapter 7. If captured in the free cash flow projections, the value of future options grants is included in the value of operations and should not be treated as a nonequity claim. Second, the value of options *currently outstanding* must

[16] Without the conversion feature, the bond would trade at a significant discount to face value, because the bond's coupon is well below its yield to maturity.

[17] Hasbro issued convertible debt that is callable when the stock price is above $27. Since Hasbro is likely to recall the bond soon, the effective time to maturity on the bond is much less than 12 years. When we tested various times to maturity, however, the changes in bond price were small.

be subtracted from enterprise value as a nonequity claim. Note, however, that the value of the options will depend on your estimate of enterprise value, and your option valuation should reflect this.

The following approaches can be used for valuing employee options:

- We recommend using the *estimated market value from option valuation models*, such as Black-Scholes or more advanced binomial (lattice) models. Under U.S. GAAP and IFRS, the notes to the balance sheet report the total value of all employee stock options outstanding, as estimated by such option-pricing models. Note that this value is a good approximation only if your estimate of share price is close to the one underlying the option values in the annual report. Otherwise, you need to create a new valuation using an option-pricing model. The notes disclose the information required for valuation.[18]

- The *exercise value approach* provides only a lower bound for the value of employee options. It assumes that all options are exercised immediately and thereby ignores the time value of the options. The resulting valuation error increases as options have longer time to maturity, the company's stock has higher volatility, and the company's share price is closer to the exercise price. Given that a more accurate valuation is already disclosed in the annual report, we do not recommend this method. However, it is still quite common among practitioners.

Exhibit 12.7 provides an example of the two valuation methods. The first method uses Black-Scholes to value both outstanding and currently exercisable options. The value of outstanding options will be less than that of exercisable options, because outstanding options include some options that will be lost if the employee leaves the company.

To estimate the value of employee stock options, you need six inputs: the current stock price, the average strike price, the stock's dividend rate, the stock's volatility, the risk-free rate, and the time to maturity. Hasbro's current share price equals $28. The other inputs are disclosed in Hasbro's 10-K for both outstanding and exercisable options. For outstanding options, the weighted average strike price equals $22, the expected dividend rate equals 1.97 percent, the volatility of Hasbro's shares equals 22.0 percent, and the average time to maturity is reported at 4.83 years. The current risk-free rate is 4.79 percent. The Black-Scholes estimator prices the average option at $9.24.[19] With 14.5 million options outstanding, the aggregate value of options is valued at $134.0 million.

---

[18] For more on the valuation of employee stock options, see, for example, Hull and White, "How to Value Employee Stock Options."

[19] Using Black-Scholes to determine the value of a single option on an average strike price will undervalue a portfolio of options with a spread of strike prices. Unless you know the spread of strike prices, you cannot measure the bias.

EXHIBIT 12.7 **Hasbro Employee Options, November 2008**

$ million

| | Black-Scholes | | |
| | Value of outstanding options | Value of exercisable options | Exercise value approach |
Company financial structure			
Enterprise value	5,050.0	5,050.0	5,050.0
Traditional debt	(556.3)	(556.3)	(556.3)
Convertible debt at 2.75% due 2021	(334.3)	(334.3)	(334.3)
Unfunded pensions	(38.3)	(38.3)	(38.3)
Employee options: value	(134.0)	(98.6)	–
Employee options: exercise proceeds	–	–	199.3
Equity value	3,987.1	4,022.5	4,320.3
Number of shares (million)			
Number of nondiluted shares	142.6	142.6	142.6
New shares issued	–	–	9.7
Number of diluted shares	142.6	142.6	152.3
Value per share (dollars)	28.0	28.2	28.4

Source: Hasbro 2007 10-K, NASD TRACE system, Black-Scholes option-pricing model.

To estimate share price, deduct the aggregate value from enterprise value, and divide by the number of undiluted shares.

Under the exercise value approach, employee options are assumed to be exercised immediately. According to Hasbro's 10-K, 9.73 million shares are immediately exercisable at an average strike price of $20.50, for total proceeds of $199.3 million. Exercise of employee options generates cash for the company and increases shares outstanding from 142.6 million to 152.3 million. Dividing equity value by diluted shares leads to a value of $28.4, slightly higher than the value under the Black-Scholes method.

Minority Interests

When a company controls, but does not fully own a subsidiary, the subsidiary's financial statements must be fully consolidated in the group accounts. Without any further adjustment, the full value of the subsidiary would be improperly included in the parent company valuation. Therefore, you need to deduct the value of the third-party minority stake in the subsidiary as a nonequity financial claim.

Because minority stakes are to a certain extent the mirror image of non-consolidated subsidiaries, the recommended valuation for minority interests is similar to that of nonconsolidated subsidiaries; see the corresponding section for more details. If the minority stake is publicly listed, as in the case of minority carve-outs (see Chapter 22), use the proportional market value owned by outsiders to deduct from enterprise value. Alternatively, you can perform a separate valuation using a DCF approach, multiples, or a tracking portfolio, depending on the amount of information available. Remember, however, that a minority interest is a claim on a subsidiary, not the entire company. Thus, any valuation should be directly related to the subsidiary and not the company as a whole.

ESTIMATING VALUE PER SHARE

The final step in a valuation is to calculate the value per share. Assuming that you have used an option-based valuation approach for convertible bonds and employee options, divide the total equity value by the number of *undiluted* shares outstanding. Use the undiluted (rather than diluted) number of shares because the full values of convertible debt and stock options have already been deducted from the enterprise value as nonequity claims. Also, use the most recent number of undiluted shares outstanding. Do not use the weighted average of shares outstanding; they are reported in the financial statements to determine average earnings per share.

The number of shares outstanding is the gross number of shares issued, less the number of shares held in treasury. Most U.S. and European companies report the number of shares issued and those held in treasury under shareholders' equity. However, some companies show treasury shares as an investment asset, which is incorrect from an economic perspective. Treat them, instead, as a reduction in the number of shares outstanding.

If you used the conversion and exercise value method to account for employee options and convertible debt and stock options, divide by the diluted number of shares.

REVIEW QUESTIONS

1. MarineCo manufactures, markets, and distributes recreational motor boats. Using discounted free cash flow, you value the company's operations at $2,500 million. The company has a 20 percent stake in a nonconsolidated subsidiary. The subsidiary is valued at $500 million. The investment is recorded on MarineCo's balance sheet as an equity investment of $50 million. MarineCo is looking to increase its ownership. The company's marginal tax rate is 30 percent. Based on this information, what is MarineCo's enterprise value? If new management announced its plan to sell the company's stake in the subsidiary at its current value, how would that change your valuation?

2. MarineCo has unfunded pension liabilities valued at $200 million, recorded as a long-term liability. MarineCo has detailed a potential legal judgment of $100 million for defective engines in its annual report. Since management estimates a 90 percent likelihood the judgment will be enforced against the engine maker and not MarineCo, they did not report a liability on the balance sheet. The company's marginal tax rate is 30 percent. If MarineCo's enterprise value is $2,600 million, what is MarineCo's equity value?

3. To finance customer purchases, MarineCo recently started a customer financing unit. MarineCo's income statement and balance sheet are provided in Exhibit 12.8. Separate MarineCo's income statement and balance sheet into the two segments: manufacturing and the customer financing unit. Assume equity in the financing subsidiary is the difference between finance receivables and debt related to those receivables. What is the return on invested capital for the manufacturing segment? What is the return on equity for the customer financing subsidiary?

4. In Question 3, we computed ROE based on an equity calculation equal to the difference between finance receivables and debt related to those receivables. Why might this ROE measurement lead to a result that is too high?

5. You are valuing a company using probability-weighted scenario analysis. You carefully model three scenarios, such that the resulting enterprise value equals $300 million in Scenario 1, $200 million in Scenario 2, and $100 million in Scenario 3. The probability of each scenario is 25 percent, 50 percent, and 25 percent respectively. What is the expected enterprise value? What is the expected equity value? Management announces a new plan that eliminates the downside scenario, making Scenario 2 that much more likely. What happens to enterprise value and equity value? Why does enterprise value rise more than equity value?

EXHIBIT 12.8 **MarineCo: Income Statement and Balance Sheet**

$ million

Income statement		Balance sheet	
Sales of machinery	1,500	Operating assets	2,200
Revenues of financial products	400	Financial receivables	4,000
Total revenues	1,900	Total assets	6,200
Cost of goods sold	(1,000)	Operating liabilities	400
Interest expense of financial products	(350)	General obligation debt	–
Total operating costs	(1,350)	Debt related to customer financing	3,600
		Stockholders' equity	2,200
Operating profit	550	Total liabilities and equity	6,200
Interest expense, general obligation	(80)		
Net income	470		

6. You are valuing a technology company whose enterprise value is $800 million. The company has no debt, but considerable employee options (10 million in total). Based on option pricing models, you value the options at $6.67 per option. If the company has 40 million shares outstanding, what is the company's equity value and value per share? What is the value per share using the exercise value approach? Assume the average strike price equals $15.

Outline

Part IV: Additional Topics

- Lecture slides on deterministic capital budgeting

- Chapter 8 of "Advanced Engineering Economics" by Park and Sharp-Bette

- Lecture slides on utility theory

- Chapter 9 of "Advanced Engineering Economics" by Park and Sharp-Bette

Deterministic Capital Budgeting

> Pure Capital Rationing with no lending or borrowing allowed

- **Primal formulation**

$$\text{max} \quad Z = \sum_{j=1}^{J} p_j . x_j$$

$$\text{subject to} \quad -\sum_{j=1}^{J} a_{nj} . x_j \leq M_n \quad , \quad n = 0, 1, ..., N$$

$$x_j \leq 1 \quad , \quad j = 1, 2, ..., J$$

$$x_j \geq 0 \quad , \quad j = 1, 2, ..., J$$

Where:

➢ p_j is the present value of project j

➢ x_j is the project selection variable

➢ M_n is the budget limit at time n

➢ N is the end of the planning period

Deterministic Capital Budgeting

- **Complementary slackness conditions**

$$\rho_n^*(M_n + \sum_{j=1}^{J} a_{nj}x_j^*) = 0 \qquad , \quad n = 0,1,...,N$$

$$x_j^*(\mu_j^* - p_j - \sum_{n=0}^{N} a_{nj}\rho_n^*) = 0 \; , \quad j = 1,2,...,J$$

$$\mu_j^*(1 - x_j^*) = 0 \qquad\qquad\qquad , \quad j = 1,2,...,J$$

➤ The complementary slackness conditions hold

at the optimal solution

Deterministic Capital Budgeting

> Pure Capital Rationing with no lending or borrowing allowed

- **Economic interpretation: the present value of a project plus the sum of the cash flows over the horizon "discounted" by the dual variables is:**

  ➤ Non-positive for a rejected project

  ➤ Exactly zero for a partially funded project

  ➤ Non-negative for a fully funded project

- **Primal formulation with one lending, one borrowing rate, and unlimited borrowing capacity**

max
$$Z = \sum_{j=1}^{J} \hat{a}_j . x_j + v_N - w_N$$

subject to
$$-\sum_{j=1}^{J} a_{0j} . x_j + v_0 - w_0 \leq M_0$$

$$-\sum_{j=1}^{J} a_{nj} . x_j - (1 + r_l)v_{n-1} + v_n + (1 + r_b)w_{n-1} - w_n \leq M_n \quad , \quad n = 1, ..., N$$

$$v_n, w_n \geq 0 \quad , \quad n = 0, 1, ..., N$$
$$0 \leq x_j \leq 1 \quad , \quad j = 1, 2, ..., J$$

Where:
- r_l is the lending rate
- r_b is the borrowing rate

638

Deterministic Capital Budgeting

- **Let us distinguish three scenarios for a project j. Using the dual formulation and complementary slackness, we obtain:**

  - The project is rejected

$$\hat{a}_j + \sum_{n=0}^{N} a_{nj} \rho_n^* \leq 0$$

  - The project is partially funded

$$\hat{a}_j + \sum_{n=0}^{N} a_{nj} \rho_n^* = 0$$

  - The project is fully funded

$$\hat{a}_j + \sum_{n=0}^{N} a_{nj} \rho_n^* \geq 0$$

- **Other insights from duality and complementary slackness**

  - ➤ Dual variables:

$$\rho_N^* = 1$$

$$(1 + r_l)\rho_{n+1}^* \le \rho_n^* \le (1 + r_b)\rho_{n+1}^* \quad , \quad n = 0, 1, \ldots N - 1$$

  - ➤ In period of borrowing

$$w_n > 0 \Rightarrow \begin{array}{c} v_n = 0 \\ \rho_n^* = (1 + r_b)\rho_{n+1}^* \end{array}$$

  - ➤ In period of lending

$$v_n > 0 \Rightarrow \begin{array}{c} w_n = 0 \\ \rho_n^* = (1 + r_l)\rho_{n+1}^* \end{array}$$

Outline

Part IV: Additional Topics

▪Lecture slides on deterministic capital budgeting

▪Chapter 8 of "Advanced Engineering Economics" by Park and Sharp-Bette

▪Lecture slides on utility theory

▪Chapter 9 of "Advanced Engineering Economics" by Park and Sharp-Bette

8

Deterministic Capital Budgeting Models

8.1 INTRODUCTION

In the previous chapter we determined that we should select from among multiple alternatives by choosing the one with the maximum net present value (*PV*) or by using the incremental approach with one of several criteria. There are two important characteristics of the problems solved in the previous chapter.

1. We could easily formulate and list all mutually exclusive alternatives of interest.

2. There is an underlying assumption of ability to borrow and lend unlimited amounts at a single, fixed interest rate. When budget limits are imposed, the borrowing ability at time 0 is restricted, and we are left with a single, fixed interest rate for future lending, or reinvestment.

In this chapter we relax these assumptions. We consider problems in which budget limits are imposed during several time periods, the projects have interdependencies, and there are different, but known, borrowing and lending opportunities. In short, we examine problems for which it would be exceedingly difficult to specify all mutually exclusive alternatives. This type of analysis is called capital budgeting. In keeping with the sense of Part Two of this book, we assume certainty with respect to all information. Linear programming (LP) is a convenient tool for analyzing such situations, and we give a brief introduction to its use in Section 8.2.

We will also see that *PV* maximization is not necessarily our best objective, for different reinvestment rates are possible. In the pure capital rationing model (Section 8.3), which allows no external borrowing and lending, this situation has been the focus of much academic controversy during the last twenty years. We include a brief review of the major arguments, not from the view of favoring any

643

one of them but rather to give the reader an important historical perspective on the subject.

The inclusion of borrowing and lending opportunities (Section 8.4) leads to more realistic operational models. In some situations the previously mentioned academic controversy disappears, and in others it reappears. Weingartner's horizon model (Section 8.5) provides the analyst with a convenient way of avoiding these issues, while yielding solutions consistent with *PV* analysis of situations allowing unlimited borrowing and lending. Bernhard's general model (Section 8.6) allows for the use of dividends and other terms in the objective function, and for a variety of linear and nonlinear constraints.

In Section 8.7 we finally consider the situation of integer restrictions, which we have avoided until now because it requires more difficult mathematical analysis. Multiple objectives are discussed in Section 8.8. Following the summary, the chapter ends with a case study illustrating the application of Bernhard's general model to a dividend-terminal-wealth problem.

8.2 THE USE OF LINEAR PROGRAMMING MODELS

Because linear programming models are so widely used in capital budgeting, we present a brief introduction here. In this section we illustrate the application of LP in a typical example. A word of caution is in order here: the example given is *not* intended to represent the best principles of capital budgeting but *rather to illustrate* the use of LP. The various methods of capital budgeting (for the deterministic case) are given in the following sections.

Example 8.1

Table 8.1 presents data for Example 8.1, which concerns five investment projects. There are budget limits of $4,400 and $4,000 at time 0 and time 1, respectively; these limits do not apply to any funds generated by the projects themselves. We note the sign convention that inflows are positive and outflows negative. Most of the projects require investment during the first two years before they return any funds. All the projects are simple investments with unique, positive, real *IRR*s, and for a sufficiently low *MARR*, say 20%, all have positive *PV*s. But from the budget limits it is clear that we cannot accept all of them; hence the capital rationing problem. Moreover, project 5 starts to provide cash inflow at time 1, when all the others require outflows, so we would like to consider this advantage of project 5. (The solution to Example 8.1 follows in the text). □

8.2.1 Criterion Function To Be Optimized
A variety of criterion functions could be optimized.

- Maximize the *PV* of the cash flows of the selected projects.
- Maximize the *IRR* of the total cash flow of the selected projects.

Table 8.1 *Data for Example 8.1*

Cash Flow at Time	Project				
	1	2	3	4	5
0	−$1,000	−$1,200	−$2,000	−$2,500	−$3,000
1	−2,000	−2,400	−2,100	−1,300	900
2	2,000	2,500	3,000	2,000	1,400
3	2,900	3,567	3,000	2,000	1,600
4	0	0	1,308	2,000	1,800
5	0	0	0	2,296	955
PV(20%)	$400	600	700	850	900
IRR, %	29.1	31.3	29.7	28.9	32.2

Budgets for external sources of funds: $n = 0$, $4,400; $n = 1$, $4,000

- Maximize the "utility" of the dividends that can be paid from the cash flows of the selected projects.
- Maximize the cash that can be accumulated at the end of the planning period.

Other functions could be used. The important thing is that the function is clearly expressed in terms of the decision variables for project acceptance or rejection and that it is (we hope) linear.

Let us see, for *illustration* purposes, the *PV* of the cash flows of the selected projects,

$$\text{Max} \sum_j p_j x_j \tag{8.1}$$

where p_j is the *PV* of project j, using $i = MARR$, and
   x_j is a project selection variable, with $0 \le x_j \le 1$.

Using a *MARR* value of $i = 20\%$, we obtain

j	1	2	3	4	5
p_j	$400	600	700	850	900

Thus Eq. 8.1 becomes, for Example 8.1,

$$\text{max } \$400x_1 + 600x_2 + 700x_3 + 850x_4 + 900x_5 \tag{8.2}$$

The project selection variables are continuous in this linear formulation. A value of $x_j = 0$ means that the project is not selected, a value of $x_j = 1$ implies

645

complete acceptance, and a fractional values implies partial acceptance. We will leave aside the question of the practicality of fractional acceptance. In some industries, such as oil and gas exploration, fractional acceptance is common practice; generally, though, it is not possible to accept fractional projects without changing the nature of their cash flows. (We will consider integer restrictions in Section 8.7.)

8.2.2 Multiple Budget Periods

The budget limits for Example 8.1 can be expressed by linear constraints on the selection variables,

$$-\sum_j a_{nj}x_j \leq M_n, \qquad n = 0, 1, ..., N \qquad (8.3)$$

where a_{nj} = cash flow for project j at time n, inflows having a plus sign, and outflows a minus sign,

M_n = budget limit on externally supplied funds at time n, and

N = end of the planning period.

Notice that M_n represents only the funds from sources other than the projects. The equation states that project outflows minus project inflows at time n must be less than the budget limit on funds from other sources at time n. A negative value for M_n implies that the set of selected projects must *generate* funds. (Equation 8.3 states that cash outflows $\leq$ cash inflows + M_n). Note that the absence of a budget limit is not equivalent to M_n being zero; the former implies a positive, unbounded M_n value. Equations of the type (8.3) are usually called budget constraints or cash balance equations. Inflows and outflows for borrowing, lending, and dividend payments may also be included; these are discussed in later sections.

Applying the equation to Example 8.1, we obtain two constraints,

$n = 0$: $\quad \$1{,}000x_1 + 1{,}200x_2 + 2{,}000x_3 + 2{,}500x_4 + 3{,}000x_5 \leq 4{,}400$

$n = 1$: $\quad \$2{,}000x_1 + 2{,}400x_2 + 2{,}100x_3 + 1{,}300x_4 - 900x_5 \leq 4{,}000 \quad (8.4)$

The advantage of project 5 at time 1 is clearly apparent here; setting $x_5 = 1$ increases the amount available for other projects by \$900. There are no stated limits for times 2, 3, 4, and 5, so we need not write constraints for these times.

8.2.3 Project Limits and Interdependencies

The limits on the selection variables given following Eq. 8.1 are presented here again.

$$x_j \leq 1, \qquad j = 1, \ldots, J \qquad (8.5)$$

The nonnegativity constraints are expressed separately:

$$x_j \geq 0, \qquad j = 1, \ldots, J \qquad (8.6)$$

It is also possible to have interdependencies among project selection variables. Some common types are the following.

1. Mutual exclusivity—when a subset of projects form a mutually exclusive set.

$$x_j + x_k + x_m \leqslant 1 \qquad (8.7)$$

The selection of one project precludes the selection of either of the other two in Eq. 8.7. Note that a complete interpretation is possible only if the x_j are restricted to integers.

2. Contingency—when execution of one project depends on execution of another.

$$x_j - x_k \leqslant 0 \qquad (8.8)$$

Here x_j cannot be selected unless x_k is also selected.

3. Complementary and competitive projects—when the selection of two projects changes the cash flows involved. For complementary projects inflows are greater than the sum of the individual project inflows; the opposite is true for competitive projects. Such situations can be handled by defining a new project for the combination and then establishing mutual exclusivity,

$$x_j + x_k + x_m \leqslant 1$$

where x_m is a combination of j and k. (If there are many such situations, the method becomes cumbersome.)

We will not impose interdependencies in Example 8.1, in order to keep the duality analysis simple at this point. That type of treatment is given in Section 8.5.

8.2.4 LP Formulation of Lorie–Savage Problem

In LP terminology, the *primal problem* formulation of the capital budgeting problem is given symbolically and numerically by Table 8.2. This version summarizes the relationships that have been presented so far in this chapter. This version of the problem is also designated as the LP formulation of the Lorie–Savage problem [15], after the two economists who stated the original form of the project selection problem. Their concern with the problem came from the inadequacies of the *IRR* method to deal with budget limitations and project interdependencies. Our analysis in the next section follows closely the work of Weingartner [20], who applied LP to the Lorie–Savage problem.

8.2.5 Duality Analysis

For every *primal problem* in linear programming, there is a related *dual problem* formulation. Table 8.3 presents both the symbolic and numeric versions of the dual problem for Example 8.1. The dual formulation is a minimization problem stated in terms of the ρ_n and μ_n. By making appropriate conversions from minimization to maximization and from $\geqslant$ to $\leqslant$, we can easily show that the dual formulation of the problem in Table 8.3 is the same as the formulation given in Table 8.2. In other words, the dual of the dual is the primal, and our specific designations are based on habit and convenience.

Table 8.2 *Primal Problem Formulation for Maximizing PV for Example 8.1 (Lorie–Savage Formulation)*

Symbolic

$$\text{Max} \sum_{j} p_j x_j \tag{8.1}$$

s.t.*

$$[\rho_n] \qquad -\sum_{j} a_{nj} x_j \leq M_n, \qquad n = 0, 1, \ldots, N \tag{8.3}$$

$$[\mu_j] \qquad x_j \leq 1, \qquad j = 1, \ldots, J \tag{8.5}$$

$$x_j \geq 0, \qquad j = 1, \ldots, J \tag{8.6}$$

where p_j = PV of project j using i = MARR,

x_j = project selection variable,

a_{nj} = cash flow for project j at time n; inflows have a plus sign, outflows have a minus sign,

M_n = budget limit on externally supplied funds at time n,

N = end of the planning period,

ρ_n, μ_j = dual variables for the primal constraints.

Numeric

$$\text{Max } \$400x_1 + 600x_2 + 700x_3 + 850x_4 + 900x_5 \tag{8.2}$$

s.t.

$$[\rho_0] \quad \$1{,}000x_1 + 1{,}200x_2 + 2{,}000x_3 + 2{,}500x_4 + 3{,}000x_5 \leq \$4{,}400$$

$$[\rho_1] \quad \$2{,}000x_1 + 2{,}400x_2 + 2{,}100x_3 + 1{,}300x_4 - 900x_5 \leq \$4{,}000 \tag{8.4}$$

$$[\mu_1] \quad x_1 \qquad\qquad\qquad\qquad\qquad\qquad \leq 1$$

$$[\mu_2] \qquad\qquad x_2 \qquad\qquad\qquad\qquad \leq 1$$

$$[\mu_3] \qquad\qquad\qquad\qquad x_3 \qquad\qquad \leq 1 \tag{8.5}$$

$$[\mu_4] \qquad\qquad\qquad\qquad\qquad x_4 \qquad \leq 1$$

$$[\mu_5] \qquad\qquad\qquad\qquad\qquad\qquad x_5 \leq 1$$

$$\text{All } x_j \geq 0, j = 1, \ldots, 5 \tag{8.6}$$

*The abbreviation s.t. stands for subject to.

The economic interpretation of the dual problem is to establish prices for each of the scarce resources so that the minimum total possible would be paid for the consumption of the resources, while ensuring that the resources used for any project cost as much as or more than the value of the project, the project PV in this case [5]. We have two categories of resources here. The first category is cash, represented by cash at time 0 and by cash at time 1; the dual variables ρ_0 and ρ_1 represent the prices, respectively. The second category consists of the projects themselves: a project is considered a scarce resource in the sense that we have the opportunity to execute only one of each. The dual variables $\mu_1, \ldots, \mu_5$ correspond to the upper-bound constraints of the projects and represent the respective prices for the project opportunities.

Table 8.3 *Dual Problem Formulation for Example 8.1, Solution to Primal and Dual*

Symbolic

$$\text{Min} \sum_n \rho_n M_n + \sum_j \mu_j \tag{8.9}$$

s.t.

$$[x_j] \quad -\sum_n a_{nj}\rho_n + \mu_j \geq p_j, \quad j = 1, \ldots, J \tag{8.10}$$

$$\rho_n \geq 0, \quad n = 0, 1, \ldots, N \tag{8.11}$$

$$\mu_j \geq 0, \quad j = 1, \ldots, J \tag{8.12}$$

where ρ_n = dual variable for budget constraint,
μ_j = dual variable for project upper bound.

Numeric

$$\text{Min} \quad 4{,}400\rho_0 + 4{,}000\rho_1 + \mu_1 + \mu_2 + \mu_3 + \mu_4 + \mu_5 \tag{8.13}$$

s.t.

$[x_1]$	$+1{,}000\rho_0$	$+2{,}000\rho_1$	$+\mu_1$				≥ 400	
$[x_2]$	$+1{,}200\rho_0$	$+2{,}400\rho_1$		$+\mu_2$			≥ 600	
$[x_3]$	$+2{,}000\rho_0$	$+2{,}100\rho_1$			$+\mu_3$		≥ 700	(8.14)
$[x_4]$	$+2{,}500\rho_0$	$+1{,}300\rho_1$				$+\mu_4$	≥ 850	
$[x_5]$	$+3{,}000\rho_0$	$-\ 900\rho_1$				$+\mu_5$	≥ 900	

$$\rho_n, \mu_j \geq 0$$

Solution

Primal variables: $x_1 = 0.22$, $x_2 = 1.00$, $x_3 = 0.0$, $x_4 = 1.0$, $x_5 = 0.16$

Dual variables: $\rho_0 = 0.3130$, $\rho_1 = 0.0435$
$\mu_1 = 0.0$, $\mu_2 = 120.0$, $\mu_3 = 0.0$, $\mu_4 = 10.9$, $\mu_5 = 0.0$

Objective function value: $1,682

If the primal problem is feasible and bounded, there is an optimal solution to both problems. At such an optimum we have, from the dual constraint,

$$\mu_j^* \geq p_j + \sum_n a_{nj}\rho_n^* \tag{8.15}$$

where the asterisk refers to values of the primal and dual variables at the optimum. We know from complementary slackness [5] that if $x_j^* > 0$, the dual constraint is met exactly, and since all dual variables are nonnegative, we have

$$0 \leq \mu_j^* = p_j + \sum_n a_{nj}\rho_n^* \tag{8.16}$$

The μ_j^* represents the opportunity value of project j, and it is equal to the PV plus the cash inflows less any cash outflows evaluated by the ρ_n^*. Hence, for all projects that are accepted fractionally or completely,

$$-\sum_n a_{nj}\rho_n^* \leq p_j \qquad (8.17)$$

Equation 8.17 states that in order for a project to be accepted, its PV must be equal to or greater than the cash outflows minus cash inflows evaluated by the ρ_n^*.

Again from complementary slackness, if $x_j^* < 1$, then $\mu_j^* = 0$. So for fractionally accepted projects (8.17) becomes

$$-\sum_n a_{nj}\rho_n^* = p_j \qquad (8.18)$$

For rejected projects we also have $\mu_j^* = 0$ and, using Eq. 8.15,

$$-\sum_n a_{nj}\rho_n^* \geq p_j \qquad (8.19)$$

In other words, the cash outflows minus cash inflows, evaluated by the ρ_n^*, exceed (or equal) the PV of the project.

We can demonstrate these conditions by using the optimal values of the LP problem given in Table 8.3. For project 1, fractionally accepted, applying (8.18) gives

$$(\$1,000)(0.313) + (2,000)(0.0435) = \$400 = PV$$

The value of cash inflows minus outflows equals the PV.

For project 2, completely accepted, applying (8.16) gives

$$\mu_2^* = \$600 - (1,200)(0.313) - (2,400)(0.0435) = \$120 > 0$$

The opportunity cost of the project is \$120, the difference between the PV and the cash outflows minus the cash inflows.

For project 3, rejected, applying (8.19) gives

$$(\$2,000)(0.313) + (2,100)(0.0435) = \$717 \geq \$700$$

Here the cash outflows minus inflows are worth more than the PV, which explains the rejection.

These types of project evaluation, or project pricing, with the dual variables, are fundamental to the LP modeling and analysis of capital budgeting problems. We will see more of this type of analysis in the following sections.

8.3 PURE CAPITAL RATIONING MODELS

The type of model given in Table 8.2 has been extensively analyzed, criticized, and modified during the last twenty years. In this section we attempt to summarize the major arguments so that the reader will obtain a historical perspective on the situation. We do not go into great detail, because the arguments are presented better elsewhere [21] and because the major conclusion to be drawn is that the pure capital rationing (PCR) model is of extremely limited applicability. This fact reinforces the fundamental notion that one must fully understand the assumptions embedded in any mathematical model before attempting to use it.

8.3.1 Criticisms of the PV Model

Among the first to criticize the *PV* model (as in Table 8.2) were Baumol and Quandt [3]. They identified three major flaws.

1. There is no provision in the model for investment outside the firm or for dividend payments.

2. The model does not provide for carryover of unused funds from one period to the next.

3. Assuming that we have an appropriate discount rate *i* for computing the *PV* of each project, this rate is valid in general only for the situation of unlimited borrowing and lending at that rate. Since we have borrowing limits implicitly stated in the budget constraints, an externally determined discount rate is inappropriate.

The first two objections can easily be overcome. For example, investment outside the firm, including lending activities, can easily be represented by new projects. Define project 6 to be lending from time 0 to time 1 at 15%. Then we set $a_{06} = -1$ and $a_{16} = 1.15$ and place no upper bound (or a very large bound) on x_6. Similarly, variables can be defined for divided payments and included in the budget constraints. We would also need to include dividends in the objective function, which implies knowledge of the discount rate appropriate for the owner(s) or shareholders of the firm in order to discount correctly the future dividends. Later, we will see some different methods for including dividends in the objective function.

The third objection is a serious one and requires more attention. To illustrate the difficulties arising from it, let us analyze Example 8.2.

Example 8.2

Table 8.4 presents the data for Example 8.2 along with the optimal LP solution. Example 8.2 is somewhat similar to Example 8.1: projects 1, 2, and 4 are the same; projects 3 and 5 are slightly changed so their *PVs* are negative; project 6 is added to the set; and the budget limits are changed.

Notice that projects 2 and 4 are completely accepted, as they were in

651

Table 8.4 *Data and Solution for Example 8.2*

Cash Flow at Time	Project					
	1	2	3	4	5	6
0	−$1,000	−$1,200	−$2,000	−2,500	−$3,000	$1,000
1	−2,000	−2,400	−2,100	−1,300	900	−700
2	2,000	2,500	3,000	2,000	1,400	−700
3	2,900	3,567	2,621	2,000	1,600	0
4	0	0	0	2,000	211	0
5	0	0	0	2,296	0	0
PV (20%)	$400	600	−150	850	−250	−70

Budgets for external sources of funds: $n = 0$, $3,000$; $n = 1$, $5,000$

Solution

Primal variables: $x_1 = 0.30$, $x_2 = 1.0$, $x_3 = 0.0$, $x_4 = 1.0$, $x_5 = 0.0$, $x_6 = 1.0$
Dual variables: $\rho_0 = 0.3189$, $\rho_1 = 0.0405$
$\mu_1 = 0.0$, $\mu_2 = 120.0$, $\mu_3 = 0.0$, $\mu_4 = 0.0$, $\mu_5 = 0.0$, $\mu_6 = 220.5$
Objective function value: $1,500

Example 8.1. The dual variables for the budget constraints, ρ_0 and ρ_1, do not have their optimal values changed much, so the pricing of projects 2 and 4 is similar.

Project 2: $\mu_2 = \$120 = \$600 - (1,200)(0.3189) - (2,400)(0.0405)$
Project 4: $\mu_4 = 0 = \$850 - (2,500)(0.3189) - (1,300)(0.0405)$

Here we have an example of a completely accepted project with $\mu_j = 0$. Project 1 is again accepted fractionally, and it prices out at zero.

Project 1: $\mu_1 = 0 = \$400 - (1,000)(0.3189) - (2,000)(0.0405)$

We can demonstrate Eq. 8.19 for a rejected project with negative *PV*.

Project 3: $(\$2,000)(0.3189) + (2,100)(0.0405) = 723 > -150$

This result is hardly surprising since project 3 has only outflows during the critical times and has a negative *PV*.

The real surprise is that project 6, with a negative *PV* of −$70, is accepted. Pricing out by using Eq. 8.16 yields

Project 6: $\mu_6 = \$221 = -70 + (1,000)(0.3189) - (700)(0.0405)$

The value of the $1,000 inflow at time 0, less the value of the $700 outflow at time 1, more than overcomes the negative *PV* and makes project 6 desirable. (The $700 outflow at time 2 is worth zero since there is no constraint on money at this time.) The extra \$1,000 when it is needed most enables us to select more of the other projects and thereby increase the overall *PV* of the projects selected. □

Project 6 in Example 8.2 has the cash flow pattern of a borrowing activity. Since its *IRR* = 26%, we are effectively borrowing at a periodic rate of 26% in order to maximize overall *PV* at 20%! This example clearly demonstrates the philosophical conflict in using an interest rate for *PV* maximization when we are faced with a budget limitation. If we have available a borrowing opportunity at a different, higher interest rate, we could be induced to borrow at a rate higher than that used for computing *PV*. The budget limits, in effect, invalidate the use of an externally determined discount rate. The inclusion of lending opportunities and dividend payments does not solve the difficulty, so various authors have attempted other approaches, some of which are discussed in the following.

8.3.2 Consistent Discount Factors

In reformulating the *PV* model to eliminate the incompatibility presented, Baumol and Quandt defined a model in which the discount rates between periods are determined by the model itself [3]. On the basis of our previous notation, their revised model is

$$\underset{x_j, \rho_n}{\text{Max}} \sum_n \sum_j a_{nj} \frac{\rho_n}{\rho_0} x_j \qquad (8.20)$$

s.t.[1]

$[\rho_n]$
$$-\sum_j a_{nj}x_j \leq M_n, \qquad n = 0, 1, ..., N \qquad (8.3)$$

$$x_j \geq 0, \qquad j = 1, ..., J \qquad (8.6)$$

The terms ρ_n/ρ_0 represent the discount factors from time 0 to time n. Whenever the discount factors are so defined, we will designate them as *consistent discount factors*. Notice the absence of project upper-bound constraints (8.5).

A typical dual constraint has the form

$$-\sum_n a_{nj}\rho_n \geq \sum_n a_{nj}\frac{\rho_n}{\rho_0} \qquad (8.21)$$

or

$$\left(-1 - \frac{1}{\rho_0}\right)\sum_n a_{nj}\rho_n \geq 0$$

But the dual variables are nonnegative, so

$$\sum_n a_{nj}\rho_n \leq 0$$

[1]The abbreviation s.t. stands for subject to.

In the primal objective function the term ρ_0 can be placed before the summation signs; thus each coefficient of x_j is nonpositive. The objective function must therefore have an optimal solution of zero with all $x_j = 0$. In addition, the solution to the dual objective function

$$\operatorname*{Min}_{\rho_n} \sum_n M_n \rho_n \qquad (8.22)$$

with $M_n > 0$ will be zero, with all $\rho_n = 0$. The zero value of ρ_0 in the denominator of the primal objective function (8.20) renders that function indeterminate.

With this line of reasoning, Baumol and Quandt rejected *PV* models. They then formulated a model with an objective function that is linear in dividend payments. We will not present this model here but instead examine the PCR line that was pursued by others.

Atkins and Ashton [1] criticized the approach of Baumol and Quandt because there were no upper-bound constraints on the projects and the consequent interpretation of dual variables was absent. The discount factors ρ_n/ρ_0 are determined by the marginal productivities of capital in the various time periods. In the absence of upper bounds on projects, any project that is accepted is also partially rejected. Hence, the discounted cash flow of that project *must* be zero.

The implication of this reasoning is that projects must have upper bounds placed on them to avoid the phenomenon of each accepted (and, at the same time, rejected) project having a *PV*, based on consistent discount factors $d_n = \rho_n/\rho_0$, equal to zero. In addition, the Atkins and Ashton model allows for funds to be carried forward at a lending rate of interest. The final modification is the interpretation of the discount factors when one of the ρ_n becomes zero: the equivalent form $\rho_n = d_n\rho_0$ avoids these difficulties.

The method for finding a *consistent optimal solution* (an optimal set of x_j and $d_n = \rho_n/\rho_0$) consists of identifying and evaluating the Kuhn–Tucker stationary points [17] of the problem. In the PCR model there are potentially many consistent solutions, whereas in the situation with lending there is only one solution. In general, this is a rather unsatisfactory procedure because of the large number of such points.

Freeland and Rosenblatt [8] pursued the PCR model (with project upperbound constraints) further and obtained several interesting results.

- The value of the objective function at a consistent optimal solution equals

$$\frac{1}{2}\sum_j \mu_j^* \text{ (property 2)}.$$

- For the PCR case (no lending or borrowing allowed) an objective function value different from zero can be obtained only if some of the M_n values have opposite signs.

- If the objective function value for a consistent optimal solution is not zero, there are alternative optimal discount factors d_n.

A more recent article by Hayes [12] on the same topic has further clarified the issue for the situation in which *all budgets are fully expended.* Hayes's analysis assumes upper bounds on projects and lending from one period to the next, but his major result does not depend on the lending activities. If the budgets are fully utilized in all periods except the last (the horizon), the optimal set of projects is independent of discount factors and may be obtained by maximizing the cash at the end of the last period (at the horizon). To see why this result is true, let us reexamine the *PV* model.

$$\text{Max} \sum_{n} \sum_{j} a_{nj} d_n x_j \tag{8.23}$$
$$\underset{x_j}{}$$

s.t.

$[\rho_n]$
$$-\sum_{j} a_{nj} x_j = M_n, \qquad n = 0, 1, ..., N - 1 \tag{8.24}$$

$[\rho_N]$
$$-\sum_{j} a_{Nj} x_j + l_N = M_N \tag{8.25}$$

$$x_j \leq 1, \qquad j = 1, ..., J \tag{8.5}$$

$$x_j \geq 0, \qquad j = 1, ..., J \tag{8.6}$$

where d_n = discount factor for time n,
l_n = cash left over at time N, the horizon,

and the other terms are as defined previously. Note that the budget constraints 8.24 and 8.25 are equalities, reflecting the assumption about cash being used up each period. The l_N term measures any leftover cash at time N, the horizon, the only time we are allowed to have excess cash in this model.

To obtain the desired result, let us split the objective function.

$$\underset{x_j}{\text{Max}} \sum_{j} a_{Nj} d_N x_j + \sum_{n=0}^{N-1} \sum_{j} a_{nj} d_n x_j \tag{8.26}$$

Now we can substitute the constraints into the objective function.

$$\underset{x_j}{\text{Max}} \, d_N(l_N - M_N) - \sum_{n=0}^{N-1} d_n M_n = \underset{x_j}{\text{Max}} \, d_N l_N - \sum_{n=0}^{N} d_n M_n \tag{8.27}$$

Since the summation in Eq. 8.27 is a constant for fixed values of d_n, it may be dropped without affecting the solution, and by dividing out the constant d_N we are left with

$$\underset{x_j}{\text{Max}} \, l_N \tag{8.28}$$

subject to constraints 8.24, 8.25, 8.5, and 8.6.

Appropriate discount factors may be obtained by the usual form $d_n = \rho_n/\rho_0$ with $\rho_0 = 1$ or any positive constant. With all budget constraints at equality, it is easy to show that $\rho_{n-1} \geq \rho_n$; therefore, no possibility exists of zero dual variables. In summary, the discount factors are irrelevant for project selection!

The foregoing result is important because it emphasizes the fact that the dual variables for the budget constraints reflect the marginal productivities of capital in the respective time periods. Since all cash flows are automatically reinvested in this closed system, any consumption choices by the owner or owners of the firm have been expressed by the values set for the M_n.

In this section we appear to have presented numerous models, summarized extensive analyses, and arrived at very little in terms of a useful *PV* model. That is precisely true. All the arguments and discussion repeatedly point to the following types of conclusions and statements.

- In any *PV* model the budget constraint dual variables must reflect the marginal productivities of capital.

- Project upper-bound constraints and lending activities must be included in order to have a meaningful formulation.

- For certain types of closed systems, in which all budgets are fully expended, the projects are selected by maximizing cash at the horizon.

We will return to this last point in Section 8.5. In the meantime, we will discuss in more detail the inclusion of lending and borrowing opportunities in the *PV* model.

8.4 NET PRESENT VALUE MAXIMIZATION WITH LENDING AND BORROWING

8.4.1 Inclusion of Lending Opportunities

We can define a lending project as an outflow of cash in one period followed by an inflow, with interest, at a later period. Define v_n to be the amount lent at time n, to be repaid at time $n + 1$ with interest r_n. We then have coefficients $a_{nj} = -1$ and $a_{n+1,j} = 1 + r_n$. We will define as many lending variables as there are time periods with budget constraints. There are no limits on lending.

Notice that we have defined only one-period loans, which is the common practice. Multiple-period lending could easily be included. The following are some typical examples, all with a constant lending rate.

Period	Case 1: Lump Sum Payment	Case 2: Interest Only During Period, Principal at End of Last Period	Case 3: Equal Payments
n	-1	-1	-1
$n + 1$	0	r	$(A/P, r, 2)$
$n + 2$	$(1 + r)^2$	$1 + r$	$(A/P, r, 2)$

The number of variables tends to become somewhat unwieldy with this approach, however, compared with the benefits derived from distinguishing between short-term and long-term lending rates. If the projects consist mainly of financial instruments, it is important to work at this level of detail [11]. Otherwise, the approximation of multiple-period lending with successive one-period lending usually suffices.

The objective function coefficients for the lending activities can be obtained by straightforward discounting at $i = MARR$. Applying this concept to case 2, we have

$$PV = -1 + \frac{r}{1 + i} + \frac{1 + r}{(1 + i)^2}$$

The resulting PV may be positive or negative, depending on whether r is greater than or smaller than i, respectively.

If one-period lending opportunities are included in the PV model, and lending is always preferred to doing nothing, we can solve an equivalent problem by simply maximizing the amount of cash at the horizon [1,8]. This result is similar to that obtained by Hayes, as described in Section 8.3.2. With attractive lending opportunities present, all budgets will be fully expended, and Hayes's result can be applied directly.

8.4.2 Inclusion of Borrowing Opportunities

We should note that the inclusion of unlimited lending opportunities still has not resolved the philosophical conflict between using an interest rate for PV maximization and having budget constraints. If borrowing opportunities are also unlimited, it appears that we have eliminated the conflict. But in that case we really do not need budget constraints and LP to solve our project selection problem. Investment projects with an IRR less than the lending rate would always be rejected, and those with an IRR greater than the borrowing rate would be accepted. The selection problem would concern only projects with an IRR between the lending and borrowing rates.

There remain two difficulties with such an approach. The first is that we rarely have unlimited borrowing opportunities at one interest rate. (In a practical sense, only an agency of the U.S. government can borrow unlimited amounts). Typically, we can borrow, but only up to a limit. Some of the models presented in the next section have this feature. The second difficulty is related to the interpretation of the interest rate used for PV calculations. If the (different) lending and borrowing rates are specified, any other discount rate must presumably reflect the time preferences of the owners of the firm. There is no philosophical conflict in having three distinct rates for lending by the firm, borrowing by the firm, and discounting to reflect the owners' time preferences. But in this case we need to include dividends in the objective function, as shown in Section 8.6 and Appendix 8.A.

We have again failed to develop a rational *PV* model. The reasons here are similar to those for the PCR case. In the face of limits on borrowing, the decisions about selecting projects must be related, through the interrelationships among project combinations and budget amounts, to the decisions for dividend payments [21]. The marginal productivities of capital from one period to the next determine the dual variables ρ_n. Any attempt to ignore these two realities in constructing a project selection model or procedure is bound to have major conceptual flaws.

8.5. WEINGARTNER'S HORIZON MODEL

Many of the conceptual issues discussed in the previous two sections can be avoided by ignoring *PV* and concentrating on accumulated cash as the objective. Such models are called horizon models. They typically include borrowing and lending activities and may have other constraints added. These models represent an empirical approach to capital budgeting and should therefore be judged mainly on this basis. The presentation in this section, which is based largely on Weingartner [20], presumes the use of LP and hence allows fractional projects.

8.5.1 Equal Lending and Borrowing Rates

The simplest type of horizon model contains budget constraints, project upper bounds, and lending and borrowing opportunities at a common, fixed rate.

Example 8.3

Table 8.5 presents the data for Example 8.3, and Table 8.6 presents both the symbolic and numeric primal formulations. The projects, 1 through 6, are the same as for Example 8.2. The budget amounts are slightly different from those in Example 8.2, being $3,000, $5,000, and $4,800 at times 0, 1, and 2, respectively. We are using 20% for both borrowing and lending, with no limits on either. The horizon is at time 2, so we are trying to maximize the accumulated cash at this time. Most of the projects, however, have cash flows after time 2, so we discount at 20% these flows back to time 2. For example, $\hat{a}_1$ represents the $2,900 inflow at time 3 for project 1, discounted at 20% for one period, or $2,900/1.2 = $2,417.

The objective function in this horizon model is $v_2 - w_2$, the accumulated cash available (for lending) at time 2, plus the value of posthorizon flows, represented by the $\hat{a}_j$. The cash balance equations 8.30 and 8.31 are similar to those for the *PV* model. A typical constraint says that cash outflows from projects, plus current lending, plus repayment with interest of previous-period borrowing, minus repayment with interest of previous-period lending, minus current borrowing must be less than or equal to the amount of externally supplied funds. The project upper bounds and nonnegativity restrictions complete the model. For simplicity, we have not included any project dependency or exclusivity constraints. (The solution to Example 8.3 follows in the text.) □

658

Table 8.5 *Data for Examples 8.3 and 8.5 (Horizon Is Time 2)*

Variable Type		Project 1	2	3	4	5	6
Cash Flow at Time	0	−$1,000	−$1,200	−$2,000	−$2,500	−$3,000	$1,000
Same for	1	−2,000	−2,400	−2,100	−1,300	900	−700
Examples 8.3	2	2,000	2,500	3,000	2,000	1,400	−700
and 8.5	3	2,900	3,567	2,621	2,000	1,600	0
	4	0	0	0	2,000	211	0
	5	0	0	0	2,296	0	0
Example 8.3 $\hat{a}_j$		$2,417	2,973	2,184	4,384	1,480	0
Example 8.5 $\hat{a}_j$		$2,230	2,744	2,016	3,767	1,356	0

	$n = 0$	$n = 1$	$n = 2$
Budgets (M_n)			
Example 8.3	$3,000	5,000	4,800
Example 8.5	$1,000	2,000	4,800
Lending rates	$n = 0 \rightarrow 1$	$n = 1 \rightarrow 2$	$n = 2 \rightarrow 3$
Example 8.3	20%	20%	20%
Example 8.5	15%	15%	15%
Borrowing rates	$n = 0 \rightarrow 1$	$n = 1 \rightarrow 2$	$n = 2 \rightarrow 3$
Example 8.3	20%	20%	20%
Example 8.5	30%	30%	30%
Borrowing limits	$n = 0 \rightarrow 1$	$n = 1 \rightarrow 2$	$n = 2 \rightarrow 3$
Example 8.5 only	None	1,000	None

The LP solution of the horizon model in Example 8.3 is straightforward and quick, requiring less than one second of time for both processing and input–output on a mainframe computer. Table 8.7 contains the solution for Example 8.3. Projects 1, 2, and 4 were accepted completely, and projects 3, 5, and 6 were rejected. In addition, there was borrowing of $1,700 at time 0 and $2,740 at time 1. At time 2 a total cash accumulation of $8,012 was available for lending.

There is more to the solution of this horizon problem than the numerical results, however. We note several features of the solution.

- The dual variables ρ_n are powers of 1.2.
- The dual variables μ_j for accepted projects are equal to the *FV*(20%) of these projects.
- Projects with positive *PV*(20%) were accepted and those with negative *PV* (20%) were rejected.

These features are not coincidental but rather are characteristic of the horizon model as presented in Table 8.6. We can verify this by examining the dual formulation, given in Table 8.8.

Table 8.6 *Primal Problem Formulation For Horizon Model for Example 8.3*

Symbolic

$$\max_{x_j, v_n, w_n} \sum_j \hat{a}_j x_j + v_N - w_N \tag{8.29}$$

s.t.

$[\rho_0]$
$$-\sum_j a_{0j} x_j + v_0 - w_0 \le M_0 \tag{8.30}$$

$[\rho_n]$
$$-\sum_j a_{nj} x_j - (1+r)v_{n-1} + v_n + (1+r)w_{n-1} - w_n \le M_n,$$
$$n = 1, 2, \ldots, N \tag{8.31}$$

$[\mu_j]$
$$x_j \le 1, \qquad j = 1, \ldots, J \tag{8.5}$$

$$x_j \ge 0, \qquad j = 1, \ldots, J \tag{8.6}$$

$$v_n, w_n \ge 0, \qquad j = 0, \ldots, J \tag{8.32}$$

where $\hat{a}_j$ = horizon time value of cash flows beyond horizon
x_j = project selection variable
a_{nj} = cash flow for project j at time n; inflows have a plus sign, outflows have a minus sign
v_n = lending amount from time n to time $n + 1$
w_n = amount borrowed from time n to time $n + 1$
r = interest rate for borrowing and lending
M_n = budget limit on externally supplied funds at time n
N = horizon, end of the planning period
ρ_n, μ_j = dual variables

Numeric

$$\max \$2{,}417x_1 + 2{,}973x_2 + 2{,}184x_3 + 4{,}384x_4 + 1{,}480x_5 + v_2 - w_2$$

s.t.

$[\rho_0]$
$$\$1{,}000x_1 + 1{,}200x_2 + 2{,}000x_3 + 2{,}500x_4 + 3{,}000x_5 - 1{,}000x_6 + v_0 - w_0 \le 3{,}000$$

$[\rho_1]$
$$\$2{,}000x_1 + 2{,}400x_2 + 2{,}100x_3 + 1{,}300x_4 - 900x_5 + 700x_6 - 1.2v_0 + v_1 + 1.2w_0 - w_1 \le 5{,}000$$

$[\rho_2]$
$$-\$2{,}000x_1 - 2{,}500x_2 - 3{,}000x_3 - 2{,}000x_4 - 1{,}400x_5 + 700x_6 - 1.2v_1 + v_2 + 1.2w_1 - w_2 \le 4{,}800$$

$[\mu_1]$	x_1	≤ 1
$[\mu_2]$	x_2	≤ 1
$[\mu_3]$	x_3	≤ 1
$[\mu_4]$	x_4	≤ 1
$[\mu_5]$	x_5	≤ 1
$[\mu_6]$	$x_6 \le 1$	

all $x_j \ge 0$, $\quad j = 1, \ldots, 6$

all $v_n, w_n \ge 0$, $\quad n = 0, 1, 2$

Table 8.7 *Solution to Examples 8.3 and 8.5*

Variable Type	Objective Function	Example 8.3, $17,786	Example 8.5, $9,210
Project selection	x_1	1.0	0
	x_2	1.0	1.0
	x_3	0	0
	x_4	1.0	0.151
	x_5	0	0
	x_6	0	0.577
Lending	v_0	0	0
	v_1	0	0
	v_2	$8,012	$5,898
Borrowing	w_0	$1,700	0
	w_1	2,740	$1,000
	w_2	0	0
Budget constraint dual variable	ρ_0	1.44	1.622
	ρ_1	1.20	1.317
	ρ_2	1.00	1.0
Project upper-bound dual variable	μ_1	577	0
	μ_2	865	137
	μ_3	0	0
	μ_4	1.224	0
	μ_5	0	0
	μ_6	0	0
Borrowing limit dual variable	β_1	—	0.017

From (8.36) and (8.37) we have $\rho_n^* = 1$. The value of $1 at time N is $1 in the optimal solution because we do not have time to do anything with it. Similarly, from (8.34) and (8.35) we obtain

$$1 + r \le \frac{\rho_n^*}{\rho_{n+1}^*} \le 1 + r, \qquad n = 0, ..., N - 1 \qquad (8.38)$$

or

$$\frac{\rho_n^*}{\rho_{n+1}^*} = 1 + r \qquad (8.39)$$

and

$$\rho_n^* = \rho_{n+1}^*(1 + r) = \rho_{n+2}^*(1 + r)^2 = \cdots = \rho_{n+N-n}^*(1 + r)^{N-n}$$
$$= \rho_N^*(1 + r)^{N-n} = (1 + r)^{N-n} \qquad (8.40)$$

The interpretation of the ρ_n^* now becomes clear: they are compound interest factors that reflect the value at the horizon, time N, of an additional dollar at time n.

Table 8.8 *Dual Problem Formulation for Horizon Model with Common, Fixed Rate for Borrowing and Lending*

$$\text{Min} \sum_n \rho_n M_n + \sum_j \mu_j \tag{8.9}$$

s.t.

$[x_j]$ $\quad -\sum_n a_{nj}\rho_n + \mu_j \geq \hat{a}_j, \qquad j = 1, \ldots, J \tag{8.33}$

$[v_n]$ $\quad \rho_n - (1 + r)\rho_{n+1} \geq 0, \qquad n = 0, \ldots, N - 1 \tag{8.34}$

$[w_n]$ $\quad -\rho_n + (1 + r)\rho_{n+1} \geq 0, \qquad n = 0, \ldots, N - 1 \tag{8.35}$

$[v_N]$ $\qquad\qquad \rho_N \geq 1 \tag{8.36}$

$[w_N]$ $\qquad\qquad -\rho_N \geq -1 \tag{8.37}$

$\qquad\qquad\quad \rho_n \geq 0, \qquad n = 0, 1, \ldots, N - 1 \tag{8.11}$

$\qquad\qquad\quad \mu_j \geq 0, \qquad j = 1, \ldots, J \tag{8.12}$

The analysis of (8.33) is similar to that of (8.10) in Section 8.2.5. If $x_j^* > 0$, the dual constraint is met exactly, and

$$0 \leq \mu_j^* = \hat{a}_j + \sum_n a_{nj}\rho_n^* \tag{8.41}$$

Substituting for ρ_n^* from (8.40), we have

$$\mu_j^* = \hat{a}_j + \sum_n a_{nj}(1 + r)^{N-n} \tag{8.42}$$

The right side of (8.42) is simply the net future value (*FV*) at time *N* of the cash flows for project *j*. The $\hat{a}_j$ term is the value of posthorizon flows discounted back to time *N*, and the summation is the forward compounding of the other cash flows. For fractionally accepted projects $\mu_j^* = 0$, and thus (8.42) equals zero. For rejected projects x_j^* and μ_j^* are both equal to zero, so

$$0 \geq \hat{a}_j + \sum_n a_{nj}(1 + r)^{N-n} \tag{8.43}$$

The horizon model with a common, fixed rate for borrowing and lending thus will accept only projects with nonnegative *FV(r)*, or *PV(r)*, and the *FV(r)* of any rejected project is nonpositive. This agreement between the LP model and the *PV* criterion reassures us that the model performs as intended. Actually, we would expect the model to perform precisely in this manner, since the unlimited borrowing and lending opportunities at interest rate r are equivalent to the assumptions underlying the *PV* criterion.

8.5.2. *Lending Rates Less Than Borrowing Rates*

Clearly, an LP model that yields the same answers as *PV* analysis is of little use. The true power of the LP model is the ability to represent a great variety of investment opportunities and restrictions, lending and borrowing opportunities, scarce resource restrictions, and so forth. In this section we modify the horizon model of the previous section by having a borrowing rate higher than the lending rate. The only modification needed in the model is in the cash balance equation 8.31, which becomes

$$[\rho_n] \qquad -\sum_j a_{nj}x_j - (1 + r_l)v_{n-1} + v_n + (1 + r_b)w_{n-1}$$

$$- w_n \le M_n, \qquad n = 1, 2, ..., N \qquad (8.44)$$

where r_l = lending interest rate,
r_b = borrowing interest rate.

The corresponding changes in the dual problem affect constraints 8.34 and 8.35, which become, respectively,

$$[v_n] \qquad \rho_n - (1 + r_l)\rho_{n+1} \ge 0, \qquad n = 0, \dots, N-1 \qquad (8.45)$$

$$[w_n] \qquad -\rho_n + (1 + r_b)\rho_{n+1} \ge 0, \qquad n = 0, \dots, N-1 \qquad (8.46)$$

Instead of (8.38) and (8.39), we obtain

$$1 + r_l \le \frac{\rho_n^*}{\rho_{n+1}^*} \le 1 + r_b, \qquad n = 0, ..., N-1 \qquad (8.47)$$

The ratio of the dual variables for the cash balance equations is now restricted to the range (including end points) between the lending and borrowing interest factors. From complementary slackness [5] we can deduce that if we are lending money at time n ($v_n > 0$), then (8.45) and the left part of (8.47) are satisfied as equality. If we are borrowing at time n ($w_n > 0$), then (8.46) and the right side of (8.47) are satisfied as equality. This makes sense, because the lending activity implies that extra dollars at time n would also be lent, leading to 1.2 times the extra dollars at the horizon as extra dollars at time $n + 1$, and so forth.

Example 8.4

We can demonstrate these results with Example 8.4, for which both data and solution are shown in Table 8.9. There are four projects, six budget limits, a

Table 8.9 *Data and Solution for Example 8.4 (Lending Rate Less Than Borrowing Rate)*

| Cash Flow | Project | | | | |
at Time	1	2	3	4	Budget
0	−600	−$1,200	−$900	−$1,500	$270
1	360	480	360	420	150
2	330	360	330	480	30
3	60	0	300	510	0
4	−150	660	270	540	−60
5	330	510	240	540	0
$\hat{a}_j$	150	300	150	330	—

$r_l = 0.2, r_b = 0.3, N = 5$

Solution

$x_1 = 1.0$	$v_0 = 0$	$w_0 = 420$	$\rho_0 = 2.754$
$x_2 = 0$	$v_1 = 0$	$w_1 = 0$	$\rho_1 = 2.119$
$x_3 = 0.1$	$v_2 = 393$	$w_2 = 0$	$\rho_2 = 1.728$
$x_4 = 0$	$v_3 = 561$	$w_3 = 0$	$\rho_3 = 1.440$
$\mu_1 = 67$	$v_4 = 490$	$w_4 = 0$	$\rho_4 = 1.200$
$\mu_2 = 0$	$v_5 = 943$	$w_5 = 0$	$\rho_5 = 1.000$
$\mu_3 = 0$			
$\mu_4 = 0$			

lending rate of 20%, a borrowing rate of 30%, and a horizon at time 5. The negative budget at time 4 means we must generate $60 to be used elsewhere in the firm. Only project 1 is accepted completely; project 3 is accepted fractionally, and the other two are rejected. There are borrowing at time 0 and lending at times 2 through 5. We can demonstrate how Eq. 8.47 indicates borrowing or lending by taking the ratios of the dual variables.

$\rho_0^*/\rho_1^* = 1.3$ borrowing at time 0

$\rho_1^*/\rho_2^* = 1.23$ neither at time 1

$\rho_2^*/\rho_3^* = 1.2$ lending at time 2

$\rho_3^*/\rho_4^* = 1.2$ lending at time 3

$\rho_4^*/\rho_5^* = 1.2$ lending at time 4 □

Everything seems to work according to theory in Example 8.4, but how do we explain the ratio ρ_1^*/ρ_2^* of 1.23, which is strictly between the limits? And if there are no restrictions on borrowing, why is project 3 accepted only fractionally? To answer these questions, let us assume two hypothetical situations in Example 8.3. First, assume everything is as before except that we borrow at time

1, forcing the ratio to be 1.3. The new dual variables can then be obtained as follows.

$\rho_5 = 1.0$

$\rho_4 = \rho_5(1.2) = 1.2$

$\rho_3 = \rho_4(1.2) = 1.44$

$\rho_2 = \rho_3(1.2) = 1.728$

$\rho_1 = \rho_2(1.3) = 2.246$

$\rho_0 = \rho_1(1.3) = 2.920$

Now let us find the corresponding value of μ_3 from Eq. 8.41. In LP terminology, we are pricing out the activity vector for project 3.

$$\$150 + (-900)(2.920) + (360)(2.246) + (330)(1.728)$$
$$+ (300)(1.44) + (270)(1.2) + (240)(1.0) = -\$103$$

The negative value means that we would not introduce project 3 into the LP solution, given the values for the ρ_n. In other words, given the other borrowing and lending activities, we are not justified in borrowing at 30% at time 1 in order to accept more of project 3.

Now assume everything is as in the original solution in Table 8.9, except that we lend at time 1, forcing the ratio to be 1.2. The new dual variables are obtained as before, and the pricing of the activity vector yields

$\rho_5 = 1.0$

$\rho_4 = \rho_5(1.2) = 1.2$

$\rho_3 = \rho_4(1.2) = 1.44$

$\rho_2 = \rho_3(1.2) = 1.728$

$\rho_1 = \rho_2(1.2) = 2.074$

$\rho_0 = \rho_1(1.3) = 2.696$

$$\$150 + (-900)(2.696) + (360)(2.074) + (330)(1.728)$$
$$+ (300)(1.44) + (270)(1.2) + (240)(1.0) = \$37$$

The positive value means that if we were lending money at time 1, given the other borrowing and lending activities, we could improve our situation by accepting project 3. The best action is to accept as much as possible without borrowing at time 1. This turns out to be 10%. What has happened is that the marginal productivity of cash at time 1 is determined by project 3.

8.5.3 Inclusion of Borrowing Limits, Supply Schedule of Funds

Another typical restriction in the horizon model is a limit on the amount borrowed at a particular time. Example 8.5 is a slight variation on Example 8.3.

665

Example 8.5

Table 8.5 presents the relevant data. The project cash flows are the same, the budgets at times 0 and 1 are reduced, the lending rate is 15%, the borrowing rate is 30%, and a $1,000 limit on borrowing is imposed at time 1. In anticipation of future borrowing at 30%, the $\hat{a}_j$ have been computed by using a discount rate of 30%. The solution for Example 8.5 is given in Table 8.7. Only one project, number 2, is accepted completely, and 4 and 6 are accepted fractionally. The only borrowing activity is at time 1, at the limit of $1,000.   □

To analyze the results of Example 8.5, we need to add one more constraint to the primal problem.

$$[\beta_1] \qquad\qquad\qquad w_1 \leq 1,000 \qquad\qquad\qquad (8.48)$$

The changes in the dual formulation are in the objective function and in Eq. 8.46.

$$\text{Min} \sum_n \rho_n M_n + \sum_j \mu_j + 1,000\beta_1 \qquad\qquad (8.49)$$

$$[w_1] \qquad\qquad -\rho_1 + (1 + r_b)\rho_2 + \beta_1 \geq 0 \qquad\qquad (8.50)$$

Instead of (8.47) we have

$$(1 + r_l)\rho_2^* \leq \rho_1^* \leq (1 + r_b)\rho_2^* + \beta_1^* \qquad\qquad (8.51)$$

The borrowing restriction at time 1 places a premium on funds at time 1 beyond that of the normal borrowing interest factor of 1.3. The nonzero value of β_1^* implies that we are borrowing the full amount and would like to borrow more. We can verify the right side of (8.51).

$$1.317 = (1.3)(1.0) + 0.017$$

What has happened in this example is as follows.

- Project 2, with the highest *IRR* of 31.26%, was accepted completely, exhausting the time 0 budget of $1,000. The cheapest method of borrowing was with partial acceptance of project 6, which is equivalent to borrowing at 26%.

- Projects 3 and 5 had negative *PV*(20%) and would not justify borrowing at 26 or 30%.

- Projects 1 and 4 have similar *IRR*s, 29.1% and 28.9%, respectively, for the original cash flows. The *IRR*s are 28.7% and 28.1%, respectively, for the $a_{0j}, a_{1j}, a_{2j}, \hat{a}_j$ flows, which is what the LP program sees. However, project 1 requires twice as much investment at time 1 as at time 0, whereas the opposite is true for project 4. Since time 1 borrowing costs 30% and the time 0 borrowing costs 26% (via project 6), preference is given to project

4. Neither project justifies borrowing at 30% in both periods, so just enough of project 4 is accepted to reach the borrowing limit of $1,000 at time 1.

It should be noted that the pricing operation with Eq. 8.41 is still valid and yields results consistent with the solution in Table 8.7.

The concept of borrowing limit can be generalized to a series of limits, each applicable to a source of loan funds at a designated rate. For example, a firm may be able to borrow an amount, say 2,000, at 22%, an additional 1,000 at 25%, and a final 1,000 at 30%, as shown in Figure 8.1. This representation is called a sloping supply schedule for funds [20]. If we let w_{kn} represent the amount borrowed at the kth step at time n, the modification to the horizon model is straightforward, as shown in Table 8.10. By convention, we order the borrowing steps in increasing order of cost r_k; the LP algorithm will naturally start borrowing at the lowest cost and move to the next step as each limit is reached.

Analysis of the dual formulation is similar to that in Example 8.5. For each w_{kn} in the primal we have a dual constraint.

$$[w_{kn}] \qquad -\rho_n + (1 + r_{kn})\rho_{n+1} + \beta_{kn} \geq 0 \qquad (8.56)$$

The dual constraint of interest is the one corresponding to the last step k at time n. If we are at the limit on the last step, we can not say anything beyond Eq. 8.56 without the actual value of β_{kn}^* from the LP solution. If we are borrowing an amount below the limit on the last step, however, we have

$$\frac{\rho_n^*}{\rho_{n+1}^*} = 1 + r_{kn} \qquad (8.57)$$

Equation 8.57 illustrates the nature of the ρ_n^* as indicators of the marginal cost of funds.

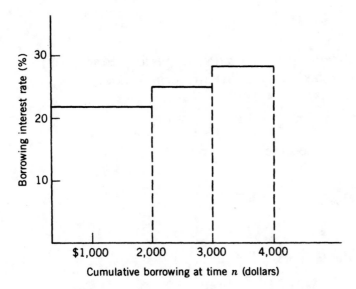

FIGURE 8.1. Sloping supply schedule of funds.

Table 8.10 *Primal Problem Formulation for Horizon Model with Sloping Supply Schedule for Funds*

$$\text{Max} \sum_j \hat{a}_j x_j + v_N - \sum_k w_{kN} \qquad (8.52)$$

s.t.

$$[\rho_0] \quad -\sum_j a_{0j} x_j + v_0 - \sum_k w_{k0} \leq M_0 \qquad (8.53)$$

$$[\rho_n] \quad -\sum_j a_{nj} x_j - (1 + r_\ell)v_{n-1} + v_n + \sum_k (1 + r_k)w_{k,n-1}$$

$$-\sum_k w_{kn} \leq M_n, \qquad\qquad n = 1, 2, \ldots, N \qquad (8.54)$$

$$[\beta_{kn}] \quad w_{kn} \leq B_{kn}, \quad k = 1, \ldots, m; \quad n = 0, \ldots, N \qquad (8.55)$$

$$[\mu_j] \quad x_j \leq 1, \quad j = 1, \ldots, j \qquad (8.56)$$

all variables ≥ 0

where w_{kn} = amount borrowed at kth step at time n,

r_k = interest rate at kth step of borrowing,

B_{kn} = limit on kth step at time n.

Other terms are as previously described

8.5.4 Dual Analysis with Project Interdependencies

The presence of project interdependencies will affect the use of (8.33) in pricing out project activity vectors in a manner consistent with the LP solution.

Example 8.6

We add a contingency relationship that project 4 cannot be performed without project 5 in Example 8.3. Then we add to the primal the form 8.8, or

$$[v] \qquad\qquad x_4 - x_5 \leq 0$$

and the dual constraints 8.33 would become

$$-\sum_n a_{n4}\rho_n + \mu_4 + v \geq \hat{a}_4$$

$$-\sum_n a_{n5}\rho_n + \mu_5 - v \geq \hat{a}_5$$

The pricing operation would reflect a penalty being applied to project 4 and a subsidy being applied to project 5. Since project 4 is so highly favorable, both 4 and 5 would be accepted. Using (8.41), we have

Project 4: $\mu_4^* = \$4,384 - (2,500)(1.44) - (1,300)(1.2)$
$$+ (2,000)(1.0) - 360 = \$864$$

Project 5: $\mu_5^* = \$1,480 - (3,000)(1.44) + (900)(1.2)$
$$+ (1,400)(1.0) + 360 = 0$$

The value of v is 360, just enough for project 5 to price out at zero, where it can be accepted. □

The mutual exclusivity constraints 8.7 would be handled in a similar manner. In practice, such constraints allow more projects to be fractionally accepted, and the typical end result is use of integer programming (Section 8.7).

8.6 BERNHARD'S GENERAL MODEL

All the features of the horizon model with borrowing constraints (Section 8.5.3) are retained in Bernhard's general model for capital budgeting [4]. Bernhard also includes dividends in a nonlinear objective function, with dividends constrained by a horizon posture restriction. In the following sections we will present the model and some general results. With few exceptions, the notation will follow Bernhard's, which is largely consistent with what we have been using. Appendix 8.A presents an application of the model to a dividend–terminal-wealth problem.

8.6.1 Model Formulation

The objective function is an unspecified function of dividends and terminal wealth.

$$\text{Max } f(D_1, D_2, \ldots, D_N, G) \tag{8.58}$$

where D_n = dividend paid at time n,
  G = time N terminal wealth, to be specified in more detail later.

It is assumed that $\partial f / \partial D_n \geq 0$ and $\partial f / \partial G \geq 0$, which imply that more dividends and terminal wealth, respectively, lead to greater utility values. Typically, f is defined to be concave.

The cash balance equations, or budget constraints, contain a liquidity requirement that reflects certain banking practices. The firm is required to maintain $C_n + c_n w_n$ in a bank account. The C_n is a constant representing basic

669

liquidity at time n, and the c_n ($0 \leq c_n < 1$) is a compensating balance fraction. The amount $C_n + c_n w_n$ earns interest at rate r_{ln}. The typical constraint is

$$
[\rho_n] \qquad - \sum_j a_{nj} x_j - l_{n-1}(v_{n-1} + c_{n-1}w_{n-1} + C_{n-1})
$$
$$
+ (v_n + c_n w_n + C_n) + b_{n-1}w_{n-1} - w_n
$$
$$
+ D_n \leq M_n', \qquad n = 0, 1, ..., N \tag{8.59}
$$

where M_n' = budget limit on externally supplied funds at time n,

l_n = lending interest rate factor at time n, $1 + r_{ln}$, and

b_n = borrowing interest rate factor at time n, $1 + r_{bn}$.

Equation 8.59 states that project outlays, minus previous-period lending, plus current lending, plus previous-period borrowing, minus current borrowing, plus current dividend cannot exceed the budget limit on externally supplied funds at time n. Regrouping terms gives

$$
[\rho_n] \qquad - \sum_j a_{nj} x_j - l_{n-1}v_{n-1} + v_n + (b_{n-1} - l_{n-1}c_{n-1})w_{n-1}
$$
$$
-(1 - c_n)w_n + D_n \leq M_n, \qquad n = 0, 1, ..., N \tag{8.60}
$$

where

$$
M_n = M_n' + (l_{n-1}C_{n-1}) - C_n
$$

Group payback restrictions state that at time n' the net outflows on the set of selected projects are recovered.

$$
[\psi] \qquad - \sum_j \sum_{n=0}^{n'} a_{nj} x_j \leq 0 \tag{8.61}
$$

Scarce material restrictions are defined for a nonmonetary resource, which could be skilled personnel, special equipment, and so forth.

$$
[\nu] \qquad \sum_j d_j x_j \leq d \tag{8.62}
$$

where d_n = amount of scarce resource consumed by project j,

d = total amount of scarce resource available.

The firm is prevented from paying excessive dividends and thus jeopardizing earning capability past the horizon. This is accomplished by a terminal-wealth horizon posture restriction. First it is necessary to define the terminal wealth. After the last dividend D_N at time N, the terminal wealth is

$$
G = M' + \sum_j \hat{a}_j x_j + v_N + c_N w_N + C_N - w_N
$$

where M' is the value at time N of posthorizon cash flows from other sources.

With the inclusion of M' and the liquidity requirement, the definition is the same as the objective function 8.29 of the horizon model. The definition is rewritten as

$$[\phi] \qquad -\sum_j \hat{a}_j x_j - v_N + (1 - c_N)w_N + G = M \qquad (8.63)$$

where M is $M' + C_N$.

The horizon posture restriction states that the terminal wealth must exceed some functional value of the dividends,

$$G \geq K + g(D_1, D_2, \ldots, D_N)$$

where $K = $ a nonnegative constant,

$g = $ a function, typically a convex one.

Rewriting, we have

$$[\theta] \qquad -G + g(D_1, D_2, \ldots, D_N) \leq -K \qquad (8.64)$$

Borrowing limits for $n = 0, 1, \ldots, N-1$, project upper bounds, and nonnegativity restrictions complete the model. Table 8.11 summarizes the objective function and constraints.

8.6.2 Major Results

With a concave objective function 8.58 and a convex constraint 8.64, the Kuhn–Tucker conditions are necessary and sufficient for optimality, and they enable us to make a number of statements about optimal solutions to the general model [17]. Table 8.12 presents the Kuhn–Tucker conditions. We present only the major results that can be obtained from them; derivations are in Bernard [4].

The pricing out of a project activity vector, analogous to (8.33), gives us

$$\mu_j^* \geq A_j^* = \sum_n a_{nj} \rho_n^* + \sum_{n=0}^{n'} a_{nj}\psi - d_j v^* + \hat{a}_j \rho_N^* \qquad (8.74)$$

where we have used the substitution $\phi^* = \rho_N^*$. The role of A_j^* in (8.74) is similar to that of PV in the horizon model.

Case 1: If $\qquad x_j^* = 1, \qquad \mu_j^* = A_j^* \geq 0$

Case 2: If $\qquad 0 < x_j^* < 1, \qquad \mu_j^* = A_j^* = 0 \qquad (8.75)$

Case 3: If $\qquad x_j^* = 0, \qquad \mu_j^* = 0 \geq A_j^*$

We should oberve that absent or nonbinding group payback and scarce material contraints imply ψ and v values of zero, and A_j^* reduces to $\sum_n a_{nj}\rho_n^* + \hat{a}_j \rho_N^*$.

Table 8.11 *Bernhard's General Model*

$$\text{Max } f(D_1, D_2, \ldots, D_N, G) \tag{8.58}$$

s.t.

$$[\rho_n] \quad -\sum_j a_{nj}x_j - l_{n-1}v_{n-1} + v_n + (b_{n-1} - l_{n-1}c_{n-1})w_{n-1} \tag{8.60}$$
$$- (1 - c_n)w_n + D_n \leq M_n, \qquad n = 0, 1, \ldots, N$$

$$[\psi] \quad -\sum_j \sum_{n=0}^{n'} a_{nj}x_j \leq 0 \tag{8.61}$$

$$[\upsilon] \quad \sum_j d_j x_j \leq d \tag{8.62}$$

$$[\phi] \quad -\sum_j \hat{a}_j x_j - v_N + (1 - c_N)w_N + G = M \tag{8.63}$$

$$[\theta] \quad -G + g(D_1, D_2, \ldots, D_N) \leq -K \tag{8.64}$$

$$[\beta_n] \quad w_n \leq B_n, \qquad n = 0, 1, \ldots, N-1 \tag{8.65}$$

$$[\mu_j] \quad x_j \leq 1, \qquad j = 1, \ldots, J \tag{8.5}$$

$$x_j, v_n, w_n, D_n \geq 0 \tag{8.66}$$

where x_j = project selection variable

v_n = lending amount from time n to $n + 1$,

w_n = borrowing amount from time n to $n + 1$

D_n = dividend paid at time n

a_{nj} = cash flow for project j at time n (inflows +)

$\hat{a}_j$ = horizon time value of cash flows beyond horizon

l_n = lending interest rate factor at time n, $1 + r_{ln}$

b_n = borrowing interest rate factor at time n, $1 + r_{bn}$

B_n = borrowing limit at time n

c_n = compensating balance fraction

M_n = budget limit on externally supplied funds at time n, adjusted for basic liquidity requirement

d_j = amount of scarce resource consumed by project j

d = total amount of scarce resource available

G = terminal wealth at time N, after paying w_N

M = value at time N of posthorizon cash flows from other sources, adjusted by basic liquidity requirement

K = nonnegative constant representing the minimum acceptable terminal wealth

ρ_n, ψ, υ, ϕ, θ, β_n, μ_j are dual variables

Table 8.12 *Kuhn–Tucker Conditions for Bernhard's General Model*

$[v_n]$ $\quad -\rho_n + l_n\rho_{n+1} \leq 0, \qquad n = 0,1, ..., N - 1$ $\hfill$ (8.67)

$[w_n]$ $\quad (1 - c_n)\rho_n - (b_n - l_nc_n)\rho_{n+1} - \beta_n \leq 0, \qquad n = 0, 1, ..., N - 1$ $\hfill$ (8.68)

$[v_N]$ $\quad -\rho_N + \phi \leq 0$ $\hfill$ (8.69)

$[w_N]$ $\quad (1 - c_N)\rho_N - (1 - c_N)\phi \leq 0$ $\hfill$ (8.70)

$[x_j]$ $\quad \displaystyle\sum_n a_{nj}\rho_n + \hat{a}_j\phi - d_j\upsilon + \sum_{n=0}^{n'} a_{nj}\psi - \mu_j \leq 0, \qquad j = 1, 2, ..., J$ $\hfill$ (8.71)

$[D_n]$ $\quad \dfrac{\partial f}{\partial D_n}\bigg|_{D_n} - \rho_n - \theta\,\dfrac{\partial g}{\partial D_n}\bigg|_{D_n} \leq 0, \qquad n = 0, 1, ..., N$ $\hfill$ (8.72)

$[G]$ $\quad \dfrac{\partial f}{\partial G}\bigg|_G - \phi + \theta \leq 0$ $\hfill$ (8.73)

SOURCE: Bernard [4].

Turning to the ρ_n^*, we let

$$\hat{b}_n = \frac{b_n - l_nc_n}{1 - c_n} \tag{8.76}$$

This $\hat{b}_n$ is the effective borrowing rate. For example, if $b_n = 1.3$, $l_n = 1.2$, and $c_n = 0.2$, in order to borrow a usable \$100, we have to borrow \$125 at 30% and put $(0.2)(125) = 25$ back in the bank at 20%. Our true borrowing cost is

$$(\$125)(0.3) - (25)(0.2) = 32.5, \text{ or } 32.5\%$$

Equation 8.76 yields the equivalent factor of 1.325. In addition, let

$$\hat{\beta}_n^* = \beta_n^*/(1 - c_n) \tag{8.77}$$

Then we can manipulate (8.67) and (8.68) to yield

$$l_n\rho_{n+1}^* \leq \rho_n^* \leq \hat{b}_n\rho_{n+1}^* + \hat{\beta}_n^*, \qquad n = 0, 1, ..., N - 1 \tag{8.78}$$

This equation is similar to (8.51), showing that compensating balance fractions do not necessarily complicate the model once we interpret them as higher effective borrowing rates.

If $v_n^* > 0$, complementary slackness indicates that the left side of (8.77) is satisfied as equality. In this case the ratio ρ_n^*/ρ_{n+1}^* equals the lending rate factor. If the company borrows, $w_n^* > 0$, and the right side is equality. Note that the ratio of dual variables is affected by the value of $\hat{\beta}_n^*$, the dual variable of the borrowing limit. If the borrowing constraint is absent or nonbinding, the $\hat{\beta}_n^*$ drops out and

673

(8.78) reduces to the analogous result 8.47 for the linear horizon model with time-varying rates.

The general model is a rather flexible framework for capital budgeting. Most of the results have been extended to the cases of linear mixed-integer programming and quadratic mixed-integer programming, respectively [18, 19]. A natural consequence of using any of these models is the need for a complete programming solution; simple acceptance criteria are possible only under very restrictive and simplistic assumptions.

8.7 DISCRETE CAPITAL BUDGETING

We have carefully avoided the issue of integer solutions until now, in order to present the concepts and theory of capital budgeting in the simpler LP framework. As we turn to discrete models, two issues face us. The first is practicality. Can we solve efficiently problems with integer restrictions? The second is the question of economic interpretation. Will the dual variables, particularly the ρ_n, play the same role in pricing out project opportunities?

8.7.1 Number of Fractional Projects in LP Solution

Before we delve into these issues, we briefly review the nature of the solutions to our example problems heretofore. Recall that in Example 8.1 we had a solution vector $\mathbf{x}^* = (0.22, 1, 0, 1, 0.16)$. Two of the five project selection variables had fractional values in the optimal LP solution. There are also two budget constraints in Example 8.1, and there are no project interdependencies. Weingartner [20] proved that in the LP formulation of the Lorie–Savage problem (the *PV* maximization in Table 8.2) the number of fractional projects in the optimal solution cannot exceed the number of budget constraints. An explanation of this fact is based on the following reasoning. If there is only one budget constraint, there need be at most one fractional project. All others would be either more preferable than the fractional one and accepted fully or less preferable and rejected completely. If there are two equally preferable fractional projects, we could adjust the investment amounts until one was completely accepted or rejected. If there are two budget constraints, it may be possible that one fractional project will exhaust the monies remaining after all fully accepted projects are funded, but more than likely two fractional projects will be needed. If there are three fractional projects in the presence of two budget constraints, one will be more (or equally) preferable, and its funding can be increased until it is accepted fully or one of the remaining two is rejected completely. The LP algorithm by nature seeks extreme points and avoids alternative optima with more variables than necessary. This type of inductive reasoning can be applied to three budget constraints and so forth.

Another way to regard the problem in Table 8.2 is as an upper-bounded LP problem [14]. A basic variable is then one whose value is allowed to be between its lower (0) and upper (1) bounds at some particular iteration. The projects' upper-bound constraints are deleted from the constraint matrix in the upper-bounded LP algorithm, and the rank of the constraint matrix is two for Example 8.1. Hence, there are at most two fractional projects in the optimal solution.

In the basic horizon model, in which the lending rate is equal to the borrowing rate for each time period and there are no borrowing limits and project interdependencies, as shown in Example 8.3, there is always an integer optimum solution. This fact is related to the equivalence between this model and the *PV* criterion. When the borrowing rate is greater than the lending rate, we can have fractional projects, as demonstrated by Example 8.4. The maximum number of fractional projects that are possible because the borrowing rate is greater is equal to the number of time periods with $r_l < r_b$, minus one. Moreover, the number of fractional projects may be increased by one for each project interdependency constraint and for each time period with a borrowing limit. The reasoning behind these last results is similar to that given for the *PV* maximization problem.

8.7.2 Branch-and-Bound Solution Procedure

Various algorithms have been developed for solving the mixed-integer linear programming problem [9]. It is beyond the scope of this text to deal with them, since many algorithms are designed for special problem structures and require a high level of mathematical sophistication on the part of the user. Instead, we will demonstrate the solution of a small problem with a branch-and-bound solution procedure which can be used by anyone with access to an LP code [17].

Example 8.7

Use Example 8.5 (Table 8.5) as a starting point and obtain an optimal integer solution. Table 8.7 shows the optimal LP solution vector $\mathbf{x}^* = (0, 1, 0, 0.15, 0, 0.58)$ and objective function value $z^* = \$9,210$. We will designate this as problem 1. The presence of two fractional project selection variables, x_4 and x_6, gives us a choice in the procedure. We will arbitrarily select x_4 and create two new problems.

Problem 2: Problem 1 with $x_4 = 0$ added as a constraint

Problem 3: Problem 1 with $x_4 = 1$ added as a constraint

We then proceed to solve problems 2 and 3 by using an LP algorithm.

Problem 2: $\mathbf{x}^* = (0.17, 1, 0, 0, 0, 0.37)$, $z^* = \$9,205$

Problem 3: $\mathbf{x}^* = (0, 0.89, 0, 1, 0, 1)$, $z^* = \$9,031$

The procedure so far has not eliminated all fractional x_i values but has, in fact, created others that did not appear in problem 1. The problem 2 solution has x_1 fractional, whereas x_1 was an integer in problem 1; the problem 3 solution has a fractional value for x_2, which was an integer in problem 1.

Undeterred, we proceed by taking problem 2 and creating from it two new problems.

Problem 4: Problem 2 with $x_1 = 0$ added

Problem 5: Problem 2 with $x_1 = 1$ added

675

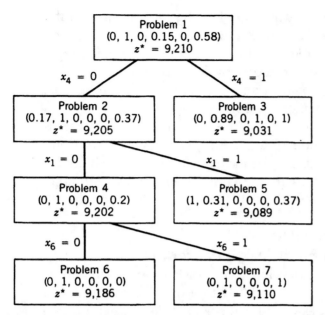

Figure 8.2. Branch-and-bound solution tree for Example 8.7. Numbers in parentheses are values of x*, the vector of project selection variables.

Figure 8.2 shows how the problems are derived from one another. The choice of problem 2 over problem 3 is based on the LP solution values, \$9,205 versus 9,031. We know that any integer solution derived from problem 3 (with added constraints such as $x_2 = 0$ or $x_2 = 1$) cannot exceed \$9,031, since the LP solution is always an upper bound on the integer solution. We think that a better integer solution is likely to be derived from problem 2. The LP solutions are

Problem 4: $\mathbf{x}^* = (0, 1, 0, 0, 0, 0.2)$, $z^* = \$9,202$
Problem 5: $\mathbf{x}^* = (1, 0.31, 0, 0, 0, 0.37)$, $z^* = \$9,089$

Because problem 4 has a better objective function value, we create from it two new problems.

Problem 6: Problem 4 with $x_6 = 0$ added
Problem 7: Problem 4 with $x_6 = 1$ added

The LP solutions are

Problem 6: $\mathbf{x}^* = (0, 1, 0, 0, 0, 0)$, $z^* = \$9,186$
Problem 7: $\mathbf{x}^* = (0, 1, 0, 0, 0, 1)$, $z^* = \$9,110$

At this point we have two integer solutions, and we can avoid further analysis of problems 6 and 7. We select the better of the two, that from problem 6 with $z^* = \$9,186$, and designate it as the incumbent (integer) solution.

Before we decide which of problems 3 and 5 to examine further, we check to see whether either can be ruled out by comparing its upper bound, or LP objective function value, with that of the incumbent. It happens that both have upper bounds less than \$9,186, and we do not examine them further. Problems

3 and 5 have been fathomed. There are no other candidate problems to examine, so we have finished and obtained the optimal solution $\mathbf{x}^* = (0, 1, 0, 0, 0, 0)$ with $z^* = \$9,186$. Figure 8.2 depicts the entire search process in tree form. □

In Example 8.7 the optimal integer objective function value is not much below the LP optimum, about 0.3%. However, we cannot generalize such characteristics, because so much depends on the projects, interest rates, and so forth. Note that a typical rounding process applied to the LP solution would give $\mathbf{x} = (0, 1, 0, 0, 0, 1)$, as in problem 7, which is suboptimal. We could conjecture that if we had branched first on x_6 instead of x_4, we might have reached the integer optimum sooner. Again, it is beyond our scope here to deal with such issues [9]. Our purpose has been to demonstrate an easily available integer solution procedure on a small capital budgeting problem.

8.7.3 Duality Analysis for Integer Solutions

Two basic approaches to duality analysis for mixed-integer linear programming have been presented in the literature. We will briefly discuss the first, more difficult method and then concentrate on the second, more straightforward method and its variations.

Recomputed Dual Variables. One method for solving mixed-integer linear programs is to use the cutting-plane procedure [9]. This approach begins with the LP optimum and successively adds constraints that delete portions of the feasible LP space but do not delete any integer solutions. Each time a constraint is added, the LP is solved again. The added constraints, called cutting planes, are derived from the current LP solution. When the current LP solution is an integer in the required variables, the procedure stops. At this point we have dual variables for both the original constraint set and the added constraints.

Gomory and Baumol [10] derived a technique for taking the dual variables for the added constraints and reapportioning them among the original constraint set. The purpose is to obtain a set of dual variables for the original problem only. (Dual variables for the cutting planes would be difficult to interpret in terms of the resources expressed by the original constraint set.) The disadvantage of this approach, apart from its complexity and the need to use the cutting-plane procedure, is that the recomputed duals are not always unique. Furthermore, the interpretation of the dual variables as measuring changes in the objective function value resulting from small changes in resource limits does not always apply in the integer case. Small changes in resource limits can cause jumps in the objective function value [20].

Penalties and Subsidies. Let us assume we have reached the LP problem corresponding to the optimal integer solution in a branch-and-bound integer procedure. (In Example 8.7 this would be problem 6, with x_1, x_4, and x_6 constrained to be zero). The LP form of the problem will contain a number of constraints that force certain project selection variables to zero and other constraints that force some project selection variables to their upper bounds. To the primal formulation of the horizon model—whether it be the basic model in Table 8.6, the model with a sloping supply schedule of funds in Table 8.10, or a model with time-dependent interest rates and project interdependencies—we would thus add

$$
\begin{aligned}
x_j &= 0, & j \text{ in } J_1 \\
x_j &= 1, & j \text{ in } J_2
\end{aligned}
\tag{8.79}
$$

where J_1 = set of projects constrained to be zero in the optimal integer solution,

J_2 = set of projects constrained to be at upper bound in the optimal integer solution.

These additional constraints will have corresponding dual variables. At first glance, the dual variables appear to be unconstrained, since the primal constraints 8.79 are equalities. We can, however, reinterpret the constraints as

$$
\begin{aligned}
x_j &\leq \epsilon, & j \text{ in } J_1 \\
x_j &\geq 1 - \epsilon \quad \text{or} \quad -x_j \leq -1 + \epsilon, & j \text{ in } J_2
\end{aligned}
\tag{8.80}
$$

where ϵ is a very small positive number. (Some LP codes check for variables set at fixed values and delete the corresponding constraints during a preprocessing stage. If this is done, it is necessary to use (8.80) instead of (8.79) to obtain information about the dual variables. An ϵ value of 0.001 or 0.0001 usually does the trick.)

In the pricing operation of a project constrained to be zero in the optimal integer solution, we then modify (8.33) as follows (assuming no project interdependencies),

$$
-\sum_n a_{nj}\rho_n + \mu_j + \gamma_j \geq \hat{a}_j
\tag{8.81}
$$

where γ_j is a dual variable, nonnegative. Rewriting, we have

$$
\mu_j^* \geq \sum_n a_{nj}\rho_n^* + \hat{a}_j - \gamma_j^*
\tag{8.82}
$$

But since μ_j^* for a rejected project is zero, the γ_j^* acts as a penalty (without Eq. 8.79 the μ_j^* was positive) to force rejection of project j.

If the project was constrained to be at its upper bound, Eq. 8.41 becomes

$$
0 \leq \mu_j^* = \hat{a}_j + \sum_n a_{nj}\rho_n^* + \gamma_j^*
\tag{8.83}
$$

In this instance the γ_j^* acts as a subsidy to enable acceptance of project j. These penalties and subsidies are a natural consequence of forcing the solution to satisfy the integrality requirements. They are known only through solving the mixed-integer programming problem. If we had solved the problem by some other method, such as the cutting-plane or enumeration method, we would still have to set up an LP model with the appropriate constraints of type 8.79 in order to extract the values of the penalties and subsidies.

We can apply these concepts to our integer solution for Example 8.5. The optimal dual variables for problem 6 are

$$\rho_0^* = 1.69 \quad \mu_1^* = 0 \quad \mu_4^* = 0 \quad \gamma_1^* = 0 \quad \beta_1^* = 0$$

$$\rho_1^* = 1.3 \quad \mu_2^* = 96 \quad \mu_5^* = 0 \quad \gamma_4^* = 0$$

$$\rho_2^* = 1.0 \quad \mu_3^* = 0 \quad \mu_6^* = 0 \quad \gamma_6^* = 80$$

The ratio analysis of ρ_n indicates borrowing at times 0 and 1, so projects 1 and 4 do not require penalties. Recall that project 4 was fractionally accepted in the LP optimum; project 1 was zero in the LP optimum but was introduced at an intermediate stage in the branch-and-bound procedure. We may verify the value of $\mu_6^* = 0$, which justifies rejection of project 6 (it was fractionally accepted in the LP optimum).

$$(\$1{,}000)(1.69) - (700)(1.3) - (700)(1.0) - 80 = 0$$

It is possible to reformulate the dual of the horizon model for an integer solution so that

- Projects forced into acceptance receive a subsidy, and projects forced into rejection receive no penalty, *or*
- Projects forced into rejection receive a penalty, but those forced into acceptance receive no subsidy.

The interested reader is referred to Weingartner [20] for further details of this method.

8.8 CAPITAL BUDGETING WITH MULTIPLE OBJECTIVES

In many situations it is not possible or desirable to evaluate different investment alternatives by one criterion, such as *PV* or terminal wealth. There are various techniques for dealing with multiple objectives, but most fall into one of three classes: goal programming, interactive multiple-criteria optimization, and nonlinear programming. In this section we provide an example of a goal-programming formulation, and we discuss the interactive approach.

Nonlinear programming can be applied if the decision maker can specify a utility function of the criteria, for example, dividends and terminal wealth. The major disadvantage of the approach seems to be the difficulty of specifying the utility function. Because each application depends so much on the utility function and on subsequent refinements in the solution algorithm, we will not

DETERMINISTIC CAPITAL BUDGETING MODELS

discuss the approach in this section. Appendix 8.A provides an example of applying a quadratic programming algorithm to a problem involving dividends and terminal wealth.

8.8.1 Goal Programming

Goal programming is a technique that enables a decision maker to strive toward a number of objectives simultaneously. The first step consists of establishing a goal for each criterion. Next, an objective function is specified for each criterion with respect to this goal. Third, weighting factors are placed on deviations of the objective functions from their goals. Fourth, the separate objective functions are combined into one overall function to be optimized [13].

Example 8.8

Table 8.13 presents data for Example 8.8. The first-year after-tax profit and employment of specialized personnel are considered to be primary goals, and terminal wealth at time 2 is considered a secondary goal. Let us assume the goals are established, respectively, as

Goal 1, first-year after-tax profits: $2,500

Goal 2, specialized personnel needed: 700 person-hours

Goal 3, terminal wealth at time 2: $4,000

These imply

$$\$2,000x_1 + 3,000x_2 + 1,700x_3 - 500x_4 \geq \$2,500$$

$$100x_1 + 100x_2 + 300x_3 + 400x_4 = 700 \text{ person-hours}$$

$$v_2 - w_2 + \$800x_1 + 600x_2 + 3,000x_3 + 1,000x_4 \geq \$4,000$$

$$(8.84)$$

Table 8.13 *Goal Programming, Example 8.8*

Coefficient Type	Project			
	1	2	3	4
First-year after-tax profit	$2,000	$3,000	$1,700	−$500
Specialized personnel needed, person-hours	100	100	300	400
Cash flow at time				
0	−$1,000	−$800	−$2,000	−$200
1	300	200	1,000	100
2	400	200	1,000	200
$\hat{a}_j$	$800	$600	$3,000	$1,000

Budgets for external sources of funds: $n = 0$, $2,000; $n = 1$, −$500; $n = 2$, −$500

680

The inequalities for profits and terminal wealth are typical of goals that can be exceeded without penalty. We now define auxiliary variables as follows.

$$y_1 = \$2,000x_1 + 3,000x_2 + 1,700x_3 - 500x_4 - 2,500$$

$$y_2 = 100x_1 + 100x_2 + 300x_3 + 400x_4 - 700 \text{ person-hours} \qquad (8.85)$$

$$y_3 = v_2 - w_2 + \$800x_1 + 600x_2 + 3,000x_3 + 1,000x_4 - 4,000$$

We are concerned with measuring positive and negative deviations, so we define components

$$\begin{aligned} y_k^+ &= y_k \quad \text{if } y_k \geq 0 \\ y_k^- &= |y_k| \quad \text{if } y_k < 0 \end{aligned} \qquad k = 1, 2, 3 \qquad (8.86)$$

Our overall objective is to minimize some weighted sum of deviations,

$$\text{Min} \sum_k (c_k^+ y_k^+ + c_k^- y_k^-) \qquad (8.87)$$

where c_k^+ and c_k^- are weighting factors for the deviations. If a \$100 profit deviation is deemed equivalent to a deviation of one specialized employee, we might set $c_1^- = 100$, $c_2^+ = 1$, and $c_2^- = 1$. Since terminal wealth is a secondary goal, set $c_3^- = 10$, an order of magnitude lower. The positive deviations for goals 1 and 3 have no adverse consequences, so $c_1^+ = 0$ and $c_3^+ = 0$. Thus, the objective function becomes

$$\text{Min } 100y_1^- + y_2^+ + y_2^- + 10y_3^- \qquad (8.88)$$

The constraints of the problem are of two types. The first type consists of goal constraints, obtained from (8.84).

$$\$2,000x_1 + 3,000x_2 + 1,700x_3 - 500x_4 - (y_1^+ - y_1^-) = \$2,500$$

$$100x_1 + 100x_2 + 300x_3 + 400x_4 - (y_2^+ - y_2^-) = 700 \text{ person-hours}$$

$$v_2 - w_2 + 800x_1 + 600x_2 + 3,000x_3 + 1,000x_4 - (y_3^+ - y_3^-) = \$4,000$$

$$(8.89)$$

The second type consists of the original set of constraints. In this example they would be cash balance equations for $n = 0, 1,$ and 2, respectively; project upper bounds; and nonnegativity constraints. An LP solution of (8.88) subject to the two types of constraints yields values for the x_j, v_n, and w_n that result in the "best" set of deviations from the goals. Assuming that lending and borrowing occur at 10%, the solution is:

$$\begin{array}{llll} x_1 = 0.483 & v_0 = 0 & w_0 = 494.2 & y_1^+ = 1,825 & y_1^- = 0 \\ x_2 = 1.0 & v_1 = 0 & w_1 = 93.0 & y_2^+ = 0 & y_2^- = 0 \\ x_3 = 0.51 & v_2 = 496.5 & w_2 = 0 & y_3^+ = 0 & y_3^- = 0 \\ x_4 = 1.0 \end{array}$$

objective function value = 0

The solution indicates that the first-year after-tax profit will be $4,325, or $1,825 above the goal of $2,500. Goal 2, specialized personnel needed, and goal 3, terminal wealth at time 2, are met exactly. Since there is no penalty for exceeding goal 1, the objective function value is 0. □

A number of variations of the goal-programming technique are suitable for particular circumstances [13]. In all of them care must be taken in formulating the goals and relative weights for deviations.

8.8.2 *Interactive Multiple-Criteria Optimization*

Another approach is to assume the operational setting of optimizing a nonlinear function of the decision variables, *without* knowing the explicit form of the trade-off (utility) function. Instead, we assume the decision maker is able to provide information about the gradient of the function. This information is then used to guide a search process over the domain of the function [6].

To illustrate the concept, let us take the three goals in Example 8.8, described in the previous section, and convert them into three criteria. We assume that we can measure each criterion by a function f_j and that we wish to maximize an overall utility function,

$$\underset{\mathbf{x}}{Max}\ U(f_1, f_2, f_3) \tag{8.90}$$

where $f_1(\mathbf{x})$ = criterion function for first-year after-tax profits,

$f_2(\mathbf{x})$ = criterion function for specialized personnel needed, and

$f_3(\mathbf{x})$ = criterion function for terminal wealth at time 2 (let $\mathbf{v}$ and $\mathbf{w}$ be included in an extended $\mathbf{x}$ vector).

We will be careful to specify the f_j as concave, differentiable functions and assume U is increasing in each f_j. Maximization of (8.90) by a steepest-ascent procedure will then lead to a global optimum [23].

The procedure begins with an initial feasible solution $\mathbf{x}^1$. At any iteration k the direction of the search is obtained from

$$\underset{\mathbf{y}^k}{Max}\ \nabla_{\mathbf{x}^k} U(f_1(\mathbf{x}^k), f_2(\mathbf{x}^k), f_3(\mathbf{x}^k)) \cdot \mathbf{y}^k \tag{8.91}$$

by letting the search direction be $\mathbf{d}^k = \mathbf{y}^k - \mathbf{x}^k$. But (8.91) can be replaced by

$$\underset{\mathbf{y}^k}{Max}\ \sum_j c_j^k \nabla_{\mathbf{x}^k} f_j(\mathbf{x}^k) \cdot \mathbf{y}^k \tag{8.92}$$

where

$$c_j^k = \frac{(\partial U/\partial f_j)^k}{(\partial U/\partial f_1)^k} \tag{8.93}$$

In many situations (8.92) is linear and can be solved by LP. In any case, if we can express f_j, we can express (8.92). What has happened is that the ratios of the partial derivatives of U with respect to f_j (which result from the breakdown of ∇U) have been replaced by trade-offs c_j^k. Each c_j^k measures the reduction in value of criterion function j that the decision maker would tolerate for one unit of increase in the value of criterion function 1, which is taken as a reference point. The trade-offs depend on the current solution and thus are indexed by the iteration counter k. They are obtained from the decision maker by an interactive procedure.

After the direction $\mathbf{d}^k$ is determined, the interactive procedure presents a number of solutions in the form of

$$f_1(\mathbf{x}^k + a\mathbf{y}^k), \qquad f_2(\mathbf{x}^k + a\mathbf{y}^k), \qquad f_3(\mathbf{x}^k + a\mathbf{y}^k)$$

where a is the step size, which is typically incremented by one-tenth of $\mathbf{d}^k$. The decision maker provides input again by selecting the preferred combination of f_1, f_2, f_3 values, without reference to the utility function U.

Given appropriate conditions on the f_j and U, the procedure will converge to a global maximum. The great advantage of the procedure is that no explicit form of the function U is required. The decision maker instead is required to provide information about trade-offs among f_j values and to indicate preferences for $f_1, \ldots, f_n$ combinations.

8.9 SUMMARY

In this chapter we have presented a number of techniques for capital budgeting under deterministic conditions. The methods are generally designed for selecting among many different investment alternatives (too many to enumerate explicitly) in the presence of budget limits, project interdependencies, and lending and borrowing opportunities. Linear programming is a major tool in the formulation, solution, and interpretation of many of the methods, either as the primary modeling technique or as a subroutine. The pricing of activity vectors is an important concept with direct economic interpretation, and we have devoted considerable space to illustrating the concept.

The models in this chapter may be grouped into three broad classifications. The first is the class of *PV* objective functions. This type suffers from some serious conceptual problems in the reconciliation of the discount rate used and the presence of budget constraints. The second class consists of horizon models; their objective is to maximize the end cash value or the terminal wealth at the end of some planning period. A number of desirable economic interpretations can be derived from such models. Moreover, models of this type are readily extended to include borrowing limits, a sloping supply schedule of funds, and integer restrictions.

The third class is characterized by objective functions containing different types of criterion variables. Bernhard's general model is the first of this type; it includes dividends and terminal wealth in the objective function. Other types

683

discussed are the goal-programming approach and interactive multiple-criteria optimization. Appendix 8.A presents an application of Bernhard's approach to a problem which has dividends and terminal wealth to consider.

REFERENCES

1. ATKINS, D. R., and D. J. ASHTON, "Discount Rates in Capital Budgeting: A Re-examination of the Baumol & Quandt Paradox," *The Engineering Economist,* Vol. 21, No. 3, pp. 159–171, Spring 1976.

2. BALAS, E., *Duality in Discrete Programming,* Graduate School of Industrial Administration, Carnegie-Mellon University, Pittsburgh, December 1967.

3. BAUMOL, W. J., and R. E. QUANDT, "Investment and Discount Rates under Capital Rationing—A Programming Approach," *Economic Journal,* Vol. 75, No. 298, pp. 317–329, June 1965.

4. BERNHARD, R. H., "Mathematical Programming Models for Capital Budgeting—A Survey, Generalization, and Critique," *Journal of Financial and Quantitative Analysis,* Vol. 4, No. 2, pp. 111–158, 1969.

5. DANTZIG, G. B., *Linear Programming and Extensions,* Princeton University Press, Princeton, N.J., 1963. (See Chapter 12 for a discussion of economic interpretation of dual problem.)

6. DYER, J. S., "A Time-Sharing Computer Program for the Solution of the Multiple Criteria Problem," *Management Science,* Vol. 19, No. 12, pp. 1379–1383, August 1973.

7. FISHER, I., *The Theory of Interest,* Macmillan, New York, 1930 (reprinted by A. M. Kelley, New York, 1961).

8. FREELAND, J. R., and M. J. ROSENBLATT, "An Analysis of Linear Programming Formulations for the Capital Rationing Problem," *The Engineering Economist,* Vol. 24, No. 1, pp. 49–61, Fall 1978.

9. GARFINKEL, R. S., and G. L. NEMHAUSER, *Integer Programming,* Wiley, New York, 1972.

10. GOMORY, R. E., and W. J. BAUMOL, "Integer Programming and Pricing," *Econometrica,* Vol. 28, No. 3, pp. 551–560, 1960.

11. HAMILTON, W. F., and M. A. MOSES, "An Optimization Model for Corporate Financial Planning," *Operations Research,* Vol. 21, No. 3, pp. 677–691, 1973.

12. HAYES, J. W., "Discount Rates in Linear Programming Formulations of the Capital Budgeting Problem," *The Engineering Economist,* Vol. 29, No. 2, pp. 113–126, Winter 1984.

13. IGNIZIO, J. P., *Linear Programming in Single and Multiple Objective Systems,* Prentice-Hall, Englewood Cliffs, N.J., 1982.

14. LASDON, L., *Optimization Theory for Large Systems,* Macmillan, New York, 1970. (See Chapter 6 for upper-bounded algorithm.)

15. LORIE, J. H., and L. J. SAVAGE, "Three Problems in Rationing Capital," *Journal of Business,* Vol. 28, No. 4, pp. 229–239, October 1955; also reprinted in Solomon, E. (ed.), *The Management of Corporate Capital,* Free Press, New York, 1959.

16. MURGA, P., *Capital Budgeting Objective Functions That Consider Dividends and Terminal Wealth,* M.S. thesis, School of Industrial and Systems Engineering, Georgia Institute of Technology, Atlanta, 1978.

17. RAVINDRAN, A., D. T. PHILLIPS, AND J. J. SOLBERG *Operations Research: Principles and Practice,* Wiley, New York, 1987. (See Chapter 4 for branch-and-bound technique. See Chapter 11 for Kuhn–Tucker conditions.)

18. SHARP, G. P., *Extension of Bernhard's Capital Budgeting Model to the Quadratic and Nonlinear Case,* School of Industrial and Systems Engineering, Georgia Institute of Technology, Atlanta, 1983.

19. UNGER, V. E., "Duality Results for Discrete Capital Budgeting Models," *The Engineering Economist,* Vol. 19, No. 4, pp. 237–252, Summer 1974.

20. WEINGARTNER, H. M., *Mathematical Programming and the Analysis of Capital Budgeting Problems,* Prentice–Hall, Englewood Cliffs, N.J., 1963.

21. WEINGARTNER, H. M., "Capital Rationing: *n* Authors in Search of a Plot," *Journal of Finance,* Vol. 32, No. 5, pp. 1403–1431. December 1977.

22. WILKES, F. M., *Capital Budgeting Techniques,* John Wiley & Sons, New York, 1983.

23. ZANGWILL, W. I., *Nonlinear Programming: A Unified Approach,* Prentice–Hall, Englewood Cliffs, N.J., 1969.

PROBLEMS

8.1. You wish to include lending activities at 8% and borrowing activities at 12% in a *PV* LP model. The interest rate used for *PV* calculations is 10%. Define the activity vectors for lending and borrowing opportunities, and write a model formulation for a time horizon of 2 years and three budget constraints.

8.2. One of the criticisms of the typical capital budgeting LP model is that only short-term (one-year) lending and borrowing is represented. Can long-term lending and borrowing be included? If so, show how by defining variables and specifying coefficients in the objective function and constraints. Would long-term lending and borrowing be more appropriate in a *PV* LP model or a horizon LP model?

8.3. In many decision environments the total number of major projects to be considered is ten or fewer. Thus, enumeration of all combinations would be feasible, since there would be $2^{10} = 1,024$ or fewer combinations. In such a case, would it make sense to use a mathematical programming approach? What information would the mathematical programming approach give that is not available from enumeration?

8.4. Formulate a *PV* LP model for selecting among the three projects described below. *MARR* = 8%. There is a budget of $13,000 at time 0, and the projects are required to generate $3,500 at time 1 and $1,200 at time 2. The life of each project is 5 years. The projects are independent except that C cannot be selected unless A is also selected. What is the value of extra budget money at time 2?

Project	Investment	Annual Cash Flow
A	$5,000	$1,319
B	7,000	1,942
C	8,500	2,300

8.5. Formulate a *PV* LP model for selecting among the three projects described below. *MARR* = 15%. There is a budget of $16,000 at time 0, and the projects are required to generate $4,000 at time 1 and $1,300 at time 2. The life of each project is 10 years. The projects are independent except that A cannot be selected unless B is also selected. What is the value of extra budget money at time 2?

Project	Investment	Annual Cash Flow
A	$8,000	$1,900
B	5,000	1,400
C	10,000	2,500

8.6. Fromulate a horizon LP model for selecting among the three projects described below, with time 2 as the horizon. There is a budget of $2,000 at time 0, and the projects are required to generate $500 at time 1 and $500 at time 2. The life of each project is 20 years. The projects are independent except that C cannot be selected unless A is also selected. The lending rate is 15% and the borrowing rate is 20%, per year. Do you see any obvious difficulty with the application of the horizon model to this particular example?

Project	Investment	Annual Cash Flow
A	$1,000	$240
B	800	190
C	1,500	310

8.7. A horizon LP model was formulated and solved for five independent projects and four budget constraints. The lending rate is 18% and the borrowing rate 25%, per year. There are no posthorizon cash flows. The solution is:

Project selection variables = (0.0, 1.0, 1.0, 0.5, 1.0)

Budget dual variables   = (1.7995, 1.475, 1.25, 1.0)

Project dual variables   = (10, 240, 310, 0, 110)

a. Indicate whether borrowing or lending occurs in each period.
b. Do you see any difficulty in interpreting the solution of this example?
c. Suppose you wish to evaluate a new independent project.

Time	0	1	2	3
Cash flow	−$1,000	−1,000	2,000	1,000

What would be your recommendation regarding acceptance?

8.8. A horizon LP model was formulated and solved for five independent projects and four budget constraints. The lending rate is 20% and the borrowing rate 25%, per year. There are no posthorizon cash flows. The solution is:

Project selection variables = (1.0, 0.0, 0.4, 1.0, 0.0)

Budget dual variables   = (1.8, 1.44, 1.2, 1.0)

Project dual variables   = (560, 0, 0, 320, 0)

a. Indicate whether borrowing or lending occurs in each period.
b. Suppose you wished to evaluate a new independent project.

Time	0	1	2	3
Cash flow	−$1,000	−1,000	2,000	1,000

What would be your recommendation regarding acceptance?

8.9. A horizon LP model was formulated and solved for five independent projects and four budget constraints. The lending and borrowing rates are

Time 0 to 1: lend at 15%, borrow at 20%

Time 1 to 2: lend at 15%, borrow at 20%

Time 2 to 3: lend at 18%, borrow at 25%

There are no posthorizon cash flows. The solution is

Project selection variables = (1.0, 0.0, 0.4, 1.0, 0.0)

Budget dual variables = (1.628, 1.357, 1.18, 1.0)

Project dual variables = (560, 0, 0, 320, 0)

  a. Indicate whether borrowing or lending occurs in each period.
  b. Suppose you wish to evaluate a new independent project.

Time	0	1	2	3
Cash flow	−$1,500	−1,500	3,500	800

What would be your recommendation regarding acceptance?
  c. What does the first project contribute to the objective function?

8.10. Formulate and solve a horizon LP model for selecting among the five following projects. The lending rate is 13% and the borrowing rate 17%, per year. There are no posthorizon cash flows.

			Project			
n	A	B	C	D	E	Budget
0	−$10,000	−$5,000	−$7,500	−$15,000	−$20,000	$30,000
1	−5,000	−12,000	−8,500	−3,000	−5,000	25,000
2	2,000	15,000	11,000	2,176	14,000	30,000
3	4,072	3,761	1,541	2,176	16,005	35,000
4	16,000	1,700	4,000	2,176	8,000	10,000
5	18,000	1,700	12,000	2,176	10,000	20,000

Verify that projects with positive future worth are accepted and those with negative future worth rejected. Verify that the ratios of the budget dual variables indicate lending or borrowing.

8.11. Rework Problem 8.10 with the inclusion of borrowing limits of $2,000 at time 0 and $2,000 at time 1, at the 17% rate. Unlimited borrowing at 20% is available at times 0 and 1.

8.12. Formulate and solve a horizon LP model for selecting among the five projects below. The lending rate is 15% and the borrowing rate 20%, per year. There are no posthorizon cash flows.

			Project			
n	A	B	C	D	E	Budget
0	−$10,000	−$20,000	−$15,000	+$5,000	−$15,000	$25,000
1	4,000	8,000	−2,000	−1,000	1,300	2,000
2	5,000	10,000	5,000	−1,000	1,700	0
3	4,400	3,000	7,300	−3,200	6,000	2,000
4	2,800	7,000	6,000	−1,150	4,000	1,000
5	1,000	6,000	7,100	−800	2,700	0

Verify that projects with positive future worth are accepted and those with negative future worth rejected. Verify that the ratios of the budget dual variables indicate lending or borrowing.

687

8.13. Rework Problem 8.12 with the inclusion of another activity, project F, with cash flow

n	0	1	2	3	4	5
Cash Flow	−\$25,000	10,000	8,000	8,000	8,000	7,000

8.14. Rework Problem 8.13 (six projects) with the inclusion of borrowing restrictions of \$10,000 per year over the planning period (5 years).

8.15. Rework Problem 8.13 (six projects) with the inclusion of a sloping supply schedule of funds. During each year the first \$5,000 of borrowing is at 20% and the next \$2,500 at 25%, and unlimited borrowing is available at 30%.

8.16. A horizon LP model was formulated and solved for selecting among the five projects below. The lending rate is 10% and the borrowing rate 20%, per year. There are no posthorizon cash flows.

	Project					
n	A	B	C	D	E	Budget
0	−\$1,000	−\$1,200	−\$900	−\$1,000	\$1,000	\$1,000
1	400	900	300	500	−400	1,300
2	800	800	500	700	−400	1,500
3	135	700	250	700	−400	200

The optimal solution contains:

Project selection variables = (1.0, 1.0, 0, 1.0, 1.0)

Budget dual variables = (1.452, 1.21, 1.1, 1.0)

a. Indicate whether lending or borrowing occurs during each time period.
b. Determine the project dual variable for project C and for Project E.
c. With a new set of budget amounts, the solution changes.

Budget amounts = (\$1,000, −1,000, 1,500, 200)

Project selection variables = (0, 1.0, 0, 1.0, 1.0)

Budget dual variables = (1.584, 1.32, 1.1, 1.0)

Explain why project A is rejected here although it was accepted previously. Express your answer in LP terms, using specific numbers.

d. If you know nothing about the budget amounts, can you say *anything* specific about the acceptance or rejection of projects in this example?
e. Describe a method for determining the optimal value of the objective function for the original problem formulation, if you know the optimal values of the project selection variables and the budget dual variables.

8.17. Construct a horizon LP example with lending rate(s) less than borrowing rate(s). Demonstrate the relationships between lending or borrowing activities and the budget dual variables and the relationships between project dual variables and project future values.

8.18. Construct a horizon LP example where at least one of the projects is accepted fractionally. Explain why it is accepted fractionally by pricing out the project activity vector.

8.19. Construct a horizon LP example with a sloping supply schedule of funds. Validate the relationships between the budget dual variables and tightness of the borrowing constraints.

8.20. Construct a horizon integer programming example. Solve it by using a branch-and-bound algorithm. Determine the subsidies and penalties attached to projects that are fractionally accepted in the LP solution, in order to force them to be integer.

8.21. Solve the goal-programming example in Section 8.8.1.

8.22. Construct an example of Bernhard's general model, using a linear objective function and a linear terminal-wealth posture restriction. Use at least four time periods and different lending or borrowing rates. Try to construct the problem so that at least one project is accepted, at least one is rejected, and at least one borrowing constraint is tight.

8.23. The ABC Company has to determine its capital budget for the coming 3 years, for which data (in thousands of dollars) are given in the following table.

End of Year	Available Investment Capital	Investment Projects					
		1	2	3	4	5	6
0	300	−50	−100	−60	−50	−170	−16
1	100	−80	−50	−60	−100	−40	−25
2	200	20	−20	−60	−150	50	−40
Discounted future revenues		150	210	220	350	200	100

At the start of year 1 the company has $300,000 available for investment; in year 2 another $100,000 becomes available, and at the start of year 3 an additional $200,000 becomes available. Project 1 requires $50,000 at the start of year 1 and another $80,000 at the start of year 2; at the start of year 3, the project yields $20,000. The yield at the start of year 3 and the discounted yields for later years amount to $150,000. The company can borrow at most $50,000 plus 20% of the money invested so far in the various investment projects at an interest rate of 12% per year. If the company deposits money at the bank, the interest rate is 8%. The company has a bank debt of $10,000, on which it pays 11% interest and which may be repaid at the start of any year. Assume that the company may undertake 100% of each project or take a participation in each project of less than 100%.

a. Formulate the capital budgeting problem by using the horizon model.

b. Find the optimal capital allocations by using a linear programming package.

c. Find the optimal capital budget, assuming that no project can be undertaken partially.

8.24. The Micromegabyte Company is a small American manufacturer of microprocessors, which are vital components in many pieces of electronic equipment, including personal computers. In a recent meeting of the board of directors, the company was instructed to engage in the development of various types of software that would go with their microprocessor products. An ad hoc committee has been formed to come up with various proposals that can be initiated in the new fiscal period. The following six proposals were considered to be competitive in the market and to have good profit potentials. Because technology in this field advances rapidly, most software products will have a market life of about 3 years.

689

End of Period	Software Projects and Their Cash Flows*					
	1	2	3	4	5	6
0	−50	−100	−70	−130	−250	−300
1	−100	−50	−100	−50	−100	−60
2	50	100	90	−100	−60	150
3	100	50	150	260	300	200
4	50	30	100	250	150	100
5	30	30	30		100	

*All units in $1,000.

The company will have at the start of year 1 (end of period 0) $500,000 available for investment; in year 2 another $200,000 becomes available, and at the start of year 3 an additional $50,000 becomes available.

The company can borrow at most $200,000 over the planning horizon at an interest rate of 12% per year. The company has to repay an old loan of $50,000 over the planning horizon. No partial payment of this loan is allowed, but the company has to pay 13% interest at the end of each year until the loan is paid in full.

Projects 1 and 3 are considered to be mutually exclusive because both projects lead to the same software development but with application on different machines. The company does not have enough resources to support more than one type of operating system. Project 2 is contingent on project 1, and project 4 is contingent on project 3. Projects 2 and 4 are graphics softwares designed to run on the specific operating system.

The company has a total of 10,000 programming hours per year for the first 2 years that can be put into the development of these software projects. Annual programming hour requirements for the projects are estimated to be as follows.

Year	Project					
	1	2	3	4	5	6
First	2,000	3,000	3,000	5,000	4,000	4,000
Second	3,000	4,000	3,000	4,000	5,000	4,000

The company can always lend any unspent funds at an interest rate of 9%. Determine the firm's best course of action with a horizon time of 4 years.

8.25. The National Bank of Maine has $1 billion in total assets, which are offset on the balance sheet by demand deposits, time deposits, and capital accounts of $650 million, $250 million, and $100 million, respectively. The bank seeks your advice on how best to allocate its resources among the following list of assets.

Bank Assets and Their Expected Rates of Return

Asset	Expected Net Return (%)
Cash and cash equivalents	0
Loans	
Commercial loans	5.5
FHA and VA mortgages	5.0
Conventional mortgages	6.2
Other loans	6.9
Investments	
Short-term U.S. government securities	3.0
Long-term U.S. government securities	4.2

In allocating its resources, the bank is now constrained by the following legal and policy considerations.

Legal restrictions

• Cash items must equal or exceed 30% of demand deposits.

• Within the loan portfolio, conventional mortgages must not exceed 20% of time deposits.

Policy guidelines (goals)

• The management does not wish its total loans to exceed 65% of total assets. Each dollar of deviation from this target will carry a penalty of 3.5 cents per period.

• Within the loan portfolio "commercial loans" are not to exceed 45% or fall below 30% of total loans, and "other loans" are not to exceed the amount of total mortgages. Deviations of 1$ from these targets will carry uniform penalties of 0.8 cent per period.

• To ensure solvency, the management desires to limit its holdings of risk assets, defined as total assets less cash items less short-term U.S. government securities, to seven times the bank's capital accounts. Each dollar of deviation will carry a penalty of 4 cents per period.

• The management wishes to earn a target profit of $50 million. It places no premium on overattainment of this profit objective, but it places a penalty of $1 on each dollar of underattainment. Set up and solve a goal programming formulation for this problem.

Outline

Part IV: Additional Topics

- Lecture slides on deterministic capital budgeting

- Chapter 8 of "Advanced Engineering Economics" by Park and Sharp-Bette

- Lecture slides on utility theory

- Chapter 9 of "Advanced Engineering Economics" by Park and Sharp-Bette

Utility Theory

- **Consider the following game:**

  - ➢ A fair coin is tossed until the first time a head occurs. If it takes n tosses to obtain the first head, the payoff to the player is $\$2^n$

  - ➢ What is the expected payoff?

  - ➢ What is the maximum amount that you would be willing to pay to play this game?

Utility Theory

- **Risk preference:**

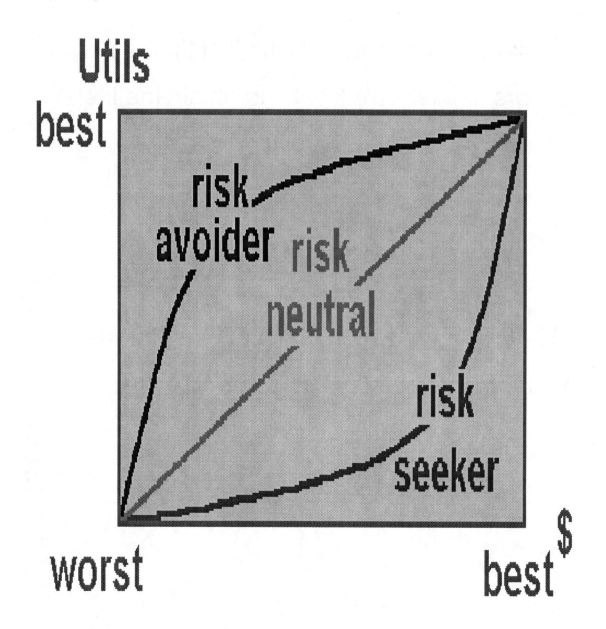

Utility Theory

- **Two famous economists: Von Neumann and Morgenstern**

  ➤ They developed a set of axioms of behavior that lead to the existence of a utility function

  ➤ Decision makers make decisions based on maximizing expected utility

Utility Theory

- **Risk averse investors have an *increasing concave* utility function**

  - $u(x) = \ln(x)$

  - $u(x) = x^{0.5}$

  - These are two examples of increasing concave

  - The increasing concavity reflects a decreasing incremental value from each incremental dollar of wealth

Utility Theory

- **Expected utility:**

  - $E[u(X)]$

- **Jensen's inequality using concavity of u :**

  - $E[u(X)] \leq u(E[X])$

  - An individual with a concave utility function u (.) would prefer to have E [X] for certain, than face the random variable X

Utility Theory

- **Certainty Equivalent:**

  - ➢ An individual will take less than E [X] for certain, rather than facing the random variable X

  - ➢ The exact amount that the individual will take is called the certainty equivalent: CE

  - ➢ $u(CE) = E[u(X)]$

  - ➢ Or: $CE = u^{-1}(E[u(X)])$

Outline

Part IV: Additional Topics

- Lecture slides on deterministic capital budgeting

- Chapter 8 of "Advanced Engineering Economics" by Park and Sharp-Bette

- Lecture slides on utility theory

- Chapter 9 of "Advanced Engineering Economics" by Park and Sharp-Bette

9
Utility Theory

9.1 INTRODUCTION

In the first two parts of this book we have assumed that decisions are made in a context of complete certainty. The decision makers are characterized as persons wishing to maximize cash flow, the present value of cash flow, or perhaps terminal cash wealth. Cash amounts at different points in time are converted to some common point in time, often time 0, by using an interest rate, and are then added to obtain *PV, FV,* and so forth.

In this third part of the book we relax these ideal assumptions in two important ways.

1. Project cash flow will no longer be regarded as certain. Instead, we will use probability concepts to describe project flows.
2. Decision makers will no longer be assumed to add (linearly) different cash flows at the same point in time or after conversion to the same point in time by use of an interest rate. Instead, small cash flows will usually be given more consideration per dollar than large cash flows.

In this chapter we give a brief introduction of the first concept, the probabilistic description of cash flows. We assume the reader is familiar with the fundamental concepts of probability theory. Probabilistic approaches to investment decisions are given extensive coverage in Chapters 10 to 13.

The principal emphasis in this chapter is on the second concept, namely the utility theory approach to combining and evaluating cash flows. Following the introduction of the concept in this section, the formal statement of utility theory is presented in Section 9.2. In Section 9.3 we discuss the properties of utility functions, followed by the procedures for assessing a utility function by empirical means in Section 9.4. An important operational method, mean–variance analysis, is shown in Section 9.5 to be based on the utility theory concept; mean–variance analysis is presented in depth in Chapters 10 and 11.

9.1.1 The Concept of Risk

We may introduce the concept of risk by asking why individual home-owners (with no outstanding mortgage or loan against their homes) would buy fire insurance. The possibility of damage from fire in a particular year is quite low, say 0.01. If the amount of damage caused by a fire is $60,000, we would say the *risk* of fire damage is a 0.01 chance (1% chance) of a $60,000 loss. If the fire insurance premium is $700 per year and the deductible amount on a loss (the amount the individual pays) is $250, then on an *expected monetary value* (*EMV*) basis an individual who buys insurance has the following yearly cost.

Event	Cost	Probability	Product
No fire occurs	$700	0.99	$693.00
Fire occurs	$700 + 250 = $950	0.01	9.50
		Expected annual cost	$702.50

Contrast this with the situation of an individual who decides *not* to buy fire insurance.

Event	Cost	Probability	Product
No fire occurs	0	0.99	0
Fire occurs	$60,000	0.01	$600.00
		Expected annual cost	$600.00

Most individual homeowners would clearly prefer to buy fire insurance in order to avoid the risk of a 0.01 chance of a $60,000 loss, even though the expected annual cost of $702.50 is greater than the expected annual cost of

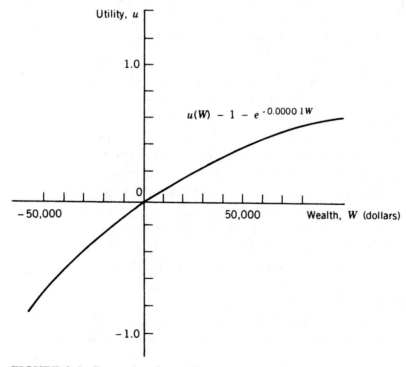

FIGURE 9.1. Example of a utility curve.

704

$600.00 without insurance. On the other hand, a large corporation with hundreds of retail outlets, facing similar risks and premiums at each outlet, might decide not to buy fire insurance. Such a corporation would become a *self-insurer*. The individual homeowner's way of evaluating the possible $60,000 loss is different from that of the large corporation, which can presumably make decisions regarding such amounts on an *EMV* basis. A $60,000 loss could be disastrous for an individual, whereas the large corporation would expect only one such loss per hundred retail outlets.

The individual's behavior, which is *not* based on an *EMV,* can be explained by the concept of *utility*. An example of a *utility function* for an individual, shown in Figure 9.1, has the following selected values. The function is

$$u(W) = 1 - e^{-0.00001W} \tag{9.1}$$

where W is the dollar amount of wealth.

Wealth, W	Utility Value
$100,000	0.63212
50,000	0.39347
10,000	0.09516
1,000	0.00995
0	0
−1,000	−0.01005
−10,000	−0.10517

The utility function in Figure 9.1 reflects a decreasing incremental value from each incremental dollar of wealth.

Following this line of argument, we can calculate an *expected utility* (*EU*) for our individual homeowner for the two decisions available: buy fire insurance or do not buy it. Let us assume the individual's total wealth, including the home, is $80,000. If the individual *buys* insurance, the *EU* of this decision for the next year is

Event	Resulting Wealth, W	Utility	Probability	Product
No fire occurs	$79,300	0.54751	0.99	0.54204
Fire occurs	$79,050	0.54638	0.01	0.00546

Expected utility = $E[u(W)]$ = 0.54750

If the individual *does not buy* insurance, the *EU* of this decision for the next year is

Event	Resulting Wealth, W	Utility	Probability	Product
No fire occurs	$80,000	0.55067	0.99	0.54516
Fire occurs	$20,000	0.18127	0.01	0.00181

Expected utility $E[u(W)]$ = 0.54697

Thus, on the basis of the *EU*, we can explain the decision of an individual homeowner to buy fire insurance even though the *expected annual cost* is higher. Large corporations also make decisions that do not result in the lowest expected annual costs, especially when potential losses are high. Such decisions can also be explained on the basis of *EU*. The difference is the scale of the cash flows; the corporation that is a self-insurer when losses are $60,000 per retail outlet might obtain insurance from an outside source when a single loss could be $25 million.

It is important to distinguish between *risk* and *uncertainty*. *Risk* applies to situations for which the outcomes are not known with certainty but about which we do have good probability information. Subsequent analysis could then be based on *EMV* or on *EU*. *Uncertainty* applies to situations about which we do not even have good probability information. In such situations other analysis techniques are appropriate, and the reader is referred to Luca and Raiffa [16].

9.1.2 Role of Utility Theory

In the preceding section we used utility theory to reconcile actual behavior with *EMV* decision making. This role of utility theory can be expanded to include behavior that is seemingly irrational because information is incomplete, because individuals have difficulties in establishing ordinal measurement scales, and because multiple-objective functions have been maximized [6]. Empirical behavior of individuals has prompted economists to construct some unusual utility functions. For example, an individual may buy insurance, normally an expected loss in a situation the individual feels offers no other choice. The same individual may buy lottery tickets, virtually always an expected loss in a situation in which the individual *does* have a choice. This type of observed behavior has led economists to hypothesize a compound-shaped utility function [7].

Utility theory can be used to justify the time value of money, as applied in Parts One and Two of this book. Furthermore, by including the effects of uncertainty in the future, we can argue for a discount rate *greater* than the equity rate or the weighted-average cost of capital presented in Chapter 5.

A very important role of utility theory is in the justification of the mean–variance method for analyzing risky cash flows. This is presented in Section 9.5.

It is important to remember that utility theory is both a *prescriptive* and a *descriptive* approach to decision making. The theory tells us how individuals and corporations *should* make decisions, as well as predicting how they *do* make decisions. The *hypothesis* aspect of utility theory should not be forgotten.

9.1.3 Alternative Approaches to Decision Making

Two related approaches other than utility theory, have been presented as constructs for decision making. They are based on principles other than expected value with a discount rate based on cost of capital. The first approach uses a risk-adjusted discount rate [2, 10]. Investment projects are assigned to risk classes, based on the uncertainty of the component cash flows. Investments in a "safe" risk class are evaluated by using an interest rate based on cost of capital, whereas investments with more uncertain cash flows are evaluated by using a higher interest rate.

The second approach is based on the concept of general states of wealth at different points in time and the implicit trade-offs an individual or corporation might make among these states [8, 14]. Although conceptually appealing, this choice–theoretic approach is difficult to implement.

9.2 PREFERENCE AND ORDERING RULES

In this section we present the formal definition of utility theory as it is commonly interpreted by economists. The theory consists of two parts: the hypothesis about maximizing expected utility and the axioms of behavior.

9.2.1 Bernoulli Hypothesis

The basic hypothesis of utility theory is that individuals make decisions with respect to investments in order to *maximize expected utility* [3]. This concept is demonstrated by the following example.

Example 9.1

An individual with a utility function $u(W) = 1 - e^{-0.0001W}$ is faced with a choice between two alternatives. Alternative 1 is represented by the following probability distribution.

Cash Amount	$-10,000	0	10,000	20,000	30,000
Probability	0.2	0.2	0.2	0.2	0.2

Alternative 2 is a certain cash amount of $5,000. The individual has an initial wealth of zero, and no investment is required for either alternative. Which alternative would the individual prefer?

For alternative 1 the expected utility is computed as follows.

Wealth, W	Utility	Probability	Product
−$10,000	−1.7183	0.2	−0.3437
0	0	0.2	0
10,000	0.6321	0.2	0.1264
20,000	0.8647	0.2	0.1729
30,000	0.9502	0.2	0.1900

Expected utility = $E[u(W)] = 0.1456$

For alternative 2 the utility is 0.3935. As this amount is greater than that for alternative 1, the certain cash amount of $5,000 is preferred to the risky alternative 1, which has a higher expected value of $10,000.

We can begin with the utility value of 0.1456 and determine a certain cash amount that is exactly equivalent to alternative 1.

$$0.1456 = 1 - e^{-0.0001W}$$

$$e^{-0.0001W} = 0.8544$$

Taking natural logarithms of both sides, we obtain

$$-0.0001W = -0.1574$$

$$W = \$1,574$$

The amount \$1,574 is called the *certainty equivalent* (*CE*) of alternative 1. Our individual would prefer any larger certain cash amount to alternative 1, would prefer alternative 1 to any smaller certain cash amount, and would be indifferent about a certain cash amount of \$1,574 and alternative 1. □

Definition. A *certainty equivalent* (*CE*) is a certain cash amount that an individual values as being as desirable as a particular risky option.

9.2.2 Axioms of Utility Theory

Individuals are assumed to obey the following rules of behavior in decision making [13, 17, 20].

Orderability. We can establish distinct preferences between any two alternatives. For example, given alternatives A and B, an individual prefers A to B, shown by A > B; prefers B to A, shown by A < B—we read the symbol < as "is less preferred than"; or is indifferent about choosing between the two, shown by A ~ B.

Transitivity. The preferences established by ordering are transitive. If A is preferred to B, and B is preferred to C, then A is preferred to C.

$$A > B \quad \text{and} \quad B > C \quad \text{imply } A > C$$

In addition,

$$A \sim B \quad \text{and} \quad B \sim C \quad \text{imply } A \sim C$$

Continuity. If A is preferred to B and B is preferred to C, there exists a probability p so that the individual is indifferent between receiving B for certain and obtaining A with chance p and C with chance $(1 - p)$. The second alternative is called a lottery involving A and C.

$$A > B > C$$

implies that there exists a p so that

$$B \sim \{(p, A), (1 - p, C)\}$$

Example 9.2

Consider the individual with utility function $u(W) = 1 - e^{-0.0001W}$. Find the probability p so that the individual is indifferent between receiving $20,000 for certain and entering a lottery with chance p of $30,000 and $(1 - p)$ of $10,000. The individual's wealth is $10,000, and there is no cost for either alternative. The comparison is between $30,000 (the initial $10,000 plus $20,000) for certain, a utility of 0.9502, and a chance p of $40,000 and chance $(1 - p)$ of $20,000.

$$u(\$40,000) = 0.9817$$

$$u(\$20,000) = 0.8647$$

$$0.9502 = (p)(0.9817) + (1 - p)(0.8647)$$

Solving for p gives 0.731. □

Monotonicity. If two lotteries involve the same two alternatives A and B, the individual prefers the lottery in which the preferred alternative has the greater probability of occurring.

$$A > B \quad \text{implies}$$

$$\{(p, A), (1 - p, B)\} > \{(p', A), (1 - p', B)\}$$

if and only if $p > p'$.

Decomposability. A risky option containing another risky option may be reduced to its more fundamental components. This axiom, often called the "no fun in gambling" axiom, is best explained by an example.

Example 9.3

Consider a two-stage lottery. In stage 1 there is a 0.5 chance of stopping and receiving nothing and a 0.5 chance of advancing to stage 2. In stage 2 there is a 0.5 chance of receiving $5,000 and a 0.5 chance of receiving nothing. This lottery may be reduced to its one-stage equivalent of

$$\$0: \quad (0.5) + (0.5)(0.5) = 0.75 \text{ chance}$$

$$\$5,000: \quad (0.5)(0.5) \qquad = 0.25 \text{ chance} □$$

Independence. A risky option A is preferred to a risky option B if and only if a $[p, (1 - p)]$ chance of A or C, respectively, is preferred to a $[p, (1 - p)]$ chance of B or C, for arbitrary chance p and risky options A, B, and C.

$$A > B$$

if and only if

$$\{(p, A), (1 - p, C)\} > \{(p, B), (1 - p, C)\}$$

for any p, A, B, and C.

The foregoing axioms have been used to derive the Bernoulli hypothesis [17, 20]. There are several different versions of the axioms. Some authors define additional ones or declare that some are embodied in others and thus superfluous.

Psychologists and behaviorally oriented economists each year write numerous papers describing experiments in which individuals systematically violate one or more of these axioms. It is not uncommon for such authors to propose a modification or elaboration of the theory [1, 4, 5, 11, 18]. This point brings us back to the *hypothesis* aspect of utility theory. The theory is an elegant mathematical way to describe real behavior, but it will always be at variance, more or less, with observed behavior.

9.3 PROPERTIES OF UTILITY FUNCTIONS

Most economists agree that an individual prefers more wealth to less. Hence, a utility function should be an *increasing*, or at the very least a *nondecreasing*, function of wealth. Other desirable properties are continuity (actually guaranteed by the axioms) and differentiability. The major question is about *risk avoidance* versus *risk seeking*.

9.3.1 Risk Attitudes

In all the examples presented so far in this chapter, the individual has been willing to accept a certain cash amount that is *less* than the *EMV* of a risky option. This type of behavior is described as *risk-averse*, or *risk-avoiding* behavior. Risk-averse utility functions, such as the one in Figure 9.1, are *concave* functions of wealth.

It has been suggested that some individuals exhibit *risk-seeking* behavior, as demonstrated by the following example.

Example 9.4

An individual is observed to buy a $5.00 lottery ticket each week. The possible prizes are represented by random variable X, and the chances of winning them are represented by probability p as follows.

$X =$	No prize	$p = 0.98889$
	$100 prize	0.01000
	$1,000 prize	0.00100
	$10,000 prize	0.00010
	$100,000 prize	0.00001

Explain the behavior of the individual.

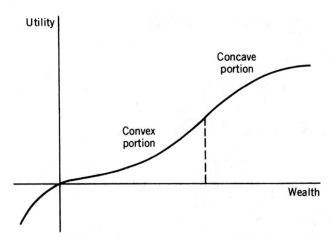

FIGURE 9.2. Utility function with a convex portion.

The *EMV* of such a lottery ticket is

$$E(X) = -5 + (0.98889)(0) + (0.01)(100) + (0.001)(1,000)$$

$$+ (0.0001)(10,000) + (0.00001)(100,000)$$

$$= -5 + 0 + 1 + 1 + 1 + 1$$

$$= -1$$

We may suggest two possible reasons for the individual to suffer the $1 expected loss each week. The first is that the purchase of a lottery ticket is a form of entertainment, similar to buying tickets to a sports event or a musical performance. The second, and more intriguing possibility, is suggested by the fact that poor people buy disproportionately more lottery tickets than middle-class and wealthy people, especially compared with other expenditures for entertainment. This fact has led many economists to suggest that the utility function for some persons may be *convex,* over a certain range of wealth, as shown in Figure 9.2. The rationale is that a poor person, in order to get out of his or her environment, is willing to take risks that a middle-class or wealthy person would not take [7]. □

We thus have a classification scheme for persons and their respective utility functions.

1. Risk-averse person: concave utility function.

2. Risk-neutral person: linear utility function.

3. Risk-seeking person: convex utility function.

Now let us reconsider the individual in Example 9.1 with utility function $u(W) = 1 - e^{-0.0001W}$. Assume that the individual has a starting wealth of $W_0 = \$20,000$ and is presented with the following lottery at no cost.

$$\{(0.5, \$10,000), (0.5, \$20,000)\}$$

711

The *CE* for the individual facing this lottery is obtained as follows.

Event, X	Resulting Wealth, W	Utility	Probability	Product
$10,000	$30,000	0.95021	0.5	0.47511
$20,000	$40,000	0.98168	0.5	0.49084

Expected utility $= E[u(W)] = 0.96595$

$$0.96595 = 1 - e^{-0.0001W}$$

$$e^{-0.0001W} = 0.03405$$

$$-0.0001W = -3.3798$$

$$CE = W = \$33,798$$

The difference between the *EMV* of $(0.5)(\$30,000) + (0.5)(\$40,000) = \$35,000$ and the *CE* of $33,798 is the *risk premium* (*RP*) the individual is willing to give up to avoid the risky option.

Risk premium, $RP = \$35,000 - 33,798 = \$1,202$

Definition [15]. A *risk premium* is an amount *RP* that solves Eq. 9.2.

$$E[u(W_0 + X)] = u[W_0 + E(X) - RP] \qquad (9.2)$$

where W_0 = the individual's wealth, a constant,
$\quad X$ = random variable representing the cash flow from a risky option,
$\quad RP$ = risk premium.

Here $W = W_0 + X$ is a random variable.

Let us recompute the *CE* for the previous lottery for an individual with the utility function of

$$u(W) = W - (0.00001)(W^2), \qquad 0 \le W \le 50,000 \qquad (9.3)$$

Event, X	Resulting Wealth, W	Utility	Probability	Product
$10,000	$30,000	21,000	0.5	10,500
$20,000	$40,000	24,000	0.5	12,000

Expected utility $= E[u(W)] = 22,500$

This corresponds to a *CE* of $34,190 (see Problem 9.7) and a corresponding *RP* of

$$RP = \$35,000 - 34,190 = \$810$$

The fact that the risk premium is different should not cause us much concern, since the utility functions for the two individuals are different. Let us recompute, however, the risk premiums for *both* individuals assuming an initial wealth of $W_0 = \$30,000$. For the individual with $u(W) = 1 - e^{-0.0001W}$, we have

Event, X	Resulting Wealth, W	Utility	Probability	Product
$10,000	$40,000	0.98168	0.5	0.49084
$20,000	$50,000	0.99326	0.5	<u>0.49663</u>

Expected utility $= E[u(W)] = 0.98747$

The *CE* is $43,796, which implies $RP = \$45,000 - \$43,796 = \$1,204$. This amount is not much different from the previous $1,202. (It actually is the same.)

For the individual with the quadratic utility function, Eq. 9.3, and an initial wealth of $W_0 = \$30,000$, we obtain

Event, X	Resulting Wealth, W	Utility	Probability	Product
$10,000	$40,000	24,000	0.5	12,000
$20,000	$50,000	25,000	0.5	<u>12,500</u>

Expected utility $= E[u(W)] = 24,500$

The *CE* is $42,930, with a corresponding $RP = \$45,000 - \$42,930 = \$2,070$.

The risk premium *increases* as the individual's wealth increases! In other words, the individual with the quadratic utility function is willing to give up *more* certain cash when faced with a risky option, as his or her wealth increases. Many economists argue that such behavior is not characteristic of intelligent investors. Instead, as their wealth increases, people should be willing to give up a *smaller* risk premium when faced with the same risky option.

9.3.2 Types of Utility Functions

Changes in the risk premium as a function of wealth are related to the behavior of the *risk aversion function* [21].

Definition. For a utility function u with first and second derivatives u' and u'', respectively, the *risk aversion function* is given by

$$r(W) = -u''(W)/u'(W) \tag{9.4}$$

where W is wealth.

Specifically, if $r(W)$ is *decreasing* as a function of wealth, the risk premium (for a given risky option) decreases as a function of wealth. Similarly, an increasing $r(W)$ implies an increasing RP, and a constant $r(W)$ implies a constant RP.

A negative exponential function such as

$$u(W) = 1 - e^{-cW}, \qquad c > 0 \tag{9.5}$$

713

has a constant risk aversion function, since

$$u'(W) = ce^{-cW} \tag{9.5a}$$

$$u''(W) = -c^2 e^{-cW} \tag{9.5b}$$

$$r(W) = c^2 e^{-cW}/(ce^{-cW}) \tag{9.5c}$$
$$= c$$

This property makes the function appealing to analysts. One does not have to know the wealth of the decision maker to perform analysis regarding *CE*s and *RP*s.

A quadratic function such as

$$u(W) = W - aW^2, \quad a > 0, \quad W \le 1/(2a) \tag{9.6}$$

has an increasing risk aversion function, since

$$u'(W) = 1 - 2aW \tag{9.6a}$$

$$u''(W) = -2a \tag{9.6b}$$

$$r(W) = \frac{2a}{1 - 2aW} \tag{9.6c}$$

and the denominator of Eq. 9.6c is less than 1.0.

In Section 9.3.1 we presented the classification of utility functions as follows.

1. Risk-averse person: concave utility function,

$$u''(W) < 0 \tag{9.7a}$$

2. Risk-neutral person: linear utility function,

$$u''(W) = 0 \tag{9.7b}$$

3. Risk-seeking person: convex utility function,

$$u''(W) > 0 \tag{9.7c}$$

We can now add the subclassifications based on the risk aversion function, Eq. 9.4.

a. Decreasing risk aversion,

$$r'(W) < 0 \tag{9.8a}$$

b. Constant risk aversion,

$$r'(W) = 0 \tag{9.8b}$$

c. Increasing risk aversion,

$$r'(W) > 0 \qquad (9.8c)$$

An example of a risk-averse utility function with constant risk aversion is the negative exponential function given by Eq. 9.5. An example of a risk-averse utility function with increasing risk aversion is the quadratic function of Eq. 9.6. An example of a risk-averse function with decreasing risk aversion is the logarithmic function.

$$u(W) = \ln(W + d), \qquad d \geq 0 \qquad (9.9)$$

In addition, some utility functions have bounded functional values, and others are meaningful only over a bounded domain (range of wealth). Other characteristics are related to the *proportion* of wealth an individual would invest in a risky option [21].

Linear combinations of utility functions, where the weights are positive and all component utility functions have the same subclassification based on Eqs. 9.8a, b, and c, maintain that subclassification [21]. This property is useful when defining a utility function of present value. For example, we can define a utility function for cash F_n received in period n, when the utility is measured at time n.

$$u_n(F_n) = (F_n)^a, \qquad 0 < a < 1 \qquad (9.10)$$

A composite utility function for the vector of cash flows $(F_1, F_2, \ldots, F_n)$ can be expressed as

$$u(F_1, F_2, \ldots, F_n) = \sum_{n=1}^{N} \frac{(F_n)^a}{(1 + i)^n} \qquad (9.11)$$

Other functional forms are possible.

9.4 EMPIRICAL DETERMINATION OF UTILITY FUNCTIONS

9.4.1. General Procedure

The most popular way to determine a utility function is by the certainty equivalent method, whereby information from an individual is elicited by asking questions about lotteries [12]. Either a *numerical* or a *functional* approach can be followed. The numerical approach is presented first, for an individual with zero wealth.

The *numerical* approach requires two reference values for starting. Pick one as $0 with zero utility and one as $1,000 with utility 1.0.

$$u(0) = 0 \qquad (9.12a)$$

$$u(\$1,000) = 1.0 \qquad (9.12b)$$

715

Now present the individual with a lottery involving the nonzero reference point (there is no cost to play).

$$\{(p, \$1,000), (1 - p, -\$1,000)\} \tag{9.13}$$

The value p that makes the individual indifferent to the lottery results in the following relation.

$$(p)u(\$1,000) + (1 - p)u(-\$1,000) = u(0) = 0 \tag{9.14}$$

This is so because the individual values the lottery with p, the same as not playing, which is equivalent to the individual's current state of zero wealth. If, for example, a value of $p = 0.60$ makes the individual indifferent about playing, then substituting from Eq. 9.12, we have

$$(0.6)(1.0) + (0.4)u(-\$1,000) = 0$$
$$u(-\$1,000) = -1.5 \tag{9.15}$$

This gives us three value points, and we continue in a similar manner.

For example, we can present the individual with a choice between a certain cash amount of $1,000 and the following lottery.

$$\{(p, \$10,000), (1 - p, \$0)\} \tag{9.16}$$

The value p that causes the individual to be indifferent results in

$$(p)u(\$10,000) + (1 - p)u(0) = u(\$1,000) \tag{9.17}$$

If $p = 0.35$, for example, substituting and solving gives

$$(0.35)u(\$10,000) + (0.65)(0) = 1.0$$
$$u(\$10,000) = 2.86 \tag{9.18}$$

Continuing in this manner, we can develop a table as shown here and graphed in Figure 9.3.

Wealth (dollars)	Utility Value
$20,000	3.40
10,000	2.86
1,000	1.00
0	0
−1,000	−1.50
−2,000	−4.00

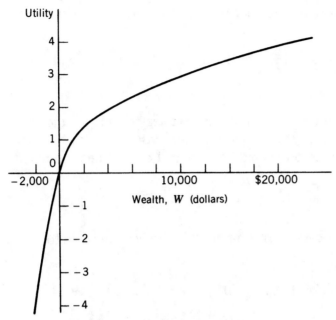

FIGURE 9.3. Typical empirically derived utility function.

The *functional* approach requires only one reference value for starting, most often $0 with zero utility. We also hypothesize the *functional* form. For example, assume the individual's utility function is Eq. 9.5,

$$u(W) = 1 - e^{-cW}, \qquad c > 0 \tag{9.5}$$

Next, we present a lottery, such as Eq. 9.13, with no cost to play, and elicit the value p that makes the individual indifferent about playing. If the same value $p = 0.6$ is obtained, we have an equation with one unknown.

$$(0.6)[1 - e^{(-c)(1,000)}] + (0.4)[1 - e^{(-c)(-1,000)}] = 0$$

$$(0.6)(e^{-1,000c}) + (0.4)(e^{1,000c}) = 1 \tag{9.19}$$

This can be solved by trial and error for $c = 0.0004$. Thus, the specific form of Eq. 9.5 is

$$u(W) = 1 - e^{-0.0004W} \tag{9.20}$$

Determining utility functions must be done with extreme care, despite the apparent simplicity of these examples. Inconsistencies and irregular-shaped functions often result. Alternative forms of lotteries are recommended by some to reduce bias in the information-gathering process [19].

9.4.2 Sample Results

In this section we present empirical results for the bids in two lottery games.

Game 1: A number of individuals (more than 10) submit sealed bids for the right to play a lottery.

$$\{(0.5, \$50), (0.5, -\text{bid})\} \qquad (9.21)$$

The highest bidder *must* play the lottery.

Game 2: A number of individuals (more than 10) submit sealed bids for the right to play the St. Petersburg game [3]. The highest bidder *must* play. In the St. Petersburg game a coin is tossed repeatedly until it turns up "heads." The payoff is

$$\$(2)^{n-1} \qquad (9.22)$$

where n is the first time heads appears. This compound lottery is equivalent to the simple lottery of

$$\{(0.5, \$1), (0.25, \$2), (0.125, \$4), \ldots, [(0.5)^n, (2)^{n-1}], \ldots\} \qquad (9.23)$$

The lottery 9.23 has an infinite number of outcomes, and its *EMV* is infinity.

$$EMV = E(X) = (0.5)(1) + (0.25)(2) + (0.125)(4) + \cdots$$
$$= 0.5 + 0.5 + 0.5 + \cdots$$

Table 9.1 shows the results of the bids made by graduate engineering students during the early 1980s. The bidders are ordered by ascending game 1 bids and, for equal game 1 bids, by ascending game 2 bids. Some of the low bids clearly reflect the artificiality of a classroom situation, or perhaps the cash amount in the pocket of a student. Similar artificial distortions can exist in a corporate environment, however, where one may be trying to calibrate a utility function by posing lottery games.

Except for the very low bids of reluctant players, the game 1 bids jump in increments of $5 or more. The lack of bids in amounts of $17 and $22, for example, might lead us to question the continuity axiom. It is apparent that some game 1 bidders—those whose bids were at least $20 (bidders 25 to 31)—thought seriously about the possibility of playing the lottery. With the exception of the highest bidder (who was willing to accept an *EMV* of zero), all showed fairly strong risk aversion. This type of result was expected.

The game 2 bids are more interesting but not so much for the degree of risk aversion shown, which was also expected. Rather, it is interesting to compare the two bids made by the same individual. For example, bidder 27 bid $25 for game 1 and $0.5 for game 2. The $0.5 bid for game 2 is equal to the first payoff in *EMV* terms, so the individual either reflects an unusual utility function or has difficulties assessing probabilities and *EMV* and *EU*. Similar low bids for game 2 were made by bidders 25 and 26. Bidders 18 and 22 offered unusually large sums to play game 2—$12 and $20, respectively.

Such difficulties in assessing *EMV* and *EU*, with resulting inconsistencies, are likely to be experienced by most individuals in society. Recall that the bids

Table 9.1 *Results of Bids for Two Lottery Games*

Bidder	Game 1 Bid	Game 2 Bid
1–5	$1	$1
6	1	2
7	1.5	1
8	2	1
9, 10	2	2
11	5	1
12, 13	5	2
14–17	5	5
18	5	12
19	10	2
20	10	4
21	10	5
22	10	20
23	15	2
24	15	4
25, 26	20	1
27	25	0.5
28	25	2.5
29	25	4
30	40	3
31	50	4

were made by engineering students with some formal training in probability and statistics. Experiments conducted elsewhere show similar inconsistencies [11, 19]. Thus, the application of utility theory must be performed with great care and caution.

9.5 MEAN–VARIANCE ANALYSIS

The *EMV* and *EU* approaches are based on probabilistic expectation over the range of possible outcomes of a risky option. In this section we present arguments for methods that are operationally different but are still based on utility concepts. These operational methods are, in general, more popular and easier to use. Therefore, a theoretical justification is attractive from a modeling point of view. We outline the main arguments and refer the interested reader to detailed sources.

9.5.1 Indifference Curves

Take the view of an investor with a quadratic utility function, as in Eq. 9.3, facing a set of alternative lotteries,

$$\{(p, 0), (1 - p, \$X)\}$$

Table 9.2 *Lotteries Toward Which an Individual Might Be Indifferent*

p	$1 - p$	X	$E(X)$	$Var(X)$, 10^6
0	1.0	$10,000	$10,000	0
0.4375	0.5625	20,000	11,250	98.4
0.5714	0.4286	30,000	12,857	220.4
0.6250	0.3750	40,000	15,000	375.0
0.6400	0.3600	50,000	18,000	576.0

NOTES: 1. Lotteries are of type

$$\{(p, 0), (1 - p, \$X)\}$$

2. Utility function is

$$u(W) = W - (0.00001)W^2, \quad W \le 50,000$$

3. All lotteries have the same $CE = \$10,000$.

with X in the range \$10,000 to \$50,000. Table 9.2 shows the lotteries, along with $E(X)$ and $Var(X)$. The $Var(X)$ is the second moment about the mean. It is equal to $E(X^2) - [E(X)]^2$. (See Section 10.2.1 for a more detailed explanation.)

These $E(X)$ and $Var(X)$ values are plotted as curve U_1 in Figure 9.4. The lotteries in Table 9.2 have been constructed so that all have a CE of \$10,000; each lottery has the same utility value, and the individual with utility $W - (0.00001)W^2$ would view them indifferently. Curve U_1 in Figure 9.4 can thus be interpreted as an indifference function relating $E(X)$ and $Var(X)$. Each combination of $E(X)$, $Var(X)$ on curve U_1 has the same utility value.

We could construct other sets of lotteries in which all in a set would have the same utility value. The result would be a family of curves $U_1, U_2, U_3, U_4, \ldots,$ one curve corresponding to each set of lotteries. Higher curves represent higher utility values.

Points A and B on curve U_3 are valued the same by the individual. A point like C or D that is not on the same curve does not have the same utility as point A. Point C is considered less desirable than point A because it has the same $E(X)$ but a higher $Var(X)$. On the other hand, point D is preferred to point A because for the same $Var(X)$ it has a higher $E(X)$. Point B is preferred to point C because of higher $E(X)$ *and* lower $Var(X)$, but by the same reasoning point D is preferred to point B. These preference rules are specified in greater detail in Chapter 11. A formal analysis [22] along these lines shows that the mean–variance approach is justified when the investor's utility function is quadratic and the probability distributions of X can be characterized by only two parameters (e.g., normal, lognormal).

9.5.2 Coefficient of Risk Aversion

We may observe some characteristics of the utility curves in Figure 9.4. First, the intersection point of a curve with the vertical $E(X)$ axis represents the

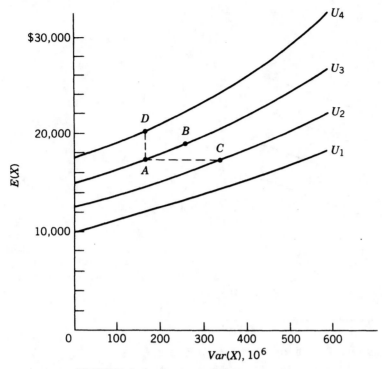

FIGURE 9.4. Utility indifference curves relating $E(X)$ and $Var(X)$.

certainty equivalent for all the points on that curve. Since such an intersection point has zero $Var(X)$, the cash outcome is certain. Second, the curves have positive slope. This reflects the fact that utility is an *increasing* function of $E(X)$ and a *decreasing* function of $Var(X)$. Third, the curves are concave. One way to explain the concavity of the indifference curves is that as risk increases, much larger increases in $E(X)$ are necessary to maintain the same level of utility for risk-averse individuals.

An approximation to the set of curves in Figure 9.4 might appear as in Figure 9.5. Here all the utility curves are linear and parallel. In Figure 9.5 we can obtain the *CE* of any point, such as Point *D,* as follows.

$$CE_D = E(D) - \lambda\, Var(D) \tag{9.24}$$

The value λ is called the *coefficient of risk aversion* (or sometimes the *risk aversion factor*). It measures the trade-off between $E(X)$ and $Var(X)$. This means that a *CE* is easier to calculate when λ is known.

Even if the linear approximation in Figure 9.5 is not appropriate, we can define λ as the *tangent* to a utility indifference curve in Figure 9.4. The value of the coefficient of risk aversion is then reasonably valid over a restricted interval. For known functional utility forms, expressions for λ as a function of the cash outcomes can be developed [9]. In practice, if we are not confident with assuming a single value of λ, then λ is varied parametrically (see Appendix 11A).

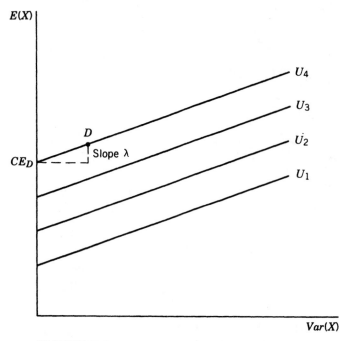

FIGURE 9.5. Approximation of indifference curves in Figure 9.4.

9.5.3 Justification of Certainty Equivalent Method

Applying Eq. 9.24 to a periodic cash flow F_n, which may be a random variable, we have

$$V_n = E(F_n) - \lambda \, Var(F_n) \tag{9.25}$$

For a series of cash flows from a project, we have in the simplest case, where λ is time-invariant and the F_n are independent random variables,

$$PV(i) = \sum_{n=0}^{N} \frac{V_n}{(1 + i)^n}$$

$$= \sum_{n=0}^{N} \frac{E(F_n) - \lambda \, Var(F_n)}{(1 + i)^n} \tag{9.26}$$

Here the interest rate i is a *risk-free* rate, which accounts for only the time value of money. This risk-free rate can be viewed as a rate at which the individual can always invest money in some risk-free projects (such as a short-term government bond). This is the amount forgone if the project is undertaken and a net income is received from the risk-free project. Thus, having a present value of the certainty equivalents greater than zero means that the project is acceptable to this investor.

Example 9.5

To illustrate the procedures involved in calculating the present value of certainty equivalents, let us examine a 5-year project with $E(F_n)$ and $Var(F_n)$ as shown in the tabulation. We assume that the λ value is known to be 0.02 for this investor. Then the certainty equivalents for the periodic random cash flows F_n are

n	$E(F_n)$	$Var(F_n)$	V_n	$PV(10\%)$
0	-400	400	-408	-408.00
1	120	100	118	107.27
2	120	225	115.5	95.45
3	120	400	112	84.15
4	110	900	92	62.84
5	120	2500	70	43.46

$$\Sigma = -\$14.83$$

Since the total present value of the certainty equivalents is negative, the investor would reject the project. □

Returning to the general case, let us assume that the utility function for cash flows distributed over time is

$$u = \sum_{n=0}^{N} c_n u_n \tag{9.27}$$

where u_n is a utility function for the random cash flow F_n occurring at time n and c_n is a constant. This expression implies that contributions to total utility are additive over time, and periodic utility values are multiplied by the constant c_n to adjust for the time preference of the events F_n. The exact form of the periodic utility functions u_n is not specified. In fact, u_n could be different functions over time or, in the simplest case, time-invariant. For our discussion, let us assume that $u_n = u_1$ for all n. A Taylor expansion can be used to generate a reasonable approximation to an expected utility function [20].

$$E(u_n) = u_n[E(F_n)] + u_n^{(2)}[E(F_n)]\,Var(F_n)/2 \tag{9.28}$$

This expression is obtained by adopting "sufficient approximation" reasoning to justify ignoring the higher moments about the mean of the cash flow in the Taylor series. If the utility function is a quadratic, however, any term $u_n^{(n)}$ (nth derivative of u_n) with $n > 3$ will be zero. Thus Eq. 9.28 becomes the exact expression of the expected utility measure. Further, the term $u_n^{(2)}$ becomes a constant for the quadratic utility function. Thus, rewriting Eq. 9.28 gives us the expression

$$E(u_n) = u_n[E(F_n)] + A_n\,Var(F_n) \tag{9.29}$$

where

$$A_n = u_n^{(2)}[E(F_n)]/2 \tag{9.30}$$

723

Returning to the total utility function given in Eq. 9.27 and taking the expected value of each side of the equation, we obtain

$$E(u) = \sum_{n=0}^{N} c_n E(u_n) \tag{9.31}$$

Substituting Eq. 9.29 into Eq. 9.31 yields

$$E(u) = \sum_{n=0}^{N} c_n u_n [E(F_n)] + \sum_{n=0}^{N} c_n A_n \, Var(F_n) \tag{9.32}$$

If a certainty equivalent can be found for each time period so that

$$u_n(V_n) = u_n[E(F_n)] + A_n \, Var(F_n) \tag{9.33}$$

the present value of this set of certainty equivalents will be equal to the expected utility of the cash flows from the investment project by letting $c_n = 1/(1 + i)^n$ [20].

9.6 SUMMARY

Utility theory is a very important concept because it helps to reconcile real behavior with expected monetary value in decision making. The typical individual has a concave utility function, reflecting an aversion to risk, which is usually measured by the variance of the cash flow. The axioms of utility theory can be used to derive the Bernoulli hypothesis of expected utility maximization. Validation experiments reveal, however, that this hypothesis is not perfectly true.

Operationally, the utility indifference curves that relate $E(X)$ and $Var(X)$ provide the theoretical basis for the popular mean–variance analysis presented in Chapter 11. The coefficient of risk aversion, heavily used in portfolio analysis, is the slope of the indifference curve. Finally, the discounted sum of certainty equivalents is shown to be an approximation (exact for quadratic utility) to the expected utility of a random future cash flow stream. All these results will be used in later chapters.

REFERENCES

1. BECKER, J., and R. K. SARIN, "Lottery Dependent Utility," *Management Science,* Vol. 33, No. 11, pp. 1367–1382, 1987.

2. BERNHARD, R. H., "Risk-Adjusted Values, Timing of Uncertainty Resolution, and the Measurement of Project Worth," *Journal of Financial and Quantitative Analysis,* Vol. 19, No. 1, pp. 83–99, 1984.

3. BERNOULLI, D., "Exposition of a New Theory of the Measurement of Risk," *Econometrica,* Vol. 22, No. 1, pp. 23–36, 1954. (Accessible translation of "Specimen Theoriae Novae de Mensura Sortis," 1738.)

4. BROCKETT, P. L., and L. L. GOLDEN, "A Class of Utility Functions Containing All the Common Utility Functions," *Management Science,* Vol. 33, No. 8, pp. 955–964, 1987.

5. CURRIM, I. S., and R. K. SARIN, "Prospect Versus Utility," *Management Science,* Vol. 35, No. 1, pp. 22–41, 1989.

6. EDWARDS, E., "The Theory of Decision Making," *Psychological Bulletin,* Vol. 51, No. 4, pp. 380–417, 1954.

7. FRIEDMAN, M., and L. J. SAVAGE, "The Utility Analysis of Choices Involving Risk," *Journal of Political Economy,* Vol. 56, No. 4, pp. 279–304, 1948.

8. HIRSHLEIFER, J., "Investment Decision under Uncertainty: Choice-Theoretic Approaches," *Quarterly Journal of Economics,* Vol. 79, No. 4, pp. 509–536, 1965.

9. JEAN, W. H., *The Analytical Theory of Finance,* Holt, Rinehart and Winston, New York, 1970.

10. JOHNSON, W., *Capital Budgeting,* Wadsworth, Belmont, Calif., 1970, Ch. 5.

11. KAHNEMAN, D., and A. TVERSKY, "Prospect Theory: An Analysis of Decision under Risk," *Econometrica,* Vol. 47, pp. 263–291, 1979.

12. KEENEY, R. L., and H. RAIFFA, *Decisions with Multiple Objectives; Preferences and Value Tradeoffs,* Wiley, New York, 1976.

13. KELLER, L. R., "Testing of the 'Reduction of Compound Alternatives' Principle," *OMEGA, International Journal of Management Science,* Vol. 13, No. 4, pp. 349–358, 1985.

14. LAVALLE, I. H., and P. C. FISHBURN, "Decision Analysis under States-Additive SSB Preferences," *Operations Research,* Vol. 35, No. 5, pp. 722–735, 1987.

15. LEVY, H., and M. SARNAT, *Portfolio and Investment Selection: Theory and Practice,* Prentice–Hall, Englewood Cliffs, N.J., 1984.

16. LUCE, D. R., and H. RAIFFA, *Games and Decisions: Introduction and Critical Survey,* Wiley, New York, 1957.

17. MACHINA, M. J., "A Stronger Characterization of Declining Risk Aversion," *Econometrica,* Vol. 50, No. 4, pp. 1069–1079, 1982.

18. MACHINA, M. J., "Decision-Making in the Presence of Risk," *Science,* Vol. 236, pp. 537–543, 1 May 1987.

19. McCORD, M., and R. DE NEUFVILLE, "'Lottery Equivalents' Reduction of the Certainty Effect Problem in Utility Assessment," *Management Science,* Vol. 32, No. 1, pp. 56–61, 1986.

20. NEUMANN, J. V., and O. MORGENSTERN, *Theory of Games and Economic Behavior,* 2nd edition, Princeton University Press, Princeton, N.J., 1947.

21. PRATT, J. W., "Risk Aversion in the Small and in the Large," *Econometrica,* Vol. 32, No. 1–2, pp. 122–136, 1964.

22. TOBIN, J., "Liquidity Preference as Behavior toward Risk," *Review of Economic Studies,* No. 67, pp. 65–85, February 1958.

PROBLEMS

9.1. Consider the homeowner in Section 9.1.1 with the utility function given by Eq. 9.1. If the deductible amount on a loss is higher than $250, the homeowner might prefer not to buy fire insurance, on an *EU* basis. Using the data in Section 9.1.1 for other factors, determine the deductible amount that would make the homeowner *indifferent* about choosing between buying and not buying insurance, on an *EU* basis.

9.2. For an individual with zero initial wealth and a utility function

$$u(W) = 1 - e^{-0.0001W}$$

find the *CE* for each of the following alternatives (probabilities of the outcomes are given).

Alternative	Cash Amount				
	−$10,000	0	$10,000	$20,000	$30,000
1	0.1	0.2	0.4	0.2	0.1
2	0.1	0.2	0.3	0.3	0.1
3	0	0.3	0.4	0	0.3
4	0	0.15	0.65	0	0.2
5	0.5	0	0	0	0.5

9.3. Solve Example 9.2 for the situation in which the individual's initial wealth is $20,000. Would you expect the probability to change as the initial wealth changes?

9.4. Consider a three-stage lottery. In the first stage there are a 0.2 chance of receiving $1,000 and a 0.8 chance of going on to stage 2. In stage 2 there are a 0.5 chance of receiving $2,000 and a 0.5 chance of going on to stage 3. In stage 3 there are a 0.2 chance of receiving $1,000, a 0.3 chance of receiving $2,000, and a 0.5 chance of receiving $5,000. Reduce this three-stage lottery to an equivalent one-stage lottery.

9.5. Construct a compound lottery and reduce it to its equivalent one-stage lottery.

9.6. Obtain information about a lottery. Calculate the *EMV* of the act of purchasing a ticket.

9.7. Derive the *CE* for an individual with initial wealth $20,000 and a quadratic utility function as given by Eq. 9.3, when facing the lottery {(0.5, $10,000), (0.5, $20,000)}. There is no cost for the lottery. Show all computations.

9.8. Can you specify a risk-seeking utility function with decreasing risk aversion? With constant risk aversion? With increasing risk aversion?

9.9. Conduct a lottery game of the type described in Section 9.4.2. Analyze the results for consistency.

9.10. Construct a set of lotteries, each with the same *CE* and similar to the ones in Table 9.2, to derive one of the higher utility curves in Figure 9.4.

9.11. Construct a set of lotteries, each with the same *CE* and similar to the ones in Table 9.2, but using the utility function given by Eq. 9.1. What is the shape of the indifference curve?

9.12. Using the worksheet provided, develop your utility function. In doing so, consider the following steps.

Step 1: Find the certainty equivalent amount *B* for a given lottery (*A* or zero with 0.5 probability each). Once the amounts *A* and *B* are specified, find the certainty equivalent amount *C* for a new lottery (*B* or zero with 0.5 probability each). Continue this procedure for the remaining lotteries. You are likely to find some inconsistencies in the certainty equivalent amounts assessed. Resolve these inconsistencies by reassessing the certainty equivalent amounts.

Step 2: Scale the certainty equivalent amounts (*A* through *J*) as a percentage of *A*. For example, if *A* = $1,000 and *B* = $300, then *A* = 100% of *A* and *B* = 30% of *A*.

726

Step 3: Plot the scaling preferences on the chart provided and smooth the curve when connecting the points plotted.

WORKSHEET FOR DETERMINING THE UTILITY FUNCTION

Certainty Equivalent

1	*A* _____ or zero	vs.	*B* _____
2	*B* _____ or zero	vs.	*C* _____
3	*C* _____ or zero	vs.	*D* _____
4	*A* _____ or *E* _____	vs.	zero
5	*E* _____ or zero	vs.	*F* _____
6	*F* _____ or zero	vs.	*G* _____
7	*A* _____ or *F* _____	vs.	*H* _____
8	*C* _____ or *E* _____	vs.	*J* _____

Scaling Preference

	Amount	%A	*U*
A			+8
B			+4
C			+2
D			+1
E			−8
F			−4
G			−2
H			+2
J			−3

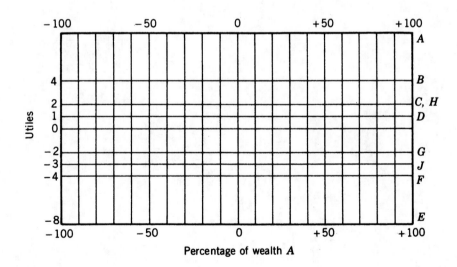